DISCARD

D0956047

WHY AMERICA MISUNDERSTANDS THE WORLD

PAUL R. PILLAR

WHY AMERICA MISUNDERSTANDS THE WORLD

National Experience and Roots of Misperception

Columbia University Press / New York

Columbia University Press
Publishers Since 1893
New York   Chichester, West Sussex
cup.columbia.edu

Library of Congress Cataloging-in-Publication Data

Pillar, Paul R., 1947–
    Why America misunderstands the world : national experience and roots of misperception /
Paul R. Pillar.
        pages cm
    Includes bibliographical references and index.
    ISBN 978-0-231-16590-7 (cloth : alk. paper) — ISBN 978-0-231-54035-3 (e-book)
    1. United States—Foreign relations.   2. United States—Foreign relations—Public opinion.
3. National characteristics, American.   4. Public opinion—United States.   I. Title.

JZ1480.P55   2016
327.73—dc23   2015016432

Columbia University Press books are printed on permanent and durable acid-free paper.
This book is printed on paper with recycled content.
Printed in the United States of America

c 10 9 8 7 6 5 4 3 2

Cover design by Diane Luger
Cover illustration by slabdsgn/Dollar Photo Club

To Lucas

CONTENTS

PREFACE

I HAVE SPENT most of a lifetime interpreting the actions and perspectives of foreign nations or managing others whose job it is to perform such interpretation. This experience has included a career with the U.S. Central Intelligence Agency and later work as an academic and independent scholar writing about foreign policy and international relations. The interpretations have not always been correct, but the effort to make them teaches some lessons that involve knowing oneself better by getting to know others. In this context, "self" and "others" can apply to nations as well as to individuals. Two lessons in particular are relevant.

One is that to understand a nation's decisions and behavior requires understanding the perspectives that the people in that nation, including its decision makers, have acquired through their shared national experience. The nation's triumphs and tragedies and the rest of its history color the images that its people and its leaders have of the rest of the world, and those images in turn guide how that nation behaves toward the rest of the world.

The other lesson is that the portion of the U.S. bureaucracy in which I formerly worked is not the principal guide for major decisions in U.S. foreign policy. The images of the world abroad that have influenced U.S. policy the most have come from other sources.

Putting those two lessons together leads to a third: that Americans' shared national experience heavily influences the way Americans perceive the outside world, which in turn has a major influence on U.S. foreign policy. In an earlier book, I described how and why the intelligence bureaucracy is not the main place to look for images that have guided major U.S. foreign-policy decisions.[1] The present book addresses one of the places we do need to look for those images. The premise is that the distinctive circumstances and history of the United States yield distinctive, important, and policy-relevant ways that Americans perceive the rest of the world.

This book unavoidably has a downbeat message in that any discussion of how perceptions are shaped by the perceiver's attributes is in large part a discussion of misperception and error. This fact does not imply, however, an overall negative outlook about the American experience or about many of the traits and attitudes that flow from it. In the course of many years of studying the troubles and flaws of other nations, I have repeatedly been reminded of why I am glad and proud to be an American.

Knowing oneself is a virtue, for nations as well as for individuals. This book has been written to add modestly to collective American virtue by helping Americans become more aware of the twists that they habitually impart to their view of what lies beyond their borders and of why they impart those twists. It also is written in the hope that such awareness will help lead in some small way to a less twisted and more accurate understanding of the world and thus to better-informed U.S. foreign policy.

I thank Anne Routon, my editor at Columbia University Press, for her support of this project. Robert Jervis, to whom I and many others are indebted for his pioneering work on misperception in international relations, read the entire manuscript and offered many helpful suggestions. My former employer, the Central Intelligence Agency, reviewed the manuscript as required to confirm that it contains no classified information, but nothing here reflects the views of either that agency or the U.S. government. I, of course, am solely responsible for any remaining errors in this book. My principal thanks go to my wife, Cynthia, for accommodating my preoccupation with working on this book and for her role in most other parts of my life that are enjoyable and fulfilling.

WHY AMERICA MISUNDERSTANDS THE WORLD

1

THE AMERICAN PRISM

THE UNITED STATES is exceptional. One can agree with that statement even without accepting the tub-thumping type of exceptionalism that regularly infuses the rhetoric of American politicians. What sets the United States apart goes beyond the ordinary differences between any two countries. Having risen to strength on a continent widely separated from most of the rest of the world, the United States has come to exert power more broadly over the entire globe than any other state ever has. Human history has seen nothing else like it.

The federal, representative, democratic republic that constitutes the American political system stands out among political inventions, even though its founders borrowed many ideas from elsewhere and it has since been repeatedly emulated. Sheer longevity distinguishes the republic, despite North America being part of the New World rather than of the Old. One can find more antiquated political relics elsewhere, but no other major power boasts as much continuity as a democracy as does the United States. The Mother of Parliaments at Westminster is older than the U.S. Congress, but at the time the United States was founded, the British political system still had a hereditary monarch who was much more than just a figurehead.

Most American politicians who trumpet the concept of American exceptionalism are selling a narrow and one-sided version of what makes the United States unique. This brand of exceptionalism can justly be criticized for being politically tendentious and for whitewashing negative aspects of U.S. behavior. It often is a crude appeal to primitive nationalism and a rhetorical promotion of policies favored on other grounds. It is a type of triumphalism based on the notion that Americans are not just different from but also better than anyone else. American exceptionalism as typically used in political discourse understates or ignores the respects in which the United States is still subject to many of the same realities and limitations that other states are.[1] Even a state that is different in important respects can still be like other states in other important respects.

Nonetheless, whatever is exceptional can be expected to have exceptional effects, for good or for ill. Although not everything important about America is different from other countries, much of what is different about it is still important. Distinctly American ways of thinking and acting matter. One indication of this is how multiple generations of observers of the American character have reached remarkably similar conclusions about the traits that constitute that character.[2] Another indication is how the very belief in American uniqueness has provided a common creed within which policy debates are conducted. Debate over imperialism at the turn of the twentieth century, for example, between those who believed that America's civilizing mission was best carried out by being the shining example of a city on the hill and those who instead wanted to charge down the hill and conquer what was below, was based on the two sides' shared assumptions about American uniqueness.[3]

Even more basic than character and creed is *perception*: how people see things and think about the nature of things. A nation's culture—which itself has been shaped by all of the physical, political, and historical circumstances that have made that nation what it is—powerfully influences its citizens' perceptions. A culture determines much of what the people who are part of that culture take to be factual knowledge.[4] American culture and everything that has gone into it constitute a prism that slants, distorts, and colors how Americans see what is around them. Sometimes the distortion is so great that they fail to see some things at all.

The distorting and coloring prismatic effects of being an American apply first of all to how Americans perceive things in their own country, which are most germane to their daily lives. But they also extend to how they perceive the world outside their national borders, especially situations and problems overseas that the United States may confront—including the nature and cause of a problem, its prognosis, the limitations and possibilities of any U.S. action, and the extent to which the problem gets noticed in the first place.

The distortion and coloration are chiefly unconscious and automatic. Americans' perceptions of the world outside the United States exemplify what psychologists have taught us about human cognition: that mental constructs based on culture and past experience shape perceptions silently but so powerfully that they often outweigh even contrary facts and evidence. The constructs, also called heuristics, are shortcuts the mind uses to cope with daily deluges of information without having to apply slow and laborious analysis to every data point.[5]

Psychologists have more to tell us about how Americans' own unusual situation affects their perceptions of the rest of the world, including what George Kennan referred to as "our inveterate tendency to judge others by the extent to which they contrive to be like ourselves."[6] The concept of projection—of ascribing one's own attributes to others—goes back to Freud. To psychoanalysts, it is a defense mechanism: a transferring of unwanted or undesirable attributes to maintain a favorable self-image.[7] It is easy to see what such projection might have to do with American exceptionalism; preserving a pristine image of America as better than any other nation encourages the sloughing off of undesirable attributes onto others, which worsens American misperceptions of the others.

One does not have to assume a national neurosis, however, for America's unusual status to contribute to Americans' misunderstanding of foreigners and foreign countries. Americans, living in a country that is so different from any others, simply have not had the experience, including domestic experience, to know any better. There has not been enough variety in the domestic experience to know better. Louis Hartz wrote of Kennan's observation, "It is peculiarly easy for us to judge others by ourselves because, especially since the Jacksonian upheaval, we have been so much alike."[8] The judging involves not only an expectation that other nations ought to emulate an American ideal but also a perception that their starting point is not fundamentally different from America's. That gets to yet another psychological mechanism that is frequently displayed in international relations: the tendency to overestimate the influence of internal characteristics on another's behavior and to underestimate the effect of the situation that the other person or nation is in.[9] Because America's situation is unique, Americans have more trouble than most in understanding the situations of others.

IMPACT ON POLICY

A myopic American public prone to mental laziness and laden with misperceptions about the outside world would be of little importance to anyone other than students of public opinion if the misperceptions did not affect U.S. foreign policy. The United States has large bureaucracies, after all, charged with using hard facts and analysis to deliver to policy makers accurate pictures of the foreign problems they must confront. But on the big U.S. foreign-policy decisions over the past several decades—those dealing with major departures such as going to war or redirecting grand strategy—the bureaucracies and in particular the intelligence agencies have had almost no influence.[10] Far more important have been the conceptions that decision makers bring with them to the job and involve their sense of how the world works and their preconceptions based on past personal experiences.

The policy makers' inbred patterns of thinking constitute one of the links between policy and the array of perceptions and misperceptions the public exhibits. Policy makers are American citizens, too. They grew up in the same culture and were shaped by the same peculiarly American circumstances and history and national experience as other Americans. They naturally tend to look at the outside world in many of the same ways. Although they may have more of an obligation to act on fact than does the average opinionated member of the general public, their heavy high-level responsibilities make the mental shortcuts all the more attractive and even necessary, and so they too tend to use oversimplification and to cling to general images they already hold.[11]

Another link between American public opinion and U.S. foreign policy is that policy makers must operate in a climate of opinion that sets significant limits to what they can do or even say, regardless of whether they would have shared the tenets of that opinion in the first place. Elected policy makers could not have attained and held power without having been responsive to American public opinion. Walter Lippmann made the point more bluntly sixty years ago: "With exceptions so rare that they are regarded as miracles and freaks of nature, successful democratic politicians are insecure and intimidated men. They advance politically only as they placate, appease, bribe, seduce, bamboozle, or otherwise manage to manipulate the demanding and threatening elements in their constituencies."[12] Although this pattern might appear in any democracy, Kennan observed that foreign policy is especially likely to be subordinated to domestic politics in the United States, where the constituencies are not parliaments but instead "particularly aggressive and vociferous minorities or lobbies."[13]

Whether vociferous minorities or other threatening elements have shaped a broader popular perception or not, that perception can acquire a significance for policy that goes beyond the mere counting of votes or the placating of a lobby. The perception becomes part of the statesman's reality for any of several reasons, such as maintaining national morale, regardless of whether the perception is true or the statesman believes it is true. In debates about the U.S.–Soviet military balance in the 1970s and 1980s, for example, an influential line of argument was that much of the American public had come to believe that the strategic balance had shifted in favor of the Soviet Union and that this was reason enough for the United States to respond with enhanced military programs of its own, whether the actual U.S.–Soviet balance had shifted as much as the public believed or not.[14]

Prevailing public perceptions can become conventional wisdom that elites as well as the general public routinely accept. The statesperson's natural tendencies to view the world in a certain way merge with his or her political need to stay within the confines that public perceptions set. The conventional wisdom in effect limits not only what the statesperson does and says but also what he or she thinks. This is what happened as the United States immersed itself in the Vietnam War. In the 1960s, a strong conventional wisdom, very difficult to buck, held that preventing a Communist takeover in South Vietnam was critical to checking a larger advance of worldwide communism. Leslie Gelb and Richard Betts note that nearly all opinion leaders inside and outside government, except for a few lonely voices, accepted this belief. "And the political trapping process," they write, "kept almost everyone in line. Public doubters would be pounced on by the press. Bureaucratic skeptics would risk their careers. Various public figures vied with each other to explain the importance of Vietnam to the American people. And the people seemed to be believers too."[15]

The U.S. foreign-policy decision-making process does a poor job of filtering out the effects of misperceptions about the outside world. The process is in one sense open, set within a democratic political system and thus vulnerable to all of the inaccuracies in public beliefs. It is in another sense closed, relying on small decision-making circles with a strong sense of mutual loyalty and thus vulnerable to the groupthink that tends to characterize such circles. Lyndon Johnson's circle, in which major decisions on the Vietnam War were made, was one of the principal inspirations for psychologist Irving Janis's development of the concept of groupthink.[16] U.S. administrations' decision-making styles have varied through the years, but four decades after Johnson's decision to go into Vietnam a decision to launch a war in Iraq was even more closed—so closed that there was no policy process at all.[17]

In the United States, the heavy use of political appointees to fill positions at echelons below the top decision makers further weakens whatever check the bureaucracy may have on the decision makers' oversimplifying, short-cutting thought processes, in addition to politicizing the bureaucracy's output.[18] The practice reduces overall professionalism in government. It also establishes a tension in which policy officials are inclined to perform end runs around the professional bureaucracy rather than to use it fully.[19]

Some observers have had difficulty finding direct evidence of public opinion influencing U.S. foreign policy.[20] But this difficulty almost certainly reflects how much policy makers share, internalize, and preemptively allow for public beliefs. The more common scholarly judgment is that public opinion has played a greater role in developing foreign and security policy in the United States than it has in almost any other country.[21]

Major changes in U.S. foreign policy most often involve the rejection of one conventional wisdom in favor of a different conventional wisdom.[22] The influence of the American experience and American culture on American conventional wisdom matters a great deal because it profoundly shapes the perceptions and thus the policies of those who make decisions on behalf of the world's superpower. This fact is too rarely understood; the textbook model of how government ought to operate—in which decision makers get their images of the outside world from an intelligence bureaucracy—is mistakenly assumed to be how it *does* operate.

PAST AND PRESENT ORIGINS
OF THE AMERICAN OUTLOOK

A combination of geography, history, and politics has carved the American prism. The process started with the nation's happy circumstance of having grown up on a continent that is rich in resources, climatologically blessed, and separated by two oceans from most of the world's troubles. This situation has in turn shaped a particular pattern of involvement with the outside world punctuated by wartime forays into other parts of the globe. The physical circumstances and the history have molded a distinctive domestic political experience, which in turn has become yet another ingredient in the culture that has molded the American outlook. The environment that surrounds the people of any nation influences their thinking insofar as it affects what they *believe* to be the nature of that environment, and their beliefs are shaped by their predispositions to view the world in some ways rather than in other ways.[23] But the predispositions themselves are in part shaped by the nation's history and culture.

The combination of experience and environment colors in two basic ways how Americans perceive what is going on in the rest of the world. One way has to do with current circumstances: the environment of today. There has not been enough continental drift since the colonial era to change the most important geographic facts about the United States. Technology obviously has affected some of the implications of those facts but has not erased the most important ones. Current circumstances also include how the American political system works today and the unsurpassed power that the U.S. superpower wields today.

At least as important as current circumstances is the cumulative effect of the nation's earlier history. That effect is intrinsic to the concept of culture, which involves beliefs and habits that are transferred from generation to generation. The experiences of previous generations of Americans have much to do with how today's Americans think and how they perceive the outside world. The evolution of the national culture is analogous in this respect to the evolution of the human brain. Psychologists tell us that much of the operation of our own brains reflects the needs and experiences of our Pleistocene ancestors.[24] Political culture, which acts as a sort of evolving national brain with regard to how members of that culture think, has similarly delayed effects.

American political culture and the outlook toward the outside world that goes with it demonstrate remarkable continuity in the sense both that today's outlook is rooted in yesterday's experiences and that many aspects of that outlook reappear throughout U.S. history. And yet most Americans have little awareness of this continuity. That lack of awareness is itself a distinctly American trait.[25] Simple ignorance of history is involved, to the extent that professional historians lament how this lack of knowledge afflicts not only the general public but also decision-making elites and how it leads to misuse of historical analogies when those decision makers do invoke history.[26] This ignorance is associated with an American proclivity to overestimate the newness of things, ranging from fascination with gadgets in everyday lives to a tendency to perceive foreign-policy problems faced today as being unlike any that have been faced in the past.[27] This proclivity is rooted in the fact that the United States is part of the New World. More specifically, it is rooted in a pragmatism that began with colonization that had many different motives—and thus did not involve importing any one ideology from the Old World—and was further developed in addressing the many practical problems of living on a frontier.[28]

The turning away from Old World ideologies was an early step toward difficulty in understanding foreign behavior and foreign issues that involve those ideologies. But this turning away did not mean that America would be a perfectly pragmatic, ideology-free land. It meant instead there was a mostly blank slate on which an American ideology could be quietly, even silently, written and form the basis for a distinctly American way of looking at the world without Americans being self-conscious about how they were looking at it.[29] Aspects of the ideology became part of conventional wisdom and part of national myths. All nations have myths, which are mainly about the nation itself but also have implications for how other nations and peoples are viewed. American myths, taken for granted by Americans and rarely the subject of national introspection, operate at least as much at an unconscious level as do the myths of other nations.[30] The paucity of self-awareness makes the distorting effects of American national myth and ideology all the greater because of a lack of conscious effort to correct for the effects.

The uniformity of thinking that underlies the automatic acceptance of American myth and conventional wisdom also underlies another tendency in American thought that impedes understanding of foreign countries. Although Americans may think of themselves as more pragmatic than ideological, they are, as Alexis de Tocqueville observed, "much more addicted to the use of general ideas than the English."[31] By "general ideas," he meant ones applicable to all humankind. Tocqueville attributed this pattern to America's being a democratic country, by which he meant one exhibiting equality. With relatively little variation among Americans, he suggested, there is little awareness of how much variation there can be between Americans and non-Americans—or, rather, in the situations they confront. This lack of awareness leads to the tendency that Kennan and Hartz noted about the application of American standards to non-Americans and to a general obtuseness regarding non-Americans' different wants, needs, and fears.

SHAPING PERCEPTIONS

No single factor explains everything about how Americans perceive the world or even most of what needs to be explained. That is as true of the subject of this book—the influence of the peculiarly American experience on those perceptions—as it is of other explanations. One can find additional explanations, for example, at the broader level of how leaders of any great power, not just the United States, tend to see the world working.[32] Other explanations are found at the narrower level of personal rather than national experiences. The views of individual members of Johnson's circle of Vietnam War decision makers were in part shaped by their particular professional experiences in earlier years.[33] Narrowing down further to the topmost decision makers, including U.S. presidents, persuasive explanations of presidential thinking have been based on that particular leader's neuroses and idiosyncrasies.[34] The collective American experience, however, has had a peculiar and powerful influence on perceptions held by Americans. It does not explain everything, but it explains a great deal.

The psychological research mentioned earlier hints at another set of explanations of how human minds in general, not just American minds, work in ways that cut corners and introduce cognitive errors. Some of those errors, as applied to international relations, are so systematic they can be the subject of generalizations about how decision makers in any country tend to perceive what other countries are up to.[35] But the psychological research itself points to the important role of nation-specific perspectives. Philip Tetlock, who has studied why expert political judgments are often wrong, clarifies why even experts do not always carefully recalculate their appraisals in the face of new evidence. A plausible explanation, says Tetlock, "is that we are naturally egocentric. In sizing up situations, we have difficulty taking other points of view seriously."[36] In sizing up situations outside their country, Americans often have difficulty taking non-American points of view seriously.

The peculiar American national experience thus interacts with humankind-wide cognitive tendencies in ways that, if we take both into account, provide fuller explanations than either could by itself. Universally applicable mental habits lead to the use of short-cuts; the specific national experience provides material from which the short-cut is built. The former helps to explain why perceptual errors are introduced; the latter explains much of the substance of the errors.

Not everything about a nation's or an individual's experience shapes later perceptions. There is simply too much in any one national or personal history for that to be the case. The mind unconsciously selects only some of the enormous amount of new information available as the basis for forming beliefs and judgments. Emotion has much to do with the selection process; it helps to determine what information is focused upon when statespersons make decisions about war and peace and when a citizenry supports or opposes such decisions.[37] Similarly, episodes in a nation's experience that are especially dramatic or traumatic—that is, evoke emotion—are most apt to provide material for the mental constructs that shape later perceptions. The basis for American perceptions surrounding recent wars can be found in large part in America's experience with earlier wars.

Anything that shapes a perception and is extraneous to the object being perceived can cause distortion and error. Some of the distortion is inevitable; preconception of some sort is needed to handle new information, and any preconception is an oversimplification. But the more idiosyncratic the basis for preconception, the more likely there will be misperception. The American experience that is the basis for how Americans see the world is idiosyncratic. The United States is more different from the rest of the world than is any other country, and that is a prime reason its citizens have difficulty in understanding the rest of the world.

Not only is the United States very different, but before it became a global power, it also had little of the sort of close and continuous interaction or competition with other countries that would have challenged American ideology and American conventional wisdom. Of course, since the United States became a global power, there has been much interaction, but these increased relations have occurred only after the United States had become so strong that the interaction has been mostly on American terms for specific American purposes, including most notably and intensely in foreign wars. Those interactions have chiseled one more facet on the American prism rather than leading to rejection of the picture projected by the entire prism. Globalization and the information revolution also have reduced the effects of geographic separation, but again on American terms. The Internet is an American creation, global pop culture is disproportionately American culture, and English is the closest thing the world has to a lingua franca. There are, in addition, the lagging effects of culturally engrained habits of thought that date from earlier American history, before the United States was a globally engaged power. Thus, today Americans and the media that they mostly read and listen to are still cognitively isolated even from other economically advanced liberal democracies.[38] Latter-day global engagement has increased the consequences of how Americans perceive the rest of the world while doing little to correct the misperceptions.

UNCORRECTED IGNORANCE

Americans today feel less need than most other people to cultivate the skills and to practice the habits that would help to correct misperceptions about the outside world. Foreign-language ability, given the ease of using English in much of the world, is one measure of this attitude. According to the U.S. Department of Education, as of 2002 only 44 percent of American high school students were enrolled in foreign-language classes. Less than 8 percent of American college undergraduates were taking foreign-language courses.[39] The associated low level of foreign-language ability in the American public was reflected in a Gallup poll indicating that only about one-fourth of Americans could converse in any language other than English.[40] Among that one-fourth, the other language for 55 percent of them was Spanish—no doubt reflecting Hispanic ethnicity of a large proportion of the respondents, for many of whom Spanish was actually a first language rather than a second. Because a poll registers only self-reported proficiency, the actual foreign-language proficiency may be even less.

The contrast with language ability in other countries, especially other developed countries, is pronounced. The head of the American Council on the Teaching of Foreign Languages says Americans are "at the bottom" of the world in foreign-language ability.[41] According to polls conducted for the European Commission, 54 percent of Europeans can hold a conversation in a language other than their native tongue. The European Union has a goal that every citizen have practical skills in at least two foreign languages; one-quarter of all Europeans already meet that standard to the point of being able to converse in two languages other than their native one.[42]

Foreign travel produces less stark but somewhat similar patterns. Americans take about 63 million trips outside the United States each year. Without further analysis and comparisons, this number sounds like a great deal. But more than half of those trips are to Canada or Mexico,[43] and of the 30 million trips taken elsewhere, many represent repeat travel by the same individuals, usually for business. According to one calculation, somewhere between 11.6 million and 14.6 million Americans traveled abroad in 2009, usually just visiting one country.[44] Compare these numbers with those from Germany, whose citizens took 76 million foreign trips of at least one night in 2007. It is impossible to tell how many different Germans traveled, but given the small proportion of the trips that were for business (9 million), there was not much repeat travel by businesspersons.[45] These greater numbers are from a country whose total population is barely more than one-quarter that of the United States.

The combination of distinctively American influences that distort perceptions and weak interactions of the sort that help to correct misperceptions yields profound and widespread American public ignorance about the outside world. Some of this ignorance can be interpreted as just one more instance of general public lack of knowledge about anything that extends beyond personal experience and popular culture and that embraces public affairs both foreign and domestic. The ignorance sometimes applies to public-policy issues that straddle the foreign and domestic realms. In a poll in 2010 that asked American respondents what percentage of the federal budget went toward foreign aid, the mean answer was 27 percent and the median was 25 percent. When asked what proportion of the budget *should* go to that purpose, the mean response was 13 percent and the median was 10 percent.[46] The actual proportion of the budget that goes for this purpose is less than one percent.

Where Americans most measurably lag behind others is in the area of simple facts about the world. A survey in 2012 asked American high school graduates ages eighteen to twenty-four to match eight names with their respective roles. Eighty-three percent could identify Mark Zuckerberg as the founder of Facebook, but only 59 percent knew Muammar Qadhafi was the recently deposed leader of Libya; 44 percent could identify Ban Ki-Moon as the United Nations secretary-general, and 34 percent named David Cameron as the leader of the United Kingdom.[47] (Someone totally ignorant of any of these people, even Mark Zuckerberg, and who merely guessed would have had a 12.5 percent chance of answering correctly.)

Other surveys have repeatedly demonstrated Americans' comparatively dismal knowledge of world geography. In one such survey in 2006 of Americans between ages eighteen and twenty-four, 47 percent could not find the Indian subcontinent on a map of Asia. Given a map of the Middle East, six out of ten people could not locate Iraq, and 75 percent could not find Israel.[48] In a similar survey in 2002, Americans in this age group were matched against counterparts in eight other countries. The Americans ranked second to last, outscoring only Mexicans.[49]

QUALIFICATIONS AND CAVEATS

Americans are not the only people whose views of outsiders are heavily colored by national history and culture. Other examples of perception-shaping national mythology are easy to find, either of the negative and tragic sort or of the positive and grandiose sort. Serbian national mythology, for example, fixates on the Serbian defeat in the Battle of Kosovo in 1389 and affects how today's Serbs view Muslims. Examples of the grandiose variety include Iranian self-perceptions rooted in the glories of an ancient Persian Empire and China as the center of the world as in the old Chinese concept of the Middle Kingdom. What is distinctive about the United States, however, makes the American variety of this phenomenon at least as pronounced as any other. In any event, the American variety is the one that matters most for U.S. interests and U.S. policy.

Nor does a single homogeneous ideology characterize how all Americans gaze at the world. Walter Russell Mead's brilliant book *Special Provi-*

dence: American Foreign Policy and How It Changed the World explores different traditions whose interplay defines the thinking underlying U.S. foreign policy. But each of these traditions itself is firmly grounded in American history and in distinctive aspects of the American experience. And each embodies patterns of thought that can encourage misperception, such as a Wilsonian tendency to overestimate the impact of democratic politics on a foreign country's external policies or a Jacksonian tendency to miss nuances while believing that even complicated problems have simple solutions.[50]

Other patterns of thought in America that supplement or cross-cut some of Mead's traditions exhibit similar distorting effects. There is, for example, what Richard Hofstadter called the "paranoid style in American politics," which he emphasized is not unique to the United States but, being a form of paranoia, by definition involves a distorted perception of threats, including foreign ones.[51] Of greater significance in the United States today is a primitive nationalism that resides chiefly in the Republican Party and is where most of the strident type of American exceptionalism mentioned earlier can be found. Anatol Lieven, who has studied this phenomenon closely, observes that this type of nationalism has given its adherents "an essentially mythological version not only of their country's history and role in the world—which is standard for most nationalisms—but of their existing society and economy. This nationalist mythology is not rooted in reality, and indeed is strikingly impervious to it."[52] This outlook was unabashedly confirmed by an anonymous aide to President George W. Bush, who noted that he and his colleagues were pleased not to be part of the "reality-based community" and said, "We're an empire now, and when we act, we create our own reality."[53]

Differences among schools of thought manifest themselves chiefly in different preferred policies, even if underlying perceptions about the outside world—our topic here—do not differ as sharply. Just as debates between imperialists and isolationists at the beginning of the twentieth century unfolded within a shared set of American exceptionalist assumptions, much debate today about where the United States should engage or withdraw is waged by opposing sides whose habits in perceiving and understanding the world have more in common with each other than the heat of the debates might suggest. Hartz noted in the mid-1950s that the distinctive American ethos he described can lead to either messianism or isolationism, with a tendency to oscillate between the two. "An absolute national morality," he wrote, "is inspired either to withdraw from 'alien' things or to transform them: it cannot live in comfort constantly by their side."[54] Most Americans share characteristically American ways of understanding—or misunderstanding—alien things, even as they disagree among themselves about the best posture to take toward aliens.

Perceptions that guide U.S. foreign policy are not an unrelenting cascade of mistaken beliefs—far from it. As strong as the specifically American distorting influences are, they still are only one set of influences. The United States could not have been as successful in the world as it has been if its lucky circumstances had not been joined to some clear-headed formulation of its policies. And clear-headed policy making requires clear and reasonably accurate images of the situations overseas that the policy is intended to confront. It is always possible to overcome the distorting effects of the American prism. The United States has had some clear-thinking leaders who have managed to do that at critical moments in the nation's history, as well as those bureaucracies with the mission of providing accurate images of the outside world.

Statements in the remainder of this book about what "Americans" think, perceive, or believe should be taken as referring to tendencies that appear in much of the thought of many citizens of the United States insofar as those thoughts are influenced by living in the United States and being part of its culture. Obviously not all Americans think in the specified way, nor are the thoughts of any one American determined wholly by national and cultural influences. The tendencies involved are not necessarily the most important influence in the formation of any one perception. But the tendencies are strong and significant.

To the extent that U.S. foreign policy has been based on accurate perceptions of the world abroad, this connection has more often been made in spite of, not because of, the peculiar tinge that the peculiar American experience imparts to such perceptions. Whatever good there is in what makes America exceptional, this is part of what is bad. This is why clear-headed thinking sometimes has difficulty prevailing. This is why when clear think-ing does prevail, it often does so only after a struggle to overcome clouded and mistaken beliefs. This is one reason why such beliefs are more prevalent in America than otherwise should be expected in an economically advanced country with a well-educated population. And it is one of the reasons why some U.S. policies, based on erroneous views of the outside world, fail. Minimizing such failure requires Americans to become more conscious of what has affected their images of the outside world, which in turn requires examination of the specific ways in which the American experience shapes those images—the subject of the chapters that follow.

2

BEHIND THE OCEAN MOATS

T HE SPECIAL SITUATION of the United States begins with its particular location on the planet, far removed from any significant and physically proximate threats. Tocqueville put at the top of his list of "accidental and providential causes which contribute to the maintenance of the democratic republic in the United States" his observation that "the Americans have no neighbors," which among other things meant they had no "conquest to dread."[1] For most of the nation's history, this physical separation has been a prime determinant of its security and one of the biggest differences from other countries' security situations. The separation was the major reason that, as the historian C. Vann Woodward observed, for much of U.S. history the country's security was not only effective but free.[2] One can find hints elsewhere of how even modest geographic separation colors national thinking about security and international relations, especially in how the island nation of Great Britain has seen advantages in an aloofness that has not been an option for continental European powers. But the barrier of the English Channel, which William the Conqueror breached in the eleventh century and which narrows to only twenty-one miles at the Strait of Dover, is minor compared to the thousands of miles of ocean that lie astride the United States.

THE NORTH AMERICAN REDOUBT

The United States does have its neighbors Mexico and Canada, of course, and it has engaged in warfare along its border with each. Southern and northern neighbors were mostly irrelevant, however, until the United States had grown strong enough to become the dominant power on the continent. Before then, the patterns of settlement were too far away from each other to collide. When in 1807 Aaron Burr was tried (and acquitted) for treason involving a murky and bizarre scheme that may have envisioned carving chunks out of both Spanish Mexico and the southwestern United States, the comically fanciful nature of the alleged plot highlighted the absence of any real threat to the United States from within the continent. When Anglo and Hispanic settlement did begin to collide, it was left to freelancing Texans to do the heavy lifting, including defeat at the Alamo and victory at San Jacinto, leading to the establishment of an independent Texas, which was annexed only later by the United States.

War between the United States and Mexico, once it had become a possibility, was for Americans less a matter of defending against a threat than of seizing an opportunity. Although some minor offensive action by Mexican forces north of the Rio Grande helped to precipitate the U.S. declaration of war, American expansionism was the dominant theme in tensions leading to the war that broke out in 1846.[3] The military outcome was a swift and efficient U.S. victory, with American combat deaths in the entire war totaling only about half the number of those who would be killed in a single day on a Civil War battlefield at Antietam Creek. The political outcome was a huge U.S. annexation of territory. After that war, military threats coming out of Mexico were limited to some raids into the United States by Pancho Villa and lesser-known guerrillas in 1916, which were related to the Mexican Revolution at the time and in which about two dozen Americans were killed.

Americans' thinking today about security in connection with their southern border reflects not any major hazard to the integrity of the nation but instead one of the ways in which the safe and advantageous physical situation of the United States skews American thinking about threats. The paucity of major security dangers permits the luxury of exaggerating and politicizing minor ones. Immigration, specifically the stanching of illegal immigration out of Mexico, is much discussed, but that is a matter of labor markets and respect for the law rather than of a threat to security. Possible terrorist threats emanating from Latin America also get bursts of attention, sometimes with reference to the activities of Lebanese Hezbollah in Argentina.[4] Alarmism about terrorists of this ilk wading across the Rio Grande is driven in part by a desire to talk up threats supposedly associated with Iran and perhaps sometimes to add an argument in favor of making a greater effort to stem illegal immigration.[5] The closest thing today to a real threat of violence coming across the border from Mexico is spillover of the activity of Mexican drug cartels, but that threat is properly regarded more as a challenge for police than as a danger of possible conquest or military invasion.[6]

As for the neighbor to the north, Canada in its own right has never been a threat to the United States. In the early days of the republic, the concern was with Britain, the sovereign power in Canada at the time. The War of 1812, which was fought in large part along the U.S.–Canadian frontier, was sometimes referred to as the second war for independence for the United States. U.S. leaders at the beginning of the war viewed Canadian territory, which the British garrisoned only lightly, less as a source of threat than as a target for capture—perhaps with annexation in mind, but more as a prize of war and a bargaining chip.[7] Other action in the war included the British attack on Washington, which was not an attempt at reconquest but rather a punitive raid, and the war's final engagement at New Orleans, which was a clear American victory.

Not long after the war, British power and especially naval power became a benevolent force for the United States. With a shared interest in preventing meddling in the New World by other European powers, the Royal Navy in effect enforced the Monroe Doctrine. Meanwhile, by the time the Canadian federation was formed in 1867, any warfare between Americans and Canadians had become inconceivable. It has long been a cliché, but one with significance, that these two countries share the world's longest undefended border.

Geographic separation from the Old World contributed in other ways to security of the U.S. homeland during the nineteenth and early twentieth centuries. At the republic's most vulnerable time during the Civil War, the isolation precluded what otherwise could have been destructive and decisive interference by European powers. The isolation also made it possible to receive great waves of immigrants, which brought growth to the country and the economy with little fear of thereby making the United States vulnerable to manipulation by a foreign neighbor.

From the Battle of New Orleans until World War I, the continental United States was untouched and unthreatened by overseas forces. This century of immunity profoundly influenced how Americans think about national security and about threats that one nation can pose to another. It was a century in which the republic went from adolescence to maturity. Many of the habits of perception Americans acquired during this large chunk of their history, regarding the outside world and how their country relates to it, endure to this day.

Even at the end of that century, physical vulnerability to outside threats was slow in coming. In the predawn darkness of July 18, 1918, a German U-boat surfaced off Orleans, Massachusetts, and used its deck gun to fire at watercraft in the harbor, sinking a tugboat. A few shells reached land, hitting harmlessly in a marsh and on a beach—the only enemy rounds to strike the United States in World War I. There were no human casualties from the encounter.

In World War II, Germany again employed submarines to try to reach the U.S. homeland, this time using them on three occasions to transport teams of saboteurs. The missions failed completely, with the leaders of the teams turning themselves in before any sabotage was carried out. In the Pacific part of the war, Japan, of course, administered a severe and shocking blow with its attack on Pearl Harbor. But Hawaii at the time was a possession in Polynesia, not a part of the United States itself. Alaska also was only a territory when Japan fought over and occupied for more than a year the Aleutian islands of Attu and Kiska, which are farther from the west coast of the United States than they are from Japan.

Concern about what Japan might do to the U.S. homeland during the war underlay the unconscionable internment of Japanese Americans and the construction of gun emplacements—the remnants of which one can visit today—to protect cities such as San Diego and San Francisco. The guns never had to be used, and Japan was scarcely able to do any more against the U.S. homeland than the Germans did. Japanese submarines shelled a military base in Oregon and an oil field in California, causing only minimal damage at each, and a submarine-launched aircraft unsuccessfully tried twice to start forest fires. During the last year of the war, Japan also sent adrift across the Pacific thousands of balloons carrying incendiary devices, again in a vain attempt to ignite widespread forest fires. On May, 5, 1945, six people on a Sunday school picnic in Oregon came across one of the devices, still unexploded. When they picked it up, it detonated and killed them, making them the only casualties in the continental United States from enemy action during World War II.

Even in this deadliest and most widespread war in human history, in which some 50 million people perished worldwide and the United States sustained more than 400,000 deaths in combat overseas, the ocean moats worked.

HABITS OF THREAT PERCEPTION

In the past sixty years, the long-range bomber and then the intercontinental ballistic missile have increased the physical vulnerability of the United States. Change in American thinking about security threats, however, has lagged behind the technological change. The long period of invulnerability ingrained in Americans certain habits of thinking about threats and about America's place in the world that persist today. The persistence is a large-scale example of how preexisting mental frameworks can trump new information and new circumstances.

Another influence on American thinking about modern weapons with intercontinental range is a tendency to compartmentalize this danger and to associate it with the Cold War, which has come and gone. This compartmentalization is indicated by how quickly American public fears about such weapons dissipated once the Soviet Union collapsed, even though as of 2013 Russia still had about 1,800 strategic nuclear weapons.[8] Fallout shelters and duck-and-cover exercises in schools have become quaint bits of history about which Americans of a certain age tell their children and grandchildren. The quick shoving away of concern about nuclear war into a seldom-examined mental attic dismays the publisher of the *Bulletin of the Atomic Scientists*, who directs attention to the doomsday clock on the *Bulletin*'s cover, intended, she says, "to inform people about the dangers that we still face from the nuclear bombs, the nuclear legacy, and the nuclear material that's still out there."[9] The journal's effort may be largely in vain. The American public had already in the 1980s begun to lower significantly its assessment of the nuclear weapons threat, even though the doomsday clock was registering then a danger at least as great as it did in the late 1960s and most of the 1970s.[10] When in its regular biennial survey the Chicago Council on Global Affairs asked Americans to name the top two or three foreign-policy problems facing the United States, "nuclear war/freeze" still got a 9 percent response in 1983, but by 1995 nothing related to nuclear war made it onto the list at all.[11]

Current American public perceptions about threats coming not from the other Cold War superpower but from rogue states and others exhibit a different dynamic. As discussed in chapter 5, a national need for bogeymen leads more to inflation than deflation of perceived threats coming from such sources, including threats with a nuclear weapons dimension. This is certainly true of perceptions about Iran, which has not even decided to build a nuclear weapon and may never acquire a delivery system with intercontinental range.[12] It is true to a lesser degree of North Korea, which does have nuclear weapons but is far away from having delivery systems that can propel them to the continental United States.[13] The point to note for now is that any threat from such antagonists has not fundamentally altered characteristic American thinking about geopolitics and long-term vulnerability. Instead, the problem now, as it was with the Soviet Union of the Cold War, is viewed as having limited duration and involving confrontation with particular malevolent regimes and is expected to go away once these regimes go away.

Something similar is true of American thinking about terrorism, a subject of significant perceptual distortion that is also addressed later. A frequent comment is that the terrorist attacks on September 11, 2001 (9/11), dispelled an American sense of invulnerability. These attacks certainly administered an enormous jolt to the American psyche that has had major implications for national policies and priorities. We are still too close to that event, however, to appreciate how it does or does not figure into larger and longer-term American habits of thinking about threats and vulnerability. These attacks, spectacular though they were, did not mark any real change in the vulnerability of the American homeland as the development of the long-range bomber or the intercontinental ballistic missile did. To the extent that terrorism, including terrorism fomented by foreigners, is a threat, it has been around much longer than strategic nuclear forces. American concern about it has been around longer as well, exemplified by the terrorism component of the Red Scare of nearly a century ago. The level of American public and political concern about terrorism has oscillated widely, depending not only on how much a recent lucky shot by terrorists has grabbed attention but also on prevailing political moods and how they shape sentiments about particular ideologies underlying terrorism.[14]

Perhaps American public sentiment about terrorism is now gradually converging with the reality that even a spectacular lucky shot does not change the fundamental facts about vulnerability. As a single shocking event recedes in time, attitudes shaped by centuries of history and immutable geographic facts come back into focus. American preoccupation with terrorism has already faded significantly in little more than a decade following 9/11, as indicated by how much some measures taken by government agencies in the name of counterterrorism—such as the National Security Agency's collection of data on telephone calls within the United States—that would have raised few eyebrows in the first couple of years after 9/11 have become subjects of public and political controversy.

In short, American perceptions toward the outside world have in large part taken shape—bearing in mind the entire course of U.S. history—in an environment mostly free from significant and continuing threats from other states. That factor alone sets the United States apart from other major powers. It is a significant reason its citizens tend to perceive the world in idiosyncratic ways.

Contrast this aspect of the American experience with, for example, that of China, the former Middle Kingdom and a large and powerful state that might have other reasons to approach the world in ways similar to those of the United States. For part of its early history China could be said to have enjoyed some physical isolation, with mountains, deserts, the sea, and sheer distance working in its favor. But even centuries ago there were persistent and serious threats from the north, to which the Great Wall, built to defend against those threats, is a monument. In World War II, much of China was occupied by an imperialist power that resided not far off the Asian mainland. Since then China has had a border war and smaller military clashes with other major powers—India and Russia, which are two of the fourteen countries with which it shares land boundaries. This geopolitical situation is far different from that of the United States.

BELIEF IN FOREORDAINED BLESSEDNESS

Geographic isolation and the security that has come with it are among several fortunate circumstances of the United States (the next chapter addresses others) that Americans have long noticed and noted. Thomas Jefferson referred in his first Inaugural Address to how the country he had been chosen to lead was "kindly separated by nature and a wide ocean from the exterminating havoc of one quarter of the globe."[15] Although noticed, however, this happy circumstance became so seamlessly incorporated into the American consciousness that it came to be regarded as part of the natural order of things. Any departure from the presumed natural order thus tends to elicit discombobulation and overreaction. This helps to explain the extent of the immediate shock of the 9/11 attacks and why most Americans overestimated on September 12 the threat that international terrorism posed to their security even if they had underestimated it two days earlier.[16] The threat itself had not suddenly increased; if anything, it had decreased in the sense that an attack that had been in the offing was, once executed, now in the past.

What Americans have seen in their country's splendid isolation is unique to the United States as well as being part of a larger natural order. This combination of specific American attributes and a more general worldview is part of what American exceptionalism is all about and why it distorts perceptions. It encourages the idea that there are some rules that apply to everyone else but not to the United States. This notion in turn has diverse consequences that go beyond issues of the homeland's physical vulnerability.

The idea of a natural order moves easily to the concept of historical inevitability and foreordination. The latter concept recurs throughout the history of American discourse about America's blessed situation. The concept often attributes that situation to providence. Many Americans more religiously minded than the deist Jefferson would be more inclined than he to attribute the "kindly separation" explicitly to divine will. This idea fits especially comfortably into the religiously infused worldview of the 46 percent of Americans who, according to a Gallup poll in 2012, believe in a biblically literal version of creationism.[17]

The idea of historical ordination, whether expressed in religious or in secular terms, as applied to the peculiarly fortunate physical situation of the United States affects in several ways how Americans tend to view the world and the place of the United States in it. Foreordained invulnerability in the homeland slides readily into the idea of invulnerability, or at least success, in other respects as well. The nation's happy location behind the ocean moats is thus an ingredient in innate, persistent American optimism.[18] That optimism has driven and sustained many positive U.S. accomplishments in the world. It also has contributed to overestimation of the prospects of success in other U.S. endeavors overseas, including offensive wars.

The notion that something as fundamental as national security rests mainly on a blessed and predetermined national condition that Americans ought simply to recognize and enjoy dulls the senses regarding other ingredients in security. It makes it harder to learn the lesson that security today is not free and does not grow on trees, even North American ones. Reliance on divine will leads to underestimating the importance of human will, including the will of non-Americans. George Kennan noted how this perceptual shortcoming was especially marked at the end of the nineteenth century, when Americans "had become so accustomed to their security that they had forgotten that it had any foundations at all outside our continent. They mistook our sheltered position behind the British fleet and British continental diplomacy for the results of superior American wisdom and virtue in refraining from interfering in the sordid differences of the Old World."[19] Beginning in the subsequent century, the presumption of superior wisdom and virtue underlay less often a withdrawal behind the ocean moats and more often an application of American power to presumably less-virtuous realms overseas.

DIVIDING HOME FROM THE WORLD ABROAD

Geographic separation has facilitated the perceived stark division between a wise and virtuous America and a rest of the world with more negative attributes. Americans have no monopoly on egocentrism, but the physical division between the homeland and other lands has lessened the ability of events to challenge egocentrically based misperceptions. The domestic world and the foreign world are more distinct for Americans than they are for most non-Americans.

This is one of the important respects in which the United States differs from continental Europe, where multiple nationalities, political systems, and religious affiliations overlap in a mottled quilt and where boundaries have frequently changed. Whatever physical attractions Europe has, its human geography is akin to a crowded communal living area in which distinctions between private and public space break down. A European creation, the Peace of Westphalia of 1648, is a landmark in establishing the concept of state sovereignty and embodied the principle that the religious affiliation of any one state is not supposed to be the next state's business. Nonetheless, distinctions between what is foreign and what is domestic have repeatedly broken down in the subsequent centuries of European history. Land and people have shifted from one sovereign to another as empires have come and gone and wars have been won and lost. Foreign and domestic threats have become meshed together as internal upheavals have become intertwined with external conflicts, as exemplified by the wars of the French Revolution. Sovereignty itself has been shifting and uncertain as supranational fixtures from the Holy Roman Empire to the European Union have been overlaid on states. America has had none of this, which is why the national homeland has a special place and sanctity in American thinking that is not found to nearly the same degree in Europeans' thoughts.[20]

The exceptionally sharp distinction between the homeland and everywhere else sustains not only an inflated perception of the wisdom and virtue of those who dwell in the former but also a contrastingly deflated perception of many who dwell in the latter. The view that anything outside America is not only messy but iniquitous underpins much of how Americans perceive the world abroad. In some respects, the closest comparison to this sort of dichotomy and to the value-laden qualities associated with what is on each side of the split is the Islamic concept of a world divided into *dar al-Islam* (the domain of Islam) and *dar al-harb* (the domain of war and chaos), but the defining distinction here is religious affiliation rather than a nation-state.

The American version of this dichotomous view of the world has at times underlain isolationism and the idea that it would be best for the United States to stay aloof from the lands of war and chaos. More often, especially in modern U.S. history, similar perceptions have supported the concept that intervention by the United States in parts of the world that are less wise and less virtuous than America can result only in the betterment of those less-advanced domains. Here the closer comparison is with European colonization and its rationales, including France's *mission civilisatrice* and Britain's white man's burden. The Englishman Rudyard Kipling, who had lived for several years in Vermont, began to write his poem "The White Man's Burden" with Queen Victoria's diamond jubilee in mind but eventually published it with a subtitle indicating it was about the United States taking possession of the Philippines.[21] Today Britain's empire is no more, and there are only hints of the French one in France's continued involvement with some of its former African colonies. The United States is the global imperial power, and there remains a strong American tendency to assume that the exercise of U.S. power in places less enlightened than America means the betterment of those places and the people who live there.

The idea of the United States conducting a civilizing mission in less civilized parts of the world was a major strand in American thinking about the annexations, including that of the Philippines, at the end of the Spanish-American War.[22] After the war, President William McKinley told a group of Methodist clergymen visiting the White House how he had prayed and paced the floor at night when trying to determine what to do with the Philippines, which military victory had placed in U.S. hands. He said that after dismissing the alternatives he finally decided "that there was nothing left for us to do but to take them all, and to educate the Filipinos, and uplift and Christianize them, and by God's grace do the very best we could by them, as our fellow men for whom Christ had died. And then I went to bed, and went to sleep and slept soundly."[23]

The annexations put the United States into the colonialism business and marked the beginning of a series of bureaucratic experiments in how to run the business.[24] It was, however—and still is—against American nature to call any of this activity "colonialism." The United States itself, after all, owes its existence to a group of colonies shaking off imperial rule. The idea of the United States as being on the anticolonial side of issues involving colonialism is a deeply engrained part of the American self-image. In any perceived division of the world between the enlightened and the backward, colonizers (insofar as they are colonizers, even if they might be friends and allies in other respects) are assigned to the latter camp along with the colonized. In this context, Americans could still view favorably their takeover of territories from the Spaniards because they perceived the takeover as removing those territories *from* the hands of an Old World colonizer.

The anticolonial self-perception is a thread running through much of U.S. history. The Latin American wars of independence in the early nineteenth century could be viewed benevolently as following the North

American colonies' lead. The Monroe Doctrine was an assertion of opposition to any effort by continental Europeans to reverse that process (with the role of the Royal Navy conveniently overlooked or downplayed). During World War II, Franklin Roosevelt vocally opposed reestablishment of French colonial rule in Southeast Asia once the war was won (although he was much more lukewarm about Dutch rule in the East Indies).[25] The American self-image has required the use of an alternative vocabulary to refer to any U.S. activity that resembles the imperialism and colonialism of others. The U.S. military has come up with the term *phase IV* to refer to tasks after the main battle that involve occupation and stabilization. When the George W. Bush administration established the Office of Reconstruction and Stabilization in the State Department, only some irreverent critics referred to it as the "colonial office."

Vocabulary matters, in part because of how it affects what the users of it perceive or fail to perceive. A national self-image that places the United States apart from European imperialism encourages Americans to overlook aspects of U.S. activities overseas that resemble what the European colonizers have done. Roosevelt opposed reassertion of French colonial role in Indochina not so much because of genuine opposition to colonialism but rather because he thought the French had been lousy colonial masters. In July 1943, he told a meeting of the Pacific War Council (the Allied group overseeing the war in the Pacific), "The French had been there for nearly one hundred years and had done absolutely nothing with the place to improve the lot of its people." The alternative he favored, which he called "trusteeship," was very much in line with the colonial idea of long-term tutelage of a backward people. Roosevelt cited as a model the Philippines, where the United States took possession in 1898 but did not set a date for independence until 1933, and even then the date set was 1945.[26] The underlying American view of Indochina as a place that could overcome its backwardness only through American guidance lingered through the intense U.S. involvement there, when Lyndon Johnson would describe North Vietnam as a "raggedy-ass little fourth-rate country" and a "piss-ant" nation.[27]

There may not have been formal establishment of U.S. colonies by that name, but other forms of political, economic, and at times military behavior by the United States have constituted a type of imperialism comparable to the European variety in the eyes of many people affected by that behavior. The perceptual shortcoming among Americans has been difficulty in understanding how and why other people see U.S. activities abroad this way. This shortcoming leads to a failure to anticipate the responses, including violent responses, that sometimes ensue from the unfavorable views that other people have of some U.S. endeavors. Those responses have run from the Filipino rebellion that lasted for several years after the United States took over the country from Spain to the insurgency and chaos in Iraq that were not part of the Bush administration's expectations when it invaded in 2003.

TERRORISM AS A FOREIGN PROBLEM

The exceptionally sharp division in the American worldview between what is foreign and what is domestic has also shaped American perceptions of terrorism. Americans, more so than Europeans and others, have viewed terrorism as overwhelmingly a foreign threat.[28] This has been the case not only with the ongoing wave of terrorism associated with religious extremists but also with earlier concerns about anarchists and leftists in the late nineteenth and early twentieth centuries, when the problem was seen as penetration of the United States by foreign radicals. The equation of terrorist threats with foreign threats is consistent with the overall American tendency to maintain a favorable, exceptionalist self-image in part by mentally projecting whatever is vile—and that certainly includes terrorism—beyond the nation's borders.

One resulting distortion in the collective American image of terrorism has been slowness in recognizing it as a subject worthy of U.S. attention rather than as a problem for foreigners to deal with. Theodore Roosevelt, who assumed the presidency when an anarchist assassinated his predecessor, was the first U.S. president to say something about the threat of international terrorism, but even in his time the United States stayed aloof from measures intended to do something about it, including measures agreed to at an international conference in St. Petersburg, Russia, in 1904. When terrorism claimed many more American victims in Lebanon in the 1980s, the subject received significant official attention, but in the American public mind it was still a foreign problem that America could avoid by avoiding the line of fire overseas.

A corollary of this pattern of thinking was the disinclination to apply the T-word to assorted radical violence in the United States in the 1970s and 1980s, even though other pejorative terms may have been used and much of the activity was akin to acts perpetrated by groups in Europe that European governments and publics had no hesitation in branding as terrorism. This disinclination facilitated inconsistency and ideological manipulation in application of the term *terrorism*—for example, violence against abortion clinics was officially characterized as terrorism when Democrats were in office but not when Republicans, with stronger anti-abortion sentiments, were in power.[29] Such conceptual confusion laid groundwork for the tendency, still evident in American discourse today, to regard terrorism erroneously not as a tactic that any violent person with a cause might use but instead as something that one particular ilk of foreigners, with one particular religious orientation, do.

The shock effect of the 9/11 attacks was accentuated by the prior relative public American inattention to terrorism and drastically increased that attention. But flawed perceptions of terrorism have continued to flow from the basic American perspective that terrorism cannot be a made-in-America problem. One flaw involves difficulty in fully appreciating the extent to which U.S. policies and relationships overseas have figured prominently in the motivations for anti-U.S. terrorism—as repeatedly indicated in the interrogations of captured perpetrators, claims of responsibility for attacks, and other statements by terrorist leaders.[30] A related shortcoming involves the influences that lead people within the United States, including U.S. citizens, to become terrorists. A natural American inclination is to think that these people have fallen under the spell of foreign, malevolent Pied Pipers. Relationships between individual American terrorists and foreign extremists have certainly existed, but in most cases that have come to light it was the American who took the initiative to create and maintain the relationship. Another inclination is to focus on training such individuals may receive from terrorist organizations abroad. Such training has occurred, but it has been an insignificant part of terrorists threats in the United States. Faisal Shahzad, a naturalized U.S. citizen of Pakistani origin who unsuccessfully attempted to detonate a firecracker-powered car bomb in Times Square in 2010, reportedly received training in northwestern Pakistan, but any such training was insufficient to make him a competent bomb builder.

In considering threats of home-grown Islamist terrorism, a reassuring but somewhat misleading thought—with enough basis for scholars to voice it but also growing out of the American view of America as too good a place to grow terrorists—is that Muslims in the United States are better integrated into society than their counterparts in many other countries with Muslim minorities. That is generally true, and the United States does not have the equivalent of the immigrant *banlieues* in France or the South Asian ghettos in Britain. But integration into the society, economy, and institutions of the United States is not the entire story as far as susceptibility to terrorism is concerned. For example, Nidal Hasan, perpetrator of a mass shooting at Fort Hood in 2009 and motivated by issues similar to those that have motivated other Islamist terrorists, was a U.S. Army major and psychiatrist, which is about as well integrated as one can be.

INSENSITIVITY TO THE FEARS OF OTHERS

The greatest perception-shaping consequence of the geographically separate and thus relatively secure U.S. situation is Americans' difficulty in appreciating the circumstances of countries not similarly blessed, which means most countries. Full understanding of the anarchical qualities of the international system and its implications comes more slowly to Americans and their leaders than it does to many of their foreign counterparts because that anarchy is not as much of a hazard to the United States as it is to others. Ironically, American political scientists have been in the forefront of explaining how the international system works, but knowledge within the academy seldom overcomes the stronger roots and more widespread influence of centuries of national experience.[31]

One concept related to international anarchy that is basic for political scientists but does not come naturally to Americans in general is the security dilemma: the sometimes dangerous situation in which steps one state might take to protect itself from what it regards as a foreign threat are seen as threatening by another state. That perception may prompt the second state to respond with steps the first state sees as threatening, leading to a spiral of instability and escalation. Security dilemmas can arise in a variety of situations, but classic instances resemble armed mobilization along a border between rival powers, with an archetype being the European crisis in the summer of 1914 that spiraled into World War I. India and Pakistan also have provided prime examples of a security dilemma more than once during their conflict-ridden history. The circumstances of the United States remove it geographically and thus conceptually far from anything like those cases.

The U.S. situation provides few reference points for Americans to understand the thoughts, calculations, perceptions, and actions of those abroad who confront security dilemmas or any kind of immediate and continuing threats. Nature's kindly separation is one of several respects in which the fortunate circumstances of the United States have deflected, or at least softened, for American statespersons many of the trade-offs and tough choices that others have had to face. Americans are thus slower than their foreign counterparts to recognize such trade-offs, especially ones that apply only to foreign states.[32] The slowness extends to understanding why other nations see threats where they do and why they take the decisions they do to respond or adapt to those threats. American failure in understanding takes the form either of unfavorably and unsympathetically interpreting the other country's actions or of being insensitive to the concerns that underlie the other country's policies.

Continental Europe again provides a sharp contrast to America's happy milieu. Those who have lived and made policy in Europe have done so in a crowded neighborhood filled with competing national aspirations and security dilemmas. The possession of provinces has been contested repeatedly, and a complex ethnic geography has fueled these contests. For many states, threats or potential threats have appeared at multiple azimuths. Smaller states have continually had to worry about how to adjust to the preferences of neighboring large ones, and the ambitions of the larger states have sometimes caused continent-wide disruption. All of this complexity has resulted in centuries of periodic warfare. Citizens and statespersons who have grown up in a culture shaped by those centuries of history and with corresponding ways of looking at the outside world come more naturally to some of the types of understanding that do not come naturally to Americans. It is no accident that the modern American statespersons who have been most adept with continental-style multipolar, all-azimuth, balance-of-power international politics have come out of that European milieu, including the German-born Heinz (later Henry) Kissinger and the Polish-born Zbigniew Brzezinski. They owe their orientation in this regard to their personal origins as well as to their political science training.

Europe has now moved beyond much of its past turmoil with its grand experiment in integration, which with the end of the Cold War has extended across the continent. That experiment itself has expanded the bounds of what Europeans can perceive more easily than most Americans, a subject to which we will return later. But the turmoil and the immediacy of threat were such a major part of the continent's history that the mental framework it left in the minds of Europeans has not been dismantled. Lurking behind European thinking about the integration experiment is awareness of what it replaced and what the continent might return to if the experiment fails.[33]

America's physical separation and the extra security that has come with it distinguish the United States even from countries that are major powers and the big fish in whatever pond they inhabit. Germany has had such a status for much of its history as a unified nation. Strong though it has been in comparison with its neighbors, its location at the center of the continent has carried with it worries about multiple immediate security threats and the specter of two-front wars. The diplomatic maestro Otto von Bismarck's way of coping with this situation was to create a complicated array of secret understandings and alliances intended to make every other country more dependent on Germany than Germany would be on the others. The arrangement was so complicated it had difficulty holding up after Bismarck's departure, but it worked for Germany as long as the maestro was around. The antithesis to Bismarck's approach was Woodrow Wilson's positing as the first of his Fourteen Points—his statement of war aims after the United States entered World War I—the principle of open covenants openly arrived at.[34] This principle reflected in part a broader American aversion to secrecy. It probably also reflected, however, a failure to appreciate fully not just what Bismarck had done but also why he had done it. Secrecy was an essential ingredient in Bismarck's system. Consistent with the open-covenants idea, Wilson believed that insofar as Germany was responsible for the war, it was not the German people who should be blamed but instead the "Prussian autocracy."[35] This perception reflected insensitivity to the geopolitical challenges that any German leader, Prussian autocrat or otherwise, necessarily faced from his seat in the middle of Europe.

While even the German Empire had to contend with security worries of the sort that the United States did not, the worries have been all the greater for lesser states. An archetypical example in preintegration Europe is Belgium. It is sandwiched between more powerful neighbors who at various times have eyed it either as a target for annexation or as a country whose neutrality would have to be violated to make war plans work. It is part of the grass that has gotten trampled as elephants have fought. The fields of Flanders became poetically emblematic of the slaughter of World War I. When it comes to how geographic circumstances shape perceptual habits, the United States is the un-Belgium.

AVERSION TO FINLANDIZATION

Low sensitivity to lesser states' need to accommodate more powerful neighbors has been a recurring pattern in American thinking. The subject acquired a name from another European country of modest size and strength: Finland. The term *Finlandization* was first used when Finland tempered its policies to avoid offending its potent neighbor, the Soviet Union. It became a dirty word with more general applicability in American discourse at different times during the Cold War. One such time was in the 1950s, when small nations' efforts at achieving neutrality were perceived as part of a Soviet effort to erode the unity of the free world. The dirty word had a resurgence around 1980, when fears were voiced that other Europeans would follow Finland's route of bowing to what was seen as a still expansionist Soviet Union.[36] Resistance to Finlandization was in part a rationale for the U.S. pursuit of Cold War policies that were favored anyway for other reasons, but the concept also helped to shape American perceptions and interpretations of any instance of a state accommodating Soviet interests.

Some three decades later, the promoters of the U.S. invasion of Iraq failed to anticipate one of that war's most important consequences: a rapprochement between Iraq and its neighbor Iran. A marked increase in Iranian influence in Iraq had not been part of the script written by the George W. Bush administration, which had labeled Iran as another node on the Axis of Evil. This development was related to some others that the makers of the war also failed to anticipate sufficiently, including the accentuation of sectarian sentiments and sectarian conflict and how the increased power of Iraq's Shia majority would open the way to better relations with Shia Iran. The failure also, however, stemmed from the more general American insensitivity to what countries and governments tend to do to cope with the sort of permanent potential threat from neighbors that the United States itself does not face. Iraq and Iran had fought a very costly eight-year war in the 1980s; when the instigator of that war, Saddam Hussein, was removed, sidling up to Iran was a natural way for his successors to try to bring more stability to their regional relations.

Rapprochement between Iran and other neighboring Arab states also has been outside many Americans' range of understanding. Those who are aware of the sectarian and ethnic differences between the countries on each side of the Persian Gulf tend to see the Arab governments on the south side as naturally hostile to Iran and Iran as hostile to them. The Gulf Arabs have certainly had major security concerns about their neighbor to the north, but this does not mean their response will be implacable and unyielding opposition. A particular American misperception, repeated endlessly in discourse in the United States about Iran's nuclear program and based in part on mis-interpretation of a leaked diplomatic cable, is that Saudi Arabia would favor U.S. military action against that program.[37] The actual Saudi view, however, as expressed by former ambassador to the United States and longtime intel-ligence chief Prince Turki al-Faisal, is that such a military attack would be "catastrophic."[38] Saudi Arabia has made efforts at rapprochement with Iran in the past, and especially since the election of the moderate Hassan Rouhani to the Iranian presidency in 2013, the smaller Gulf Arab states have been conducting a version of Finlandization by warming their own relations with Tehran.[39]

Debate in the United States over a crisis that erupted in 2014 when political upheaval in Ukraine led to a forceful Russian annexation of the Crimean Peninsula demonstrated some of the same slowness in under-standing geopolitical realities—realities common to much of the world but not to North America—about living next to powerful and poten-tially threatening neighbors. The crisis got Cold War juices flowing again within much of the American commentariat. It was discussed in terms of a contest between Russia and the West in which if one side was win-ning, the other must be losing. Much of the debate demonstrated insuf-ficient sensitivity to the necessity for close and extensive relations with its larger neighbor if Ukraine was to be peaceful and prosperous and to how accommodating some Russian interests, including the status of eth-nic Russians within Ukraine, also was a necessary part of resolving the crisis. The concept of Finlandization was trotted out pejoratively again in American commentary.[40]

As with many other debates on many other issues, there was insightful comment to offset in part the misunderstanding, misperception, and insen-sitivity, and some policy makers showed evidence of understanding many of the important nuances in the situation. Both Brzezinski and Kissinger—the old strategists whose thinking had continental European roots—explicitly invoked Finland as a *positive* model for the future of Ukraine.[41] The less insightful tendencies in the public discourse, however, imposed political constraints on the policy makers, leading to feckless rounds of sanctions and retribution.

DIVERGENT PERCEPTIONS OF U.S. ACTIONS

The American difficulty in appreciating foreign fears and concerns about more powerful states extends in particular to difficulty in appreciating fears and concerns about the most powerful state of all: the United States itself. This deficiency is in one respect another instance of a security dilemma, in which each side sees its own actions as less threatening than the other side sees them. Security dilemmas are not unique to relationships involving the United States, but the United States is especially prone to this kind of insensitivity. One reason for this inclination is that its size and power inevitably mean it has more impact on other states than other states have on it.[42] Another reason is the decidedly benign national self-image that Americans, for reasons to be explored further in later chapters, tend to have even more than other people do and that is inconsistent with the idea that U.S. actions might be negative and threatening. Yet another reason again involves geographic proximity: the U.S. ability to project power at a distance enables it to overcome distance while affecting other states, whereas most of those states lack the power to act similarly in the reverse direction. Power-projecting America becomes in effect another large, worrisome neighbor, but Americans do not fully realize the implications of this definition of the United States because they do not have comparable worries in return.

Foreigners have several legitimate reasons to worry about the exercise of U.S. power in their neighborhoods. In addition to a history of U.S. actions that have sometimes genuinely damaged the interests of those not categorized as U.S. enemies, conflicts of interest can arise even between supposed allies. It always is prudent to allow for uncertainty about future U.S. behavior. The power and presence of the United States are such that it can even inflict damage inadvertently.[43] The United States is the elephant that may be unaware of how it can hurt smaller creatures merely by rolling over, but the smaller creatures are aware and necessarily so.

The disconnect between foreign perceptions of the United States and the corresponding American perceptions begins with the question to what extent the United States even takes into account how its actions affect foreigners. A survey by the Pew Research Center in 2013 asked residents of thirty-eight countries, "How much does the United States consider your country's interests?" In a majority of the nations polled, those who responded "not too much" or "not at all" outnumbered those who replied "a great deal" or "a fair amount." This was true of almost all the European and Middle Eastern countries surveyed as well as of U.S. allies in the Far East, such as Japan, South Korea, and Australia. In Canada—an immediate neighbor where the rolling elephant does not even have to project power at a distance to have a major impact—66 percent replied "not too much" or "not at all."[44]

This is quite different from how Americans see things. The Pew Center asked in 2002 and 2004 a more generic version of the same question: "Does U.S. foreign policy consider [the] interests of others?" Large majorities of Americans who were polled—75 percent in 2002 and 70 percent in 2004—replied either "a great deal" or "a fair amount." The results in the eight foreign countries surveyed yielded virtually the opposite result, with the comparable numbers for "a great deal" or "a fair amount" ranging from a high of 44 percent in Britain to a low of nine percent in Turkey (both in 2002) and most of the others in between 20 and 30 percent.[45] These results do not directly demonstrate American obtuseness about foreigners' sentiments; it would be possible, after all, for an American to be fully aware that foreigners evaluate U.S. foreign policy differently than he does himself. But the differences in the numbers are huge, and the very fact that many citizens of foreign countries feel as they do about U.S. policy is itself evidence against the proposition that U.S. policy gives much consideration to those foreign citizens' interests. The polling results likely reflect American misperceptions about foreign perceptions—an American insensitivity to how foreigners believe the United States is insensitive to their interests.

The pattern persists when questions turn from merely taking others' interests into account to how the United States directly affects those interests or may threaten them. In a Pew poll in 2009, majorities in every one of the twenty-four countries surveyed said that the United States influences the respondent's country "a great deal" or "a fair amount." Pluralities in nineteen of those countries said that this influence is bad rather than good.[46] A poll two years later asked another selection of foreign respondents whether they worry that the United States might become a military threat to their own country. The proportion who said they were "very" or "somewhat" worried about this was 46 percent in Jordan, 54 percent in Egypt, 59 percent in Turkey, 67 percent in Pakistan, 71 percent in Indonesia, and 91 percent in the Palestinian territories. Most of these numbers were not even as large as they were a few years earlier, when the figure for Jordan was 67 percent.[47]

Such foreign fears and negative sentiments about the United States, even in countries deemed to be friends of the United States, are most of the time not part of most Americans' perception of the outside world. The fears and sentiments are too inconsistent with a positive national self-image—which can be found in any country but is especially well entrenched in exceptionalist America—to be on Americans' radar. A jolting event, the most prominent example of which was the 9/11 terrorist attacks, occasionally forces awareness of negative sentiments about the United States, but the response in most Americans' thinking is to attribute the failure of understanding to foreigners (and perhaps to U.S. bureaucracies) but not to themselves. President George W. Bush expressed the thoughts of many of his countrymen when he said a month after 9/11: "I'm amazed that there is such misunderstanding of what our country is about, that people would hate us. I am, I am—like most Americans, I just can't believe it. Because I know how good we are, and we've go to do a better job of making our case."[48]

The frame of mind Bush manifested is shared not only by most of the American public but also by most of the political class and even much of the intellectual elite. Stephen Walt observes, "This self-congratulatory view of America's global role is routinely echoed by scholars and pundits alike, thereby reinforcing Americans' sense of their own benevolent global role."[49] He points to the late Samuel Huntington as an eminent American political scientist who argued in the early 1990s that U.S. global primacy is a fundamentally benevolent and even necessary influence across the globe.[50] "In short," concludes Walt, "Americans see their country as a positive force in the world, but the rest of the world is decidedly ambivalent."[51]

One consequence of this disparity in perceptions is the frequent belief that if there is trouble with how foreigners react to U.S. policies, the problem is less in the substance of the policies themselves than in the explanation or selling of those policies—"making our case," in Bush's words. This belief has led to endless consternation about U.S. public diplomacy, to repeated and mostly futile efforts to improve it, and to persistent faith in the idea that the global response to U.S. policies would be markedly better if only Washington could find the right sales technique.[52] Meanwhile, possible redirection of the policy itself gets that much less attention.

Bush's "war on terror" exhibited all of these tendencies and reflected insufficient and typically American insensitivity to how foreigners react to the assertion of American power projected across the oceans and into their neighborhoods. A poll of the United States and eight foreign countries (Britain, France, Germany, Jordan, Morocco, Pakistan, Russia, and Turkey) in 2004 asked whether the "war on terror" was a sincere effort to reduce terrorism. Among American respondents, 67 percent said yes and 25 percent no. The only other country that yielded a result close to this was Britain, where 51 percent said yes and 41 percent no. In Russia, a plurality (48 percent to 35 percent) said no, and in all the other countries large majorities said no.[53]

The same poll also asked about four possible motives for the United States to pursue the "war on terror": to control Mideast oil, to target unfriendly Muslim governments, to protect Israel, and to dominate the world. Americans gave the lowest positive responses on each of the four—none higher than 18 percent. Again, however, the responses in most other countries were far different from those of Americans. Respondents saying yes to the "to dominate the world" motivation included 13 percent in the United States, 24 percent in Britain, 44 percent in Russia, 47 percent in Germany, 53 percent in France, 55 percent in Pakistan, 60 percent in Morocco, and 61 percent in both Jordan and Turkey.[54]

Such results suggest either widespread unawareness among Americans of how the actions of their own country are viewed abroad or, to the extent there is awareness, a belief that the only problem is with "making our case" rather than with the actions themselves or with the policies that underlie them. Consistent with this pattern, Americans show little belief that U.S. actions have had anything to do with establishing the conditions or motivations for terrorism. Asked in 2004 whether "there is anything that the United States did wrong in its dealings with other countries that might have motivated the 9/11 terrorist attacks," most Americans, by a margin of 51 percent to 38 percent, said no. Even fewer Americans (28 percent) believed there was any way in which the United States was "unfair" in its dealings with other countries that might have motivated the attacks.[55] The relative importance of the different risk factors underlying international terrorism have long been subject to political and scholarly debate, but the poll results show a marked American unawareness of the significant ways in which the global reach and actions of the sole remaining superpower elicit responses and resentment that are very much related to terrorist motivations.[56]

The recurring American tendency to overestimate how favorably U.S. actions in someone else's backyard will be received and to underestimate the ill will such actions may elicit has underlain failures in planning for U.S. initiatives overseas. One of the most conspicuous failures in recent times was the expectation among those who made the Iraq War that the American presence in Iraq would be broadly welcomed. Speaking in the same vein as many other promoters of the war, Vice President Dick Cheney said on the eve of the U.S. invasion of Iraq that there was "no question" but that Iraqis "will welcome us as liberators."[57]

The Iraq War was an admittedly extreme example of failure of policy planning in which policy makers intentionally walled themselves off from insights and expertise inside or outside the bureaucracy that could have helped them to anticipate better the hostile responses they would subsequently encounter in Iraq.[58] This insouciant approach, however, was grounded in and reflected in an unusually clear way the broader American tendency to expect that when the United States treads in other neighborhoods, the neighbors' reactions will be more favorable than they actually turn out to be. When Mitt Romney said in a speech in 2012 that "there is a longing for American leadership in the Middle East," to many Arabs this was what a *New York Times* journalist described as a "laugh line."[59] Although the statement was made in an electoral campaign and was intended as criticism of an incumbent president, there is every indication that it reflected a sincere belief held by Romney and most of his audience.

SLOW LEARNING

The splendid physical isolation of the American homeland not only underlies characteristically American ways of thinking about threats, vulnerability, and invulnerability but also retards any learning from others—learning that would help to correct misperceptions in American thought. There is less of the interaction, including forced interaction, that fuels such learning. The physical separation also contributes to Americans' relative ignorance about the rest of the world discussed in the previous chapter.

The separation exacerbates the tendency, rooted in the ideology of American exceptionalism, to believe that the United States is not only different from but also better than everyone else. Being better includes being more knowledgeable and closer to the truth.[60] American public discourse, especially at the most exceptionalist-infused end of the political spectrum, includes strong criticism of anyone who suggests that America lags behind other countries in anything and can learn from those other countries.[61]

The resistance to learning from foreigners has affected how Americans approach international terrorism, even though in official dealings there are few other subjects in national security that require international cooperation as much as does counterterrorism. This resistance in part reflects the apparent popular belief that terrorism started with 9/11. It also, however, reflects widespread ignorance of how long and how extensively other nations thousands of miles away have been confronting and combating international terrorism—for example, what European governments were doing to combat violent leftist radicalism in the 1970s and 1980s, when those governments made changes in legal regimes and police powers that would be echoed only years later in the United States. When after 9/11 America lectured foreigners on being "for us or for the terrorists" in a U.S.-led "war on terror," this posture betrayed a provincialism and arrogance that understandably annoyed and dismayed many foreigners who had been deal-ing seriously with terrorism for years.[62]

Ensconced behind the ocean moats, Americans have not been pushed to correct the distortions in what they see caused by the American prism—not only those related to the physical separation itself but also those stemming from other aspects of the American experience, discussed in later chapters.

3

ABUNDANCE AND POWER

THE UNPARALLELED STRENGTH of the United States, based on its tremendous endowment of resources, has further shaped a distinctively American way of looking at the world. As with America's physical separation from troubles and threats elsewhere on the globe, its power has rested on an extraordinarily fortunate geography. That geographical circumstance was the beginning of a story of many things coming easily to Americans and consequently of Americans viewing things differently from those who never had it so good.

THE BOUNTEOUS LAND

A combination of climate, geology, and biology made it possible for an unusually rich and powerful nation to arise in North America. The lower forty-eight states are centered on a temperate latitude that, spared the diseases of the tropics and the barrenness of more frigid lands, has constituted a belt along which a disproportionate amount of humanity's advances have occurred. In the center of the North American part of that belt lies some of the most fertile soil on earth. The soil developed from conditions that were a bit too dry for a forest but still moist enough not to be a desert. Instead, tall grasses with long roots lived and, when they died, added to the depth and richness of the soil. As late as the latter part of the nineteenth century, there was still so much of this wonderfully rich land available that it was being given away to anyone willing to settle on it and till it. Among other effects, this opportunity attracted immigrants, who added to the population and power of the United States. The opportunity was drastically different from the more typical circumstances in countries many of these immigrants left. There, agriculture often involved farm plots being divided into parcels too small for children to live on and many children having to find something else to do.

The wealth of the Americans' land was by no means limited to the prairie. The vast forests that covered much of the country were themselves a valuable resource and were profligately exploited—and after exploitation of the forests there was still more land to till. There were the hydrocarbon resources that included huge coal deposits and enough petroleum for the United States to become the birthplace of the oil industry. It is no accident that the rise of the United States into a global power coincided with the rise of fossil fuels as the dominant source of energy. Beyond hydrocarbons, there were other mineral resources, such as iron ore, that could conveniently be transported over large fresh-water lakes and married with the coal to make the steel that was a big part of why the United States became an industrial powerhouse.

It was not just the riches of the land that made the Americans' situation special, however; there was also so little competition for it. The original settlers from Europe found a continent that was far more sparsely populated than what they had known. Estimates of the pre-Columbian population of the New World vary widely, but the best evidence suggests that all of North America had fewer than 2 million people at the time of the European voyages of discovery.[1] The land was not empty, but starting from an Old World frame of reference it seemed close enough to being so that the concept of expanding into empty land became a new frame of reference for Caucasian colonizers and settlers. There have been few other instances of people being able to see themselves as entering a vacant cornucopia—one of the few was when the

Native Americans' ancestors traversed the Bering land bridge and entered a continent with no human competitors at all, not even Neanderthals.

As the United States later expanded from the original thirteen colonies, various distractions and troubles kept outside powers from competing for the remaining land. The United States in 1803 picked up the entire western half of the Mississippi River basin, known as the Louisiana Purchase, for four cents an acre when Napoleon Bonaparte's France was preparing for war with Britain and, for reasons related to a slave revolt in Haiti, lost interest in retaining Louisiana. Florida dropped into the U.S. lap when Spain—still exhausted by the Peninsula War and losing its grip on its entire Western Hemisphere empire—ceded the territory in the Adams–Otis Treaty of 1819. The United States amicably secured what would become its Pacific Northwest in a treaty with Britain in 1846 that split the jointly administered Oregon country, tying up the last territorial loose end left from the Revolutionary War and the War of 1812. This acquisition, together with the large cession of land from militarily defeating a weak Mexico and the later Gadsden Purchase, rounded out the territory that would become the lower forty-eight states. The United States obtained Alaska for two cents an acre in 1867 when the Russians, having recently lost the Crimean War and expecting that in a new war they probably would lose Alaska to Britain anyway, were eager to unload the territory.

The land has been bounteous for Americans, and the land came to Americans remarkably easily.

THE FRONTIER AND AMERICAN OPTIMISM

The riches of the U.S. homeland were bound to have a deep impact on the American character. American as well as foreign observers have long noticed this impact. Appreciation for the richness of the land and what it meant for the future of the United States dates back to the beginning of the republic.[2] Tocqueville identified the rich continent as another of the factors that maintained American democracy.[3]

One of the most significant analyses on this subject was first presented in a paper in 1893 by a young historian at the University of Wisconsin, Frederick Jackson Turner. His contribution became known as the "frontier thesis": the concept that from early colonial times until his own time successive American generations' pushing of a frontier westward moved Americans farther away from European influence and was a central factor in shaping American attitudes. Turner said that free land was at the heart of the frontier's formative influence. An ideal that is "fundamental in American thought" and was "developed in the pioneer era," he wrote, is "that of individual freedom to compete unrestrictedly for the resources of a continent— the squatter ideal." Among the characteristics of American thought that stemmed from the influence of the frontier experience is "that practical, inventive turn of mind, quick to find expedients; that masterful grasp of material things, lacking in the artistic but powerful to effect great ends."[4]

The latter inference identifies a distinctively American habit of thinking that has affected how Americans perceive matters they have touched overseas as well as at home. It is a habit that minimizes obstacles to accomplishment and promotes the belief that with enough dedication and cleverness the United States can "effect great ends" wherever it tries to do so. This outlook has fostered a failure to perceive many of the obstacles that have frustrated U.S. endeavors to effect desired ends abroad.

The core of Turner's idea was not limited to the physical locale of the Western frontier. In a later essay, he observed how captains of American industry regarded themselves as "pioneers under changed conditions."[5] Still later, David Potter modified and expanded Turner's thesis in observing that it was not just the frontier that cultivated the distinctively American attitudes in question, although it was at the frontier that the attitude formation was most apparent because that was where, for most of the nation's history, mobility and abundance were most apparent. Overall abundance in America was itself the key influence. The entire expanding economy was important. Mobility often involved moving not just to the western frontier but also, especially from the start of the twentieth century, to the cities.[6]

Turner's thesis had much appeal when he first proposed it. The concept meshed well with the expansive, muscle-flexing national mood of the times.

His ideas came to have considerable influence in the study and teaching of U.S. history before they received a more critical look around the time of the Great Depression.[7] Broader American public attitudes among people who know nothing of historiography have exhibited a somewhat parallel pattern. Although the United States has had periodic panics, recessions, and depressions, most of its history has given its citizens a basis for faith in an overall upward trajectory of growth and prosperity. For most of this history, the economic as well as the physical circumstances of the American people have fostered confidence and optimism sufficient to set them apart from other people. The economic historian Robert Heilbroner observed, "Just as in our own case optimism reflects an experience with history in which any less confident and bold philosophy would have failed to measure up to reality, so in the case of the rest of the world the absence of a native optimism mirrors an experience with history very different from ours."[8]

The impact of the American experience on the frontier (the literal frontier, not the figurative one in industrial cities) was extended and strengthened by its incorporation into American popular culture. By the mid–twentieth century, the Western had become a major genre of American literature, cinema, radio, and television. This channel for direct awareness of the subject amplified the more indirect ways in which an experience that ended generations earlier has shaped later Americans' attitudes. The Western genre in its various art forms also has amplified some of the themes that have affected American thinking about U.S. encounters with the rest of the world. They include the themes of a civilizing mission in less-civilized places and of American toughness ultimately prevailing. They also include, notwithstanding the moral ambiguity of some films by John Ford and others, the idea of white-hatted Americans embodying goodness as they fight against bad guys.

America's unusual material abundance has been a major root of American exceptionalism, along with everything exceptionalist attitudes entail regarding distorted or mistaken beliefs about how America's encounter with the rest of the world should be expected to work. The beliefs include the exceptionalist ideas that the United States is somehow not subject to the same sorts of obstacles and limitations or even the same rules as other nations. The abundance of the previously sparsely populated homeland cultivated the concept of Manifest Destiny: the idea that the successful expansion of America and American influence was bound to happen. Belief in a predestined future leaves little room for doubt, for learning from others, or for perceiving things that get in the way of realizing that future. Abundance also has dulled awareness of the need to make hard, resource-constrained choices and fostered the belief that such choices can be avoided through further economic expansion.[9]

The rich land has been central to the more religious interpretations of the notion of a foreordained American future. Especially in the early days of the United States, it fostered the beliefs that America's riches were God-given and that the nation was playing a millenarian role. Richard Hughes writes that "the land itself struck many as a Garden of Eden . . . here was virgin land that seemed to have come forth from the hand of God."[10] A belief that a future is not only bound to happen but also directed by a divinity makes it even more difficult to perceive things that get in the way of that future.

The direct impact of these attitudes on U.S. foreign affairs became especially significant about the time Turner was developing his thesis. In 1890, the superintendent of the census announced that the western frontier was "closed," which meant there no longer was a discernible line beyond which the population density was less than two persons per square mile. But Manifest Destiny was by then so firmly a part of the national outlook that it would not stop at a frontier or at the ocean's edge. It kept right on going overseas, with the nation being seen as destined not only to populate and civilize its own land but also to bring its civilizing influence to other lands abroad. Thus ensued the Spanish-American War, McKinley's self-comforting decision to take in the Filipinos, and the start of America's building of an empire. Just as Americans did not view their overseas dependencies as colonies, however, neither did they see themselves as imperialists or their nation as having an empire. Euphemistic vocabulary tended to disguise the reality. The difference in self-image in this regard between Americans and Europeans—including the English, the French, and others for whom empire builder was very much a part of their self-image—has been stark.[11] In the late nineteenth century, the difference was all the more striking given that the early days of America's empire building came only a few years after the most feverish phase of the European scramble for colonies in Africa.

POWER AND PERCEIVED VIRTUE

The power and the ability to project power that have ultimately been rooted in America's wealth are the other half, along with the separation that the ocean moats provide, of a great asymmetry in how the United States relates to the rest of the world. The United States can touch and affect the lives of others, for good or for ill, much more than others can touch the United States. This has been the case from the earliest days of the republic once the British colonial rulers were expelled after the Revolutionary War through the later years of Americans' intense interaction with the rest of the world.

Americans' relatively happy and easy experience of growing rich and strong on their own continent also has affected American perceptions about that interaction by further exaggerating a self-image of Americans as pure of heart, consistently well intentioned, and consistently beneficial in their influence. This connection is made most readily by those with a religious perspective, which includes a large proportion of the American population. If God bestowed on Americans an abundant land that made them powerful, then they evidently are a chosen people who are doing God's work in their activities overseas.

The connection is less direct and conscious for those with a more secular perspective, but the psychological tendency to group positive things together helps to make the connection for them. Americans must have been doing something right, the thinking goes, to have used their resources to build the free and prosperous country that is the United States, and they likewise must be doing right by others overseas. Americans' awareness, dating back to the republic's early years, of how fortunate they have been to inhabit their particular spot on the planet does not correct this oversimplified perspective as much as it otherwise would because of the universal psychological tendency to attribute failure to circumstances but success to one's own character. Forgetfulness about how much the good fortune of having the land has had to do with subsequent success and prosperity has become increasingly a factor as each American generation has been farther removed from those who felled the trees or broke the prairie soil.

The result today is an American population that, along with George W. Bush, thinks it knows "how good we are"—with "good" embracing intentions and character as well as ability and the perceived goodness applying to the impact the United States has on the rest of the world. The beliefs involved are at the core of American exceptionalism, and they include the idea that the United States is not only very different from other countries but also better than other countries. When a poll of Americans in 2010 asked, "Because of the United States' history and its Constitution, do you think the U.S. has a unique character that makes it the greatest country in the world?" it received 80 percent affirmative responses.[12] A different poll in 2013 got a similar response to the question whether "the United States is unique and unlike any other nation," with 72 percent agreeing or strongly agreeing. The result was more mixed on the question whether "the United States is *morally* better than most other countries": 11 percent strongly agreed, 24 percent agreed, 22 percent were undecided, 30 percent disagreed, and 13 percent strongly disagreed.[13] Given that disagreement with this proposition did not necessarily imply a belief that the United States was either inferior or equivalent to other countries on this dimension but only that there was insufficient basis for making a moral judgment, it is noteworthy that only a minority expressed disagreement. Probably the most salient aspect of this result is that more than one-third of the Americans polled were willing to make a judgment and to deem the United States superior not only in power and wealth but also in morality.

This outlook, rooted at least in part in the material good fortune and success of the United States, exacerbates the misunderstandings about foreigners' reactions to the exercise of American power, discussed in the previous chapter. Those misunderstandings involve insufficient anticipation of and incorrect interpretations of negative responses to the exercise of that power, whether those responses come in the form of insurgencies, terrorist attacks, or something else. The stronger one's belief in the innate and inherent goodness of one's own country's actions is, the more one is likely to be surprised by such responses.

Almost every nation exhibits to some degree such amour propre, but only the United States has experienced the circumstances that have given rise to it to the high degree seen in American exceptionalism. And because the United States has been able to project power more than any other nation, it is in that ability where the most opportunities for misunderstanding have arisen in interactions with the outside world and where the misunderstandings matter the most.

PUSHING ASIDE THE NATIVES

The rich continent that met European-descended Americans seemed close enough to empty that it was easy to think of it as having been bestowed on them by providence. But of course it was not really empty. The subjugation of those already living there became another formative part of U.S. history that has imparted a distinctly American way of looking at contests that different peoples abroad have waged over different lands. The most distinctive part of the U.S. experience was how easily the Native American population was marginalized.

The relevant patterns were established early in the colonial period. In the first colony, Virginia, European settlers used a mixture of combat and conciliation to deal with the native population. Issues arose among colonists in the seventeenth century as to what the mixture should be. A faction favoring more combat and less conciliation even staged a revolt, known as Bacon's Rebellion, against the authorities in Jamestown. The overall mixture of tactics, however, had already begun the process of marginalization. Settlers traded extensively with some tribes they treated as allies. Their trades included guns, which enabled these tribes to defeat and enslave rival tribes. War and the diseases introduced through trade with the Europeans caused the populations of all of the tribes to decline and made it increasingly harder for them to resist expanding European settlement. By the early eighteenth century, nearly every Native American community in Virginia and other southern colonies was in an inexorable downward spiral of disease, debt, slavery, and war. Bacon's Rebellion was suppressed, but the Baconites in effect won the larger argument over what should be done with the natives.[14]

Later combat against other tribes farther west would be a bit more of a challenge. The ability of the Plains Indians in particular to make effective use of horses and guns in the Indian Wars during the latter half of the nineteenth century made the contest interesting—so interesting, in fact, that this encounter became a salient part of American culture and a major subtheme in the Western genre of performing and literary arts. Generations of American kids have played cowboys and Indians, and it was clear to most of them with which side they were, or should be, most identified. The interesting aspects of this fight not only further extended the lasting impact of the frontier experience on American thought but also made it easier to believe that it had in fact been a real fight and not a pushover. This episode in U.S. history thus further strengthened beliefs in an American ability to prevail even against what Americans like to think have been difficult challenges.

Compared with countless other contests between different peoples over a piece of land, however, the one that began in tidewater Virginia and ended three centuries later in Arizona was nothing close to an even contest. The marginalization of Native Americans, as painful as it was for the ones marginalized, was not one of the harder things that other Americans have done. Most Americans thus have little basis in their own nation's experience for understanding how ubiquitous these contests for land are in the rest of the world and how genuinely tough the contests can be. They have little basis for appreciating the intensity of antagonisms and feelings associated with such struggles and how much wider trouble can stem from them.

Americans' national experience is probably a contributing though not the chief factor in their inattention to such conflicts. Relative American inattention to many territorial conflicts abroad—whether they have involved Greeks against Turks, Armenians against Azerbaijanis, or other fighting pairs—has not been consequential enough for U.S. interests to lead to postmortem hand-wringing over why more attention was not paid to those conflicts. The events leading to World War II in Europe certainly were highly consequential and have been the subject of much recrimination and regret, although the postmortems have focused largely on Hitler's ambitions and why they were not more correctly interpreted. As important as the Nazi dictator's own malevolent goals, however, was why his ideology found a receptive audience. Part of that ideology was the concept of lebensraum or living space. Much of what would become World War II was a fight between Germans and Slavs, initiated by Germans who had less space than they had before the territorial cessions they were forced to make after World War I. Understanding these issues as well as the strength of motivations and emotions surrounding such issues comes less naturally to Americans than it does to residents of the crowded European continent. Ironically, one could have found in the Nazis' idea of lebensraum some parallels to the American idea of Manifest Destiny insofar as it involved a self-styled superior people populating a continent. But for Americans to make such connections would have involved too much of a role reversal—between those wearing white hats and those wearing black ones—and would have smelled too much like moral equivalence for this realization to have aided American understanding of Nazi expansionism. Instead, the prospect of reversed roles probably impeded understanding.

Another atrocity that would stimulate after-the-fact hand-wringing was the genocide in Rwanda in 1994. Postmortem American attention has again focused on why the perpetrators' malevolent intentions were not recognized or why U.S. bureaucracies did not respond with greater alacrity. Largely missing from even the after-the-fact discussion of the tragedy, let alone from American thinking before the genocide, is that Rwanda was a prime example of how intense a conflict between two ethnic groups can get when they are competing for scarce land. It has been left to academic specialists to observe how the genocide and other ethnic violence in Rwanda have been grounded in land scarcity that has made it difficult for the production of food to keep pace with the population growth.[15] Such explanations are foreign in every sense of the word to Americans, for whom land was not scarce and any competition for it was one sided.

UNDERESTIMATING THE ADVERSARY

The nature of the Indian Wars and the marginalization of Native Americans have shaped American perceptions of later adversaries. The battles were frontier battles, and the opponents were considered savages. The effects on American thinking about other opponents—especially ones who, like the Native Americans, were ethnically much different from the dominant ethnicities in the United States—have persisted in spite of other factors that to some extent have corrected such thinking. One such factor present from the early days of the republic was a view that although Native Americans were savages, noble qualities could be found in them. Another corrective was hard-headed thinking among some military professionals who realized that not all enemies are alike. One of the more cerebral early U.S. military officers, Henry Halleck (who later would become general in chief of Union forces in the Civil War), focused on strategy toward potential opponents outside North America because frontier fighting against Native Americans and Mexicans, in his words, "needed little attention because against such adversaries the strength of America was more than adequate."[16] Yet another corrective, long overdue, was the later attention to the civil rights of Native Americans as citizens of the United States who should be considered as worthy as any other citizens.

The persistence, despite these corrective influences, of national thought patterns born in the frontier wars is reflected in how Americans who applied the relevant imagery to games of cowboys and Indians they played as boys later applied the same imagery to wars they fought as men. American soldiers in foreign wars have referred to enemy territory as "Injun country," a frontier land inhabited by savages. Such vocabulary was often used in the Vietnam War and contributed to disparaging views of the adversary not only from the top, as in Lyndon Johnson's dismissal of the "piss-ant nation," but at ground level, as in scurrilous references to "gooks." This kind of ethnic bias flowed from the same set of attitudes that also bolstered the sense of the United States as being on another mission to bring civilization to a less-civilized people.

More directly relevant to misperception and more consequential for U.S. interests was how the tendency to view the enemy as coming from a lower order of civilization encouraged underestimation of the enemy's determination and staying power. Thinking of the adversary against a background of savages who hide behind trees and scurry into the forest at the first shots makes it all the harder to appreciate how much the adversary can be driven by the sort of nationalism associated with modern nation-states. Although the United States and specifically its military leaders appreciated in some respects the time and cost that would be required to have a chance at winning a counterinsurgency in South Vietnam, as of late 1964 Johnson's advisers underestimated the pressure that would be required to get the insurgency's sponsors in the Democratic Republic of Vietnam (North Vietnam) to back down. The authors of the *Pentagon Papers* concluded that this error stemmed from a misreading of determination in the North: "Underlying this optimistic view was a significant underestimate of the level of the DRV commitment to victory in the South, and an overestimate of the effectiveness of U.S. pressures in weakening that resolve."[17] The secretary of defense at the time, Robert McNamara, wrote years later, "We underestimated the power of nationalism to motivate a people (in this case, the North Vietnamese and Vietcong) to fight and die for their beliefs and values—and we continue to do so today in many parts of the world."[18]

THE OTHER CHOSEN PEOPLE

One of the best examples of Americans applying to a current international problem a mindset forged in their own national experience of easily overrunning a continent and pushing aside the people who already lived there concerns the conflict between Israelis and Palestinians. A major feature, now several decades old, of U.S. foreign relations has been the extraordinary relationship with and deference to the State of Israel—a relationship unmatched by U.S. ties to any other nation, even long-standing traditional allies. The unquestioned and unquestioning U.S. backing of Israel has included billions of dollars in annual aid to a country that itself has the twenty-fifth highest per capita income in the world as well as the casting of lonely votes and vetoes in the United Nations against resolutions critical of Israeli policies. Meanwhile, sympathy for the Palestinians as a people under foreign military occupation is harder to find in the United States than in much of the rest of the world.

The chief explanation for this anomaly in U.S. foreign relations is to be found in how power and fear work in contemporary domestic American politics.[19] That is not the entire story, however. The effectiveness of lobbying on this set of issues benefits from an American predisposition to accept the messages the lobbyists convey.

The narratives of how Israelis and white Americans built their respective nations have significant parallels. Both countries are nations of immigrants. The origins of each include the fleeing of religious persecution in Europe, which in the case of European Jews involved one of the deadliest instances of such persecution in history. Both peoples built their countries through settlement and development of the land and a subsequent transition in emphasis from agriculture to industry.

The impressive prosperity and well-being that both peoples achieved gave rise to two thoughts among each regarding the reasons for success. One was confidence in the people's own inventiveness and ability, with a tendency to view their own nation's traits as superior to those of others. The American sense of superiority that was part of America's self-proclaimed civilizing mission overseas had a parallel in the belief held by the founding father of Zionism, Theodor Herzl, that a Jewish state in Palestine would be a European bulwark against Asia or, as Herzl put it, "a vanguard of culture against barbarianism."[20] Another perceived reason for success was a belief that divine will must be involved. For Israelis, the underlying concept was the ancient one of Jews being God's chosen people. For Americans, it was the more religious interpretations of Manifest Destiny and the role of providence in bestowing upon them a rich continent.

Contentious issues involving Israel today, centered on occupation of the West Bank, have additional parallels with the American frontier experience. Settlers on the West Bank are populating a frontier for Jewish Israelis. They resist, displace, and sometimes have to fight off unhappy natives, just as American frontiersmen did. The distinction between civilians and military as well as the activities of each sometimes get blurred on the West Bank, just as they did on the American frontier.[21]

Culturally and demographically, it was natural that most Americans would more readily identify with Ashkenazi (European-origin) Jews, who dominated early Zionism and Israeli politics for much of the country's history, than they would with Middle Eastern Arabs. The parallel aspects of the two national narratives, however, have probably been at least as important in shaping the dominant American mindset about current conflicts involving Israel.

Americans have long seen such parallels, even before the modern State of Israel was a gleam in Zionists' eyes. The comparisons Americans were making in the early days of their own republic were to the ancient Israelites of the Old Testament, the ones who battled Amalekites and Philistines rather than Arabs. Pilgrims and Puritans in what would become Massachusetts thought of their settlements as the "new Israel."[22] Until 1787, undergraduates at Harvard were required to study Hebrew.[23] The novelist Herman Melville wrote in 1850, "We Americans are the peculiar, chosen people—the Israel of our time; we bear the ark of the liberties of the world."[24] As Canaan was the promised land for the Israelites, so too was America seen as the promised land for European-origin Americans, and the Puritans even called it "Canaan."[25]

American believers, well read in the Old Testament, had these parallels engrained in their thinking by the time Melville was writing. When modern Israel came along, transferring the parallels to it was easy. Even if the transfer was not conscious and explicit, it flowed naturally from a pattern of thought that was well entrenched and grounded in Americans' own experience and their interpretation of that experience. American perceptions of Middle Eastern history have come more from the Bible, which tells stories of Israelites inhabiting the land that is now in dispute, than from any accounts of the later fourteen centuries in which Arabs have lived there.[26]

Disproportionate American support for the Israeli side of the dispute over Palestine is thus overdetermined for reasons of ethnicity and theology as well as politics and history. These determinants have outweighed any sympathy for those under occupation or denied political rights. Our concern here, however, is not just with sympathies and support but with perceptions and understanding—with what Americans believe to be true and what might predispose them to false beliefs. The explanation for American beliefs, on this issue as on many others, is to be found first of all in the sympathies. Factual beliefs follow emotional sentiments, and perceptions follow preferences, at least as much as the other way around. This is in part a matter of seeking internal consistency in one's own mindset and reducing cognitive dissonance.[27] It is also in part a matter of believing sources we like more than ones we don't like. Americans who are forming beliefs about the Israeli–Palestinian conflict are not filling in a blank slate; they are hearing about this subject from their own politicians and from Israel itself and its supporters through the vigorous public diplomacy that the Israelis call *hasbara*. Americans believe much of what they do about this conflict, including what is false as well as what is true, in large part because those beliefs are consistent with the objectives and policies of the side they are predisposed to support. This tendency has repeatedly resulted in widely accepted but factually incorrect American perceptions about the conflict, even concerning recent events. In one of the most recent rounds of periodic combat between Israel and Hamas in the Gaza Strip, for example, the prevailing American belief—reflected in a congressional resolution of support for Israel—was that Israel's use of force in mid-2014 was a response to Hamas's firing of rockets into Israel. In fact, the sequence of events was the other way around.[28]

Predisposition also applies more directly, however, to the substance of some of the beliefs, with roots again running back to the Americans' experience of settling and populating their own promised land. Of particular salience here are the beliefs early Americans had about how much of a presence the preexisting population had on the land and, related to that, how realistic that population's nationalist aspirations were. As Europeans and their descendants settled North America, the Native American population never constituted enough of a presence to be widely seen as the basis for a separate nation-state that would limit the expansion and help set the boundaries of the United States. This fact was mostly a simple matter of relative numbers. The already-thin native population in what would become the United States thinned further after European colonization began. The indigenous people suffered a rapid and drastic decline in population—possibly as much as 50 percent—due mainly to diseases the Europeans had imported.[29] The population recovered as immunities developed but never came close to keeping pace with growth of the white population. In the 2010 census, only 0.9 percent of the U.S. population was recorded as being wholly American Indian or Alaska Native, with another 0.7 percent identifying themselves as a mixture of that category and some other.[30] Even those most troubled by past injustices to and current social and economic problems of Native Americans recognize U.S. territorial expansion as a fait accompli. There never has been talk of a "two-state solution" involving Native Americans.

The demographic realities associated with the establishment and expansion of the modern State of Israel have been much different. At the time of the Balfour Declaration of 1917, in which the British government committed itself to the establishment of a "national home" for the Jewish people in Palestine without prejudice to "the civil and religious rights of existing non-Jewish communities" there, the Arab population of Palestine was about ten times that of the Jewish population. Estimates vary, but there were about 58,000 to 70,000 Jews and around 700,000 Arabs.[31] In the United Nations plan in 1947 to partition Palestine, the population of the projected Jewish state—despite rapid Jewish immigration in the three decades after Balfour's pronouncement—would have been 45 percent Arab, whereas the projected Arab state would have been only one percent Jewish.[32] The demographics were further revised in the subsequent war in Palestine, in which Jewish forces captured substantially more territory than had been allotted to their side in the partition plan and many Arabs were either expelled or fled from what became the State of Israel.

The similarities and differences between American and Israeli experiences in establishing and building a nation in a new land have combined to foster myopic and incomplete American perceptions of the struggle over land in Palestine that continues to this day. With the American experience appearing to have so much in parallel with that of Israel, a natural tendency has been to think that *all* aspects of Israel's experience parallel America's, including the parts involving marginalization of an indigenous population too small to make a plausible claim to a state of its own. As with attitudes toward Native Americans today, verbal deference may be given to the rights of those marginalized. The basic American framework for perceiving the situation in Palestine, however, is less one of a struggle for land between two comparable and comparably deserving peoples and more one of a single chosen people making the desert bloom or the prairie yield and expanding their writ from sea to sea or from sea to river.

To a large degree, Americans have bought into the Israeli mythology of "a land without a people for a people without a land," which seems to echo some of the American mythology of expanding onto an empty continent. We see manifestations of this mythology in many statements about the Israeli–Palestinian conflict from American politicians, which, as always with anything having to do with Israel, stem in large part from certain harsh realities of domestic politics but also have resonance among the voting citizens who hear the statements. Some statements are badly erroneous depictions of the history and demography of the region in question. In a speech on the Senate floor in 2002, Senator James Inhofe said that in the days before the Balfour Declaration "nobody really wanted this land." A Palestinian nation, said Inhofe, "did not exist. It was not there. Palestinians were not there. Palestine was a region named by the Romans, but at that time it was under the control of Turkey, and there was no large mass of people there because the land would not support them."[33] Inhofe, although declaiming more persistently on this theme than some others, has not been alone in making such assertions. Former history professor and Speaker of the House Newt Gingrich said while running for president in 2012 that the Palestinians are an "invented people."[34] One of Gingrich's competitors for the presidential nomination, former senator Rick Santorum, declared that Palestinians do not exist at all and that everyone living in the West Bank is an Israeli.[35] That genuine ignorance—not just campaign rhetoric—is behind such statements is revealed in private comments that parallel the public ones. A journalist witnessed a U.S. senator in the 1980s, for example, asking a Saudi official where the Palestinians had come from "to begin with."[36]

As with many other matters involving Israel, American discourse is more constrained and distorted than discourse among Israelis themselves. Israel's founding fathers fully realized that the Zionist project involved a contest between two nations for the same land and freely acknowledged this fact well before the main battles were fought. David Ben Gurion said in a speech in 1919, "There is a gulf, and nothing can fill that gulf. . . . I do not know what Arab will agree that Palestine should belong to the Jews—even if the Jews learn Arabic. . . . We, as a nation, want this country to be ours; the Arabs, as a nation, want this country to be theirs."[37] What for most Israelis is confined to mythology and *hasbara* is for many Americans a perception of fact—the erroneous perception of the expansion of a chosen people into a land without a people. We are seeing in this American misperception of reality the influence not only of current domestic politics but also of past American experience.

With Americans having fallen into the habit of accepting the Israeli narrative of the Israeli–Arab conflict and having little awareness of the Palestinian narrative, further mistaken beliefs arise out of the untested trust they place in anything they hear that favors the Israeli version. This process has been going on since the founding of Israel. A story that quickly caught on during the 1948 war, for example, was that Palestinian Arabs left their homes because Palestinian leaders had broadcast instructions for them to do so to give Arab armies a clear shot at driving Jews out of Palestine. There was no truth to the story, but it became a part of Israeli lore and was widely accepted in the United States.[38]

Misunderstanding of the underlying demographic reality in the dispute over Palestine has fostered misunderstanding of the diplomatic history of that dispute. Americans perceive Arab postures toward the founding of the State of Israel chiefly as perverse and unreasonable rejection of the Israelis rather than, as Ben Gurion observed it, as unsurprising resistance to the loss of what the Arabs considered their own homeland. The reasonable nature of the original Arab rejection of Zionism in the 1940s, given the demography of Palestine at the time—a rejection long since abandoned by mainstream Arabs after Israel became an established and permanent fact—has hardly crept into American consciousness.[39] Similarly, the prevailing American perception of what happened when the two sides appeared to come close to an agreement in 2000 and early 2001 is that, as Inhofe puts it, the Israeli government "offered the most generous concessions to Yasser Arafat that had ever been laid on the table," but Arafat "stormed out of the meeting" to launch a premeditated campaign of terrorism and rioting. Competing narratives of that chapter of the peace process persist, but as Jeremy Pressman's careful analysis of the negotiations shows, the Israeli offer "neglected several elements essential to any comprehensive settlement," and the Palestinian side "favored a genuine two-state solution and did not seek to destroy Israel by insisting on the right of return or through the second intifada."[40]

American perceptions of an ongoing issue—Israeli colonization of the West Bank—are shaped not only by Americans' general affinity for the Israeli side of the conflict but also by more direct correspondences with the U.S. expansionary experience. Most Americans extend to Israelis the same privilege they have extended to their own country in not calling the process "colonization." Even in criticism of Israeli actions, the gentler term *settlements* is used. And the building of these settlements harks back again to the American experience of westward expansion and acquisition of land. Santorum made this connection explicit when he rationalized Israeli retention of land seized in the war of 1967 as comparable to the United States retaining Texas and other territories it seized from Mexico upon winning the Mexican War.[41] Americans are conditioned not to notice the other aspects of Israeli activity in the West Bank, besides construction of settlements, that point toward permanent expansion of Israel—such as appropriation of land and demolition of Palestinian housing.[42] Predisposed perception can be a matter of what is not perceived as well as of what is.

OVERLOOKING CHALLENGES THAT OTHERS FACE

The American nation as a whole has had little reason to worry about having enough vital resources, in particular essentials such as food and energy. The abundance of food grown in the United States is reflected in its being the largest agricultural exporter in the world. As for energy, in addition to vast coal deposits the United States had enough petroleum to be a net exporter of oil until 1946. Oil-price shocks and foreign embargoes in the 1970s put energy security on the national agenda for the first time. The habits and attitudes born amid abundance, however, were by then firmly engrained, as reflected in continued profligacy in the use of petroleum even after these concerns arose. More recently, the development and rapid application of technology to release oil and gas trapped in shale by fracturing the rock is leading the United States to become again a net exporter of petroleum products.[43] Celebration over the shale-oil revolution and its implications is more a matter of returning to old, comfortable American ways of thinking about energy resources than of embarking on a totally new way of thinking.

Abundance in an essential resource such as hydrocarbons has numerous effects, of course, on American thoughts and perceptions about many issues of public policy, including conservation and the environment. Our present concern is with how this aspect of abundance affects American perceptions and understanding of foreign countries' situations and behavior. The principal effect is slowness in comprehending how nations not blessed with similar abundance may be driven even to acts of desperation by the need to secure resources.

This was the case with respect to understanding Japan's situation leading up to World War II and how acutely Japan felt threatened by the prospect of not having enough oil. In late 1941, a subcabinet committee led by Assistant Secretary of State Dean Acheson applied rules about frozen financial assets in a way that created a de facto embargo of U.S. oil exports to Japan, which precipitated Japan's launching of what became World War II in the Pacific.[44] The direct Japanese objective was to seize oil resources in Southeast Asia, with a simultaneous preemptive blow against the U.S. fleet at Pearl Harbor being part of the supporting strategy.

President Franklin Roosevelt may already have been maneuvering to move the United States into the war since Hitler had begun his aggression in Europe, and there are indications that Roosevelt and many other officials understood at some level that the supply of oil was very important to Japan. The events of 1941 suggest, however, something less than full appreciation of just how important it was. This story is not solely one of messy bureau-cratic decision making leading to the imposition of an oil embargo through decisions at the assistant secretary level. Moreover, the American public appreciated Japanese motivations even less than U.S. officials did. When the attack at Pearl Harbor came, it thus seemed all the more despicable and incomprehensible unless the most nefarious qualities were attributed to the Japanese. This popular perception was useful in enlisting public support for the U.S. war effort, but in an important respect it involved misperception of how the war came about.

Acheson later claimed to have been out of the information loop and unaware of Japanese messages that others in the government were read-ing. He wrote in his memoir that he "knew little, as we tightened the eco-nomic blockade of Japan, of the tension it was producing there." Acheson is probably correct in his more general observation that officials in the State Department and in the government generally "misread Japanese inten-tions. This misreading was not of what the Japanese military government proposed to do in Asia, not of the hostility our embargo would excite, but of the incredibly high risks General Tojo would assume to accomplish his ends. No one in Washington realized that he and his regime regarded the conquest of Asia not as the accomplishment of an ambition but as the survival of a regime."[45] Such a realization would have come more easily to people who themselves had to worry about where they would get their next barrel of oil.

Abundance and the paucity of external impediments to prosperity have led Americans to look inward for explanations for their happy economic circumstances. The absence of hardships imposed either by nature or by adversaries is taken for granted; the attribution of success, at the level of either the nation or the individual, to character and culture is a reassuring and flattering brush stroke on the American self-image. The riches of the North American continent and the mobility that its residents have enjoyed have led Americans to think of failure to advance economically as largely a matter of individual responsibility. Even during the Great Depression, those who did not advance tended to blame themselves.[46] The associated misperception of situations abroad involves an assumption that similar explanations account for other nations' economic lot, with a tendency to underestimate the effect of—or to fail to see at all—other constraints to growth and prosperity.

Presidential candidate Mitt Romney provided an example of this assumption in a speech in Jerusalem in 2012. Referring to the disparity (which he actually understated) between the per capita gross domestic product of Israel and that of areas managed by the Palestinian Authority, Romney's explanation for it was that "culture makes all the difference"—by which he meant that something akin to the Protestant work ethic drove Israeli enterprise but was missing from Arab culture.[47] He made no mention of the numerous physical, legal, and resource impediments, within a few miles of where he was standing, to Palestinian economic activity that were part of the Israeli occupation, ranging from denial of building permits to prohibitions on Arab use of transportation networks. Of course, Romney's motivation for saying what he did undoubtedly had something to do with the audience and pocketbooks to which he was appealing (he was speaking at a fundraiser attended by prominent Jewish American backers). Moreover, he was a very wealthy man who repeatedly demonstrated in other ways during the campaign his difficulty in comprehending the circumstances of those less well off. But his remarks suggested a view that was both sincerely held and characteristically American. He specifically likened the economic disparity between Israel and the Palestinian territories to the one between the United States and Mexico, with culture being his explanation for both. An irony in Romney's comments is that cultural traits were indeed being displayed, but more in the outlook that underlay the comments themselves than in any differences between Israelis and Arabs in economic performance.

The tendency to believe that whatever has come easily to Americans should come easily to others (at least if they are not retarded by an inferior culture) can lead to a variety of mistaken expectations. Some concern the transferability of America's experience in economic development. In the early 1960s, after his first visit as vice president to South Vietnam, Lyndon Johnson was seized with the idea of developing the Mekong River basin to provide hydroelectric power and other benefits. As president, he made this idea, before major escalation of the war, a large part of the mark he hoped the United States would leave on Vietnam. "We're going to turn the Mekong into a Tennessee Valley," he said.[48] Johnson had confidence in not only the concept's transferability and effectiveness but also its attractiveness to the North Vietnamese as an alternative to more war.

Other mistaken expectations, such as ones pertaining to the development of unconventional weapons, lead to exaggerated threat perceptions. The pace and extent of nuclear proliferation is an example. Ever since John Kennedy spoke of the possibility that by the 1970s there would be as many as twenty-five nation-states armed with nuclear weapons, American discourse on the subject has tended to err on the high side of subsequent nuclear developments. This disparity reflects in part a preference to focus on worst cases rather than on most likely cases. A slower-than-expected pace of proliferation is due in part to restraint embodied in international treaties and institutions devoted to nonproliferation and to decisions by national governments to eschew a course that on balance they consider disadvantageous. But the high-side errors also reflect insufficient appreciation of how the relevant technology—even though the United States was able to develop it decades ago with the Manhattan Project—is still exceedingly difficult for most others to master. Recent and repeated prognostications of a cascade of nuclear proliferation in the Middle East if Iran were to develop a nuclear weapon take little account of how hard it would be for the most likely prospective proliferators to do the trick.[49]

Similar patterns underlie a strong preoccupation with and fear of terrorist groups' possible use of chemical, biological, radiological, or other unconventional weapons. The preoccupation has consistently outpaced what actual terrorists have managed to do on this front.[50] This discrepancy has persisted even though the experience of the 9/11 attacks—which had nothing to do with such unconventional weapons—should have imparted different lessons. (The widespread prior assumption that mass casualties would have to involve unconventional weapons made 9/11 that much more of a surprise for many Americans.) The persistence is due in part to deliberate manipulation of the issue for other reasons, such as the selling of the Iraq War, in which the idea of weapons of mass destruction falling into the hands of terrorists was a major theme. It is also due in part to the fascination and intrigue associated with exotic methods of killing people. But a further significant reason is an underestimation of the technical challenges involved in using such methods effectively.[51]

POWER PROJECTION AND ITS EFFECTS

With no other country as powerful as the United States, its citizens have little basis for empathizing with those who face a superior power and may resent as well as fear what that power can do to them. Other states can mount challenges, including local military challenges, to U.S. influence in different parts of the world, but only the United States has on a global scale what Barry Posen calls "command of the global commons."[52] The United States has unmatched ability to use the instruments of its power at a distance and thereby to affect profoundly the lives of people in different parts of the globe. This ability, based ultimately on the homeland's wealth and resources, thus contributes to Americans' inability, described in the previous chapter, to comprehend fully how and why foreigners may develop negative sentiments toward the United States and what it does overseas, notwithstanding Americans believing they know "how good we are."

Foreigners and foreign governments with negative sentiments toward the exercise of U.S. power have numerous options for countering that power besides mounting local military challenges. Stephen Walt has described many different strategies foreign states use to counter U.S. power, ranging from balking and "soft balancing" to blackmail.[53] To a scholar such as Walt, the resulting pattern is one in which the power of even the world's sole superpower is held much more in check than may at first be apparent. To most Americans, who have not done the scholarly cataloging of responses and whose thinking about such things is influenced more by a national experience of growing and largely unchecked power, the pattern is much less obvious. They tend to view individual instances of resistance in isolation as separate problems to be resolved or overcome. They thus do not fully understand the overall limits on American power—as suggested by popular support for some of the very policies that have engendered the negative responses that Walt has studied. Americans may not understand the consequences of specific U.S. endeavors overseas because of their insufficient appreciation of the negative sentiments these actions cause or the options foreigners have for acting on those negative sentiments or both.

A modern U.S. endeavor that especially epitomizes both the reach of American power and Americans' slowness in comprehending its consequences is the use of armed, unmanned aerial vehicles, commonly called drones, to kill suspected terrorists. Missile strikes from drones are the ultimate in long-distance, push-button, remote-control warfare. Operators in the safety and comfort of a base in the United States are thousands of miles removed from whatever bloodshed results in a remote land when an operator pushes the firing button. This combination of great physical separation and the power to make major and even deadly things happen at far remove replicates at the tactical and personal level what is taking place at the larger level of policy and strategy. The drone strikes have had positive and relatively easy to count effects by taking ill-intentioned individuals out of commission. Far harder to count and more prone to escaping notice or at least proper consideration are whatever anger and resentment result from civilian casualties. Such anger and resentment can undermine the counterterrorist objective by fostering anti-American extremism.[54] The heavy U.S. reliance on drone strikes reflects in one sense the limits of American power in that U.S. policy makers see the strikes as the only way to touch targets in especially remote places at an acceptable cost. It also symbolizes, however, both the unmatched long reach of American power and the insufficiently appreciated consequences that the application of this power can have.

THE UNSEEN LIMITS OF POWER

Americans' extraordinary success in building at home the most powerful nation in history has fostered a tendency to believe that with enough effort and determination the United States can accomplish just about anything abroad. The United States cannot really do that, and any such belief involves profound misperceptions. The misperceptions are in part directed inward and involve the nature of American power itself. But they also point outward and involve a failure to see obstacles and difficulties that American power encounters overseas and a misjudgment of how malleable foreign situations are and how susceptible to change they are through American efforts.

These patterns of belief are reflected in a further tendency in American discourse to assess U.S. foreign policy in terms of almost anything that happens, for good or for ill, around the globe regardless of whether it is the work of the United States or subject to significant U.S. influence. To the extent Americans presume that the United States has the power to resolve problems throughout the world, unsolved problems are taken as a deficiency of U.S. policy. Thus, scorecards on the foreign policy of whoever is the incumbent U.S. president are routinely filled out with plus marks for anything good that happens in the world and minus marks for anything bad. Some of this type of scorekeeping reflects the usual playing of politics in which both claims of credit for one's own side and accusations of failure by one's opponents are exaggerated. But some of it stems from a more broadly shared exaggeration of the scope of American power. This type of policy scorekeeping in turn helps to sustain a tendency to overlook the limits on that power.

Warfare has provided some of the most dramatic and costliest examples of this inability to see those limits and appreciate them fully. The United States has hardly been alone in overreaching its power during war and hitting up against the limits with sometimes disastrous results. History's other examples range from the Athenian expedition to Sicily during the Peloponnesian War to the invasions of Russia by Bonaparte and Hitler. Only with the United States, however, has the attempted application of power had a global scope. American attitudes about the application of power overseas are also uniquely rooted in a now long history of successfully subduing a continent, which has yielded habits of mind that go well beyond individual leaders' megalomania. Those attitudes were not negated even by the difficult choices and limits to power that the United States encountered in winning wars such as World War II because the limits and hard choices were forgotten more easily than the victorious outcome.[55]

The launching of the Iraq War in 2003 is one of the most salient and searing as well as one of the most recent illustrations of these habits of thought. The blindness to the limitations of this application of U.S. military power was due largely to the extraordinarily closed nature of the process leading to the decision to initiate this war—to the extreme of there being no policy process at all. The policy makers deliberately isolated themselves from sources of insight that could have helped to correct their blindness.[56] Getting the country to go along with this expedition was largely a matter of assiduous cultivation of a rationale for war that involved mythical alliances between Saddam Hussein and terrorist groups. Contributing significantly, however, both to the policy makers' thinking and to public acceptance of a major offensive war was unfounded optimism about what U.S. military power could accomplish in a far-off land. The optimism was enhanced by the glow of the still-recent victory in the Cold War and what was regarded as a not so momentary unipolar moment following the Cold War. The optimism was rooted more fundamentally in the longer history of easily won national success.

So it was that on the eve of the Iraq War a public figure such as former Reagan administration official Kenneth Adelman argued that the war would be a "cakewalk."[57] The optimism of those who made the war was reflected in rosy predictions in private as well as in public. One of the most enthusiastic promoters of the war, Deputy Secretary of Defense Paul Wolfowitz, was telling senior army officers a month before the war that they should plan on the U.S. military presence in Iraq being down to 30,000 to 34,000 troops just a few months after the invasion.[58] Actual U.S. troop strength in Iraq would peak at 168,000 in late 2007, four and a half years into the war. Wolfowitz made numerous other statements about things he "imagined" would go well for the United States in Iraq.[59]

That the optimism about Iraq was rooted in part in America's easily won success on a resource-rich continent was illustrated by Wolfowitz's repeated references to Iraq's oil wealth as a reason to expect that the war could be fought on the cheap. "There is a lot of money there," he told Congress in February 2003, that could be put to better use "instead of building Saddam's palaces."[60] A month later he told another congressional committee that "Iraq can really finance its own reconstruction."[61] Like Texas, like Iraq. This was another instance in which one similarity with the American experience—in this case, being blessed with ample petroleum—was extended inaccurately into an assumption of other similarities.

The most basic respect in which the successful U.S. experience of growing and expanding in North America to become a strong nation has shaped U.S. citizens' attitudes about the application of power on other continents is found in the American belief that if there is a problem overseas, the United States should be able to solve it. Robert McNamara, in reviewing his own and his colleagues' failures during the Vietnam War, wrote, "We failed to recognize that in international affairs, as in other aspects of life, there may be problems for which there are no immediate solutions. For one whose life has been dedicated to the belief and practice of problem solving, this is particularly hard to admit."[62] It is hard also for many other Americans to admit, and many never do admit it.

4

THE SUCCESSFUL SOCIETY

A MERICANS' RELATIVE SUCCESS and the ease with which that success came have involved not only favorable physical and geographic circumstances but also a domestic society that has suffered fewer of the sorts of disruptions and destructive divisions that have beset many other countries. This is easy to forget amid political gridlock in Washington and a related partisan and ideological competition that has become more intense and uncompromising in recent years. That competition, however, overlays a more fundamental, long-standing consensus about politics and society that Louis Hartz wrote about more than half a century ago and is centered on the tenets of liberal democracy.[1] The day-to-day competition is a game Americans are at liberty to play because the players agree on enough else that their lives do not depend on the outcome of the competition. (The Civil War was the one big, violent exception to this pattern—a completion in the nineteenth century of unfinished business from the founding of the republic in the eighteenth.) The world's history of military coups, insurrections, internal wars, and other domestic disorders not only in less-developed countries but also in Europe and the rest of the developed world is a reminder of how the working of domestic society in the United States has been as much a part of what makes America exceptional as is the external application of U.S. power. Even if the United States is not altogether unique in this regard, its domestic success is part of what fosters a distinctive American way of looking at the rest of the world.

America's success in ordering and organizing a domestic society is related to the good fortune of its physical and geographic situation in at least a couple of respects. One is the lack of the sort of cross-border patterns of habitation that have bred irredentism or other forms of instability in many other places, such as among Germans in the Sudetenland, Kurds in Iraq and Turkey, and Russians in Ukraine. Concentrations of ethnic minorities exist in some parts of the United States, but they are not the basis for aspirations to secede or to revise international boundaries. Another element of good fortune is how an abundance of resources avoids fierce competition over scarce resources. Land has been the most conspicuous but not the only resource in question. Land to be had for free is the opposite of ownership of land and land reform as a focus of severe ill will and communal strife. The latter has figured prominently in the histories of many other countries, from Russia to Rwanda, from Algeria to Zimbabwe.

What could have been a fly in the smooth American ointment was the status and handling of the indigenous population in the face of settlement and conquest by a different people who themselves (or their relatively recent ancestors) had come from afar. This is the kind of interaction that in many other countries has produced enduring internal conflict, resentment, and strife. We see the consequences today in, for example, the division between those of Spanish and native ancestry as a prominent political fault line in Latin American countries such as Bolivia and Peru and in a similar division between Chinese and longer-established local ethnic groups in Southeast Asian nations such as Malaysia.

History did not turn out that way in the United States, however, in part because of the aforementioned small numbers of Native Americans in this portion of North America and in part because the indigenous people were marginalized so quickly that they never were a complicating factor in the developing American consensus and American community. Part of the consensus then—before more modern attitudes developed much later—was that the indigenous people were inferior barbarians who *should* be marginalized. Although Bacon's Rebellion in early colonial Virginia stemmed from disagreement over policy toward the natives, by the late seventeenth century public debate on the subject had largely ceased.[2] That pattern continued through the eighteenth century and into the nineteenth. At the very time that citizens of the young republic were developing so much of a consensus and sense of community that they called that period the Era of Good Feelings, Andrew Jackson was using military force to bash Creeks and Seminoles. After Jackson became president, his message to Congress about the native peoples was "that those tribes can not exist surrounded by our settlements and in continual contact with our citizens is certain. They have neither the intelligence, the industry, the moral habits, nor the desire of improvement which are essential to any favorable change in their condition. Established in the midst of another and a superior race . . . they must necessarily yield to the force of circumstances and ere long disappear."[3]

America's history and the special circumstances associated with it have helped to create and sustain a remarkable experiment in representative democracy. The United States was ahead of almost the entire rest of the world in conducting this experiment, and it is distinctive in the length of time its political structure has endured. The United States has been unusually successful in the long-term organization of a modern society. And at least as pertinent to Americans' attitudes, its citizens believe it is even more successful in that regard than it actually is.

The principal consequence of this aspect of the American experience is a difficulty in comprehending how hard it is for similar experiments to be repeated and to take hold in other countries. Americans lack a basis for appreciating the extent to which internal divisions and conflicts that they have largely been spared tend to complicate or preclude representative democracy or to feed chronic instability.[4] Meanwhile, the ethnic, racial, religious, and other dimensions of Americans' own experience with domestic politics and society have imparted other distinctive details to the picture that has emerged from the American prism.

FAITH IN MELTING POTS

A long-standing part of Americans' collective self-image has been that in America people of different ethnic origins swirl together smoothly to produce a new demographic blend. One of the first to write in this vein was John Hector St. John de Crèvecoeur, who was born to French nobility, served with French colonial forces in the French and Indian War, and then settled as a farmer in New York. During the latter part of the Revolutionary War, he published *Letters from an American Farmer*, in which he posed the question "What is an American?" The kernel of his answer was that Americans "are a mixture of English, Scotch, Irish, French, Dutch, Germans, and Swedes. From this promiscuous breed, that race now called Americans have arisen."[5]

Scholars today have left as an open question exactly how assimilated or blended people of different ethnic origins really are in the United States.[6] A melting pot clearly has been at work, with ethnic identities in many immigrant families greatly diluted after just two or three generations of cultural immersion and intermarriage. The United States also has had, however, a substantial history of nativism, which has recent echoes in debates over immigration policy.[7] Most important for the present purpose is the widespread and firm American *belief* that America has indeed been a melting pot and that the pot has worked well, regardless of whatever details data may reveal about the actual degree of assimilation.

Confidence in the working of America's own melting pot has led to overestimation of the ability of different ethnic groups in other countries to integrate and to work together to build stable and peaceful societies. Associated with this tendency is an underestimation of the large role that ethnic nationalism plays in politics around the world. Moreover, as Jerry Muller observes, "Americans also find ethnonationalism discomfiting both intellectually and morally."[8] They are slow to recognize that the roots of ethnically based nationalism grow deeper than most other ways of organizing politics and society.[9] The most consequential demonstrations of this lack of recognition have arisen when the United States has attempted large-scale political engineering in other lands.

The clearest expression of the American perspective can be found in the statement of national-security strategy that the George W. Bush administration issued in September 2002, which declared, "America's experience as a great multi-ethnic democracy affirms our conviction that people of many heritages and faiths can live and prosper in peace."[10] Six months after issuing this document, the same administration launched the Iraq War, which would sink into a mire of ethnic and sectarian strife and bloodshed. The confidence—the policy makers' confidence, rooted in a larger American attitude—in the ability of people of different heritages and faiths to live in peace and prosperity was in this case strong enough to overcome more informed perspectives about how toppling the regime in Iraq was likely to open the door to intense communal conflict. The latter perspectives included that of the U.S. intelligence community, which before the war indicated that the communities of different heritages and faiths in Iraq would be at each other's throats as they contended for power after the dictator was overthrown, leading to violent conflict if an occupying force were not sitting on them.[11]

The evolution of the U.S. military expedition in Afghanistan from a counterterrorist operation to a long-term nation-building program exhibited some of the same incongruity between Americans' expectations and aspirations on the one hand and an ethnically divided reality on the other. There was not the same Pollyannaish ambition that the promoters of the Iraq War had about building a liberal democracy in Mesopotamia, but as the American operation in Afghanistan ground on into a second decade, the belief that something close to a multiethnic democracy could be established sustained the American motivation to persevere. Political fault lines in Afghanistan are even more purely ethnic than in Iraq, and whatever stability has been achieved in the past has been based on intercommunal deal making rather than on the melting-pot effect. Such deal making is not a process that Americans tend to understand or appreciate, having had little experience with it outside of its limited role in a few big-city political machines.

THE RACIAL EXCEPTION

The status of African Americans has constituted a conspicuous unmelted blob in much of the history of the American melting pot. The racial exception to American exceptionalism began with the quite different way, compared to every other group, in which blacks came to America: as slaves.[12] The division between races has played a large role in U.S. history, to the extent that it led to a civil war that represented by far the greatest threat the American republic has ever had to its integrity. The legacy of race as a defining distinction in the American experience is strong and has been a fundamental category for understanding and judging other people, especially among Americans of European descent.[13]

That the distinction between black and white races has had such a special role in U.S. history has kept it separate from other ethnic distinctions in the American mind. As a criterion for perceiving different demographic groups and forming conclusions about these groups' ability or inability to live harmoniously together, race has been in a class by itself. The divisive role race has played in U.S. history thus has ironically tended not to detract from the larger faith in the efficacy of melting pots. That faith may actually have been strengthened by seeing how the integration of whites of different national origins has seemed easy when compared to the integration of blacks and whites.

Race also is a conspicuously more visible distinction than most other ethnic or sectarian divisions. To an American eye, Arabs and Kurds look alike, as do Serbs and Croats, but blacks and whites definitely do not. The easy physical identifiability involved in the racial division is another reason the prominence of that division for Americans has not erased their tendency to underestimate the difficulty of integrating different ethnic communities in other lands.

The salience of race in the American consciousness at times leads Americans to assign it too large a role in their explanations of conflicts overseas, at the expense of understanding other aspects of those conflicts that are at least important. When an interviewer asked Lyndon Johnson during the

Vietnam War to explain why J. William Fulbright, the chairman of the Senate Committee on Foreign Relations, had come to oppose the war, Johnson replied, "It's some little racial problem." The president said that the Arkansas senator "cannot understand that people with brown skins value freedom too," and he went on to criticize Fulbright for opposing civil rights legislation in the United States.[14] Johnson's reply was a tactically convenient way to change the subject from the war and from the loss of public and political support for it to his domestic program. The reply also reflected, though, how much easier it was for Americans to invoke racially based explanations than to understand that the Vietnam War was less about the yearning of brown-skinned people for freedom than about a nationalist movement and a yearning for self-determination.

Race has been a major dimension in perceptions of conflict in the Darfur region of western Sudan, which has been a favorite cause of American actors and other celebrities. The conflict is seen as between Arabs and black Africans, with the former having the support of the regime in Khartoum and generally being perceived as the culprits responsible for the human suffering in Darfur. Although this image fairly depicts to some extent the lines of conflict in Darfur, the conflict is more complex and involves the divergent interests of farmers and seminomadic livestock herders. All Sudanese are African, nearly all Darfurians are Muslim, and intermarriage has reduced even the physical differences between "Arabs" and "black Africans."[15] Many Americans who have expressed interest in the Darfur conflict have not laid eyes directly on either.

Most, though by no means all, of the malevolent legacy of America's troubled racial history has now been overcome, thanks mainly to Johnson's and others' efforts to deal with it by force of law. This partial success has probably enhanced the American faith in the universal efficacy of melting pots by being taken as a lesson that even the most bitter and visible ethnic divisions can be overcome. If blacks and whites in America can be integrated, goes the thought, so can anyone. Substantial, visible progress in racial integration since the 1960s is within the living memory of many Americans today. It is easy for them to forget that it took a century to get from the Civil War and the abolition of slavery to the civil rights legislation of the 1960s and thus to fail to apply the relevant lesson to ethnic divisions in other countries.

The intensity and salience of America's past racial problems also would lead many Americans to reject the premise of this chapter: that the United States, for a combination of reasons, has not had to struggle with as many and as serious domestic disruptions as most other countries. "We fought a civil war over secession and slavery, didn't we?" would be the likely response to this assertion. A single salient issue or even a single wrenching event can produce so much glare that it obscures the larger picture. The phenomenon is similar to how the shock and salience of 9/11 led many Americans to believe incorrectly that the United States was way ahead of everyone else in facing the threat of international terrorism and in devising legal and security mechanisms for dealing with it. Regarding ethnic divisions, Americans again resist believing there are lessons to be learned from abroad, and there is again a lack of self-awareness of how America's exceptional circumstances affects Americans' perceptions of conflicts abroad.

MIXED EFFECTS OF RELIGION

The role of religion in current American thinking about overseas problems is more complicated than the effects of ethnicity and race. The historical role of religion in America also has been complicated from the early days of settlement along the eastern seaboard. Religious freedom was a major theme and motivation for many of the original colonists, for whom the physical separation of crossing the Atlantic also involved a doctrinal separation from the Church of England. Several of the colonies, however, had their own distinct religious identities—for instance, Catholics in Maryland, Quakers in Pennsylvania, and Congregationalists in Massachusetts.

The degree of overall religiosity in America has also varied significantly over time. The American colonies were widely affected by the evangelical movement known as the First Great Awakening in the first half of the eighteenth century, but the United States later came into being in the hands of the mostly secular-minded Founding Fathers, who codified a separation of church and state. The U.S. Constitution makes no mention of religion or of God except for prohibiting in the First Amendment the making of any law regarding an establishment of religion. The days of the Founding Fathers marked a perigee of the role of religion in the American public consciousness.

Since those days, the trajectory of religious influence on American attitudes has been uneven but upward. Besides passing through the Second and Third Great Awakenings of the nineteenth century (and what some consider a fourth, beginning in the latter half of the twentieth century), Americans found certain beliefs of revealed religion to be natural complements to the national self-image that other aspects of their circumstances and history had nurtured. This was especially true regarding the idea of providence as underlying America's blessedly fortunate physical circumstances and historical success. The conjoining of God's will with not only those circumstances but also with the American people's will was a theme increasingly heard in the late nineteenth century from figures such as William Jennings Bryan. A similar combination would appear, with particular reference to foreign relations, in the writings and speeches of Woodrow Wilson and John Foster Dulles in the twentieth century and continue through George W. Bush in the twenty-first.[16]

Providence also had played a role in much thinking among European great powers as they were expanding their empires, but the carnage of World War I tore apart most of the perceived connection with the divine and destroyed it altogether in Germany.[17] In the United States, by contrast, the tie between divine will and national destiny was left largely undamaged by the war. During the Cold War, the tie was strengthened further in American minds with the dominant theme of U.S. foreign policy being a struggle against godless communism.[18]

The Establishment Clause of the Constitution would hardly give an accurate idea of the role religion plays today in not only the civic culture but also the political life of the United States. The place of "In God We Trust" on U.S. currency is not a matter of controversy except among a few seldom-noticed atheists. Asking for God's blessing on the United States is a required closing line for any major address by a U.S. president. Courts allow religious beliefs of persons in the private sector to overrule portions of statutes providing for public services.[19] A leading candidate for the Republican presidential nomination in 2012, former senator Rick Santorum, said that John F. Kennedy's speech in 1960 in which Kennedy pledged not to impose his Catholic faith on the nation if elected president made Santorum "want to throw up."[20]

The current place of religion in the thoughts of Americans, as compared to non-Americans, can be summarized in two patterns readily apparent in cross-national polls that have asked people about the importance of religion in their lives. First, Americans do not define themselves in religious terms as much as do people in most less-developed countries, where religion is typically a matter not only of faith but of substate community identification. An individual American does not locate his or her place in national society in the same way that a Hindu or Muslim in India would, with religion being the primary distinguishing attribute. But, second, Americans are significantly more religious overall than their counterparts in other developed countries. In a series of polls taken between 2006 and 2009 that asked respondents whether religion is important in their daily lives, 38 percent of all those polled in twenty-seven developed countries said yes; in the United States, the figure was 65 percent.[21]

Notwithstanding the religious dimension of divisive domestic issues in the United States such as abortion, religion in the theological sense has become a significant element of the civil religion of the United States. Even when not explicitly mentioned, it is part of how many Americans relate their nation as a whole to the rest of the world. It thus helps to shape American perceptions of the rest of the world in several ways.

A sense of righteousness, or lack of righteousness on the part of others, is a component of those perceptions. President George W. Bush again functioned as a spokesman for the outlook in question, with his pronouncements made all the more sincere by his personal religious history. In a private meeting with religious leaders, after mentioning that "I was a sinner in need of redemption and found it," Bush described the United States as a nation that was "sinned against."[22] This manner of looking at the international relations of the United States exacerbates tendencies to overlook actions by the United States—the perceived righteous side—that stimulate or provoke harmful actions by others. It also encourages the downplaying or overlooking of any legitimate grievances or understandable impulses among the "sinners."

The rise of religiosity in America has coincided with and been related to the American habit of looking at foreign policy in moral terms. Arthur Schlesinger Jr. observed how what he described as the "realism of the revolutionary generation" faded during a century without any direct U.S. involvement in Europe's struggles—a century that nurtured the myth of American innocence and righteousness—after which "the moralization of foreign policy became a national penchant." This moralization led to an unfortunate undermining of diplomacy, noted Schlesinger, given that diplomacy is all about adjusting conflicting interests rather than about confronting evil with good.[23] In terms of misperceptions, this comment could be rephrased by noting that moralization of foreign policy impairs the ability to understand the conflicting interests at stake and to see possibilities for reconciling or compromising those interests. Other observers have noted how Americans have a stronger sense of moral absolutism than Europeans or even their next-door neighbors in Canada.[24]

The sociologist Daniel Bell commented in the middle of the twentieth century, "One of the unique aspects of American politics is that while domestic issues have been argued in hard-headed, practical terms, with a give-and-take compromise as the outcome, foreign policy has always been phrased in moralistic terms." One of the possible explanations Bell offered for this pattern was that "perhaps being distant from the real centers of interest conflict allowed us to employ pieties, rather than face realities."[25] Since the 1950s, about which Bell was writing and in which he discerned an "end of ideology," American domestic politics have become markedly less practical, more ideological, and more moralistic. The damage has been obvious in the form of political gridlock, congressional paralysis, and a lack of comity. This result indirectly supports Bell's point that indulging in pieties rather than being practical and realistic is an affordable luxury only when there are no immediate practical problems to address. In foreign relations, even by the 1950s a globally involved United States was no longer distant from centers of conflict relevant to its own interests. The sheer power of the United States helped to overcome what might otherwise have been even heavier damage from this outdated indulgence in moralism, but a price for this indulgence has nonetheless been paid, including in the form of misperception and misunderstanding of many of those foreign conflicts.

The strictly religious aspect of the American civil religion is a major ingredient in the American tendency to view the world in a rigidly divided, Manichean manner, in which those on the other side are not just adversaries and not even just sinners, but embodiments of evil. The term *Manichean* has a non-Christian, albeit religious, origin, but the American outlook can be traced to Jesus's words, as related in Matthew 12:30 and Luke 11:23 and long repeated by American preachers, about being either for him or against him.[26] The clearest American echo of those words was in the "either with us or with the terrorists" rhetoric voiced during the younger Bush's administration. The Manichean outlook has impaired understanding of many other situations faced by many other administrations, however—basically any situation, of which there are many in the world, in which lines of contention do not divide the players cleanly into two sides, much less distinguish clearly between good and evil. During the Cold War, such situations included the Vietnam War, in which some of the most important drivers of events were not part of a worldwide lineup of Communists versus non-Communists. In the contemporary Middle East, they include simultaneous civil wars in Syria and Iraq; the United States declared an objective of dispatching the regime in Syria, but the strongest challengers to that regime are Islamist radicals who also are seen as the greatest threat in Iraq. American attempts to define politics in the Middle East as a single, overarching contest between radicals and moderates keep failing amid a more complex reality.

American interpretations of international terrorism illustrate the tendency to apply the good-versus-evil template as well as the shortcomings of that application. George W. Bush, the incumbent president at the time of the 9/11 attacks, spoke in terms that described the perpetrators of those attacks as satanic. He referred to Osama bin Laden as "the evil one" and to his colleagues as "evil ones" or "evildoers." He later quoted a survivor from the World Trade Center who described the sound of the collapsing twin towers as "like the roar of the devil."[27] For the majority of the American public who believe that the devil exists and that people can be possessed by the devil,[28] such vocabulary has a specific, substantive, religiously infused meaning.

Perceiving terrorism in terms of the evil nature or evil spirits of individual terrorists implies a highly truncated and distorted understanding of the phenomenon of international terrorism. It leads to the ignoring of, if not the explicit rejection of, the role that political, economic, and social circumstances play in determining the incidence of terrorism, including who is most likely to resort to it or to sympathize with those who do, where it is most likely to arise, and what causes it to wax or wane.[29] Much public discussion in the United States of counterterrorism, especially in the years following 9/11, has accordingly tended to regard any attention to these circumstances as a wimpy digression from the need to confront the evildoers forthrightly. Narrow focus on individual terrorists' malevolence also leads to a mistaken belief that terrorism can be defeated by eliminating a fixed group of evil individuals called "the terrorists"—somewhat like exorcising evil spirits from an individual. This perspective impedes understanding of terrorism as a tactic that different sorts of people of widely different religious persuasions have used for many different purposes for millennia.

Divine will also has entered American views of democratization and of political and civil liberties in foreign countries. In one of the televised debates during his campaign for reelection in 2004, President Bush said, "I believe that God wants everybody to be free. That's what I believe. And that's one part of my foreign policy. In Afghanistan I believe that the freedom there is a gift from the Almighty."[30] Bush, a Republican, was one of the two most avowedly religious presidents in recent decades; the other was Jimmy Carter, a Democrat. Bush's expressed sentiments, however, reflected the inclinations of substantial portions of the American citizenry articulated at different times and in different ways. The image of the long U.S. nation-building effort in Afghanistan as being the delivery of God's gift of freedom recalls Melville's words from a century and a half earlier about Americans being a chosen people bearing "the ark of the liberties of the world."

Belief that one is carrying out a divine mission naturally leads to underestimation of obstacles to completion of the mission and overestimation of the likelihood of successfully completing it. Believers tend to be confident that if God wants something, He will get His way. In this respect, religious faith has been one of several ingredients contributing to overly optimistic American expectations about the establishment of liberal democracy in Afghanistan, in the Middle East after the Arab Spring, and elsewhere. As such, it also contributes to recriminations and political criticism of the stewardship of incumbents when liberal democracy is not smoothly established in such places. Botching a democratization program is bad enough; messing up a gift from God is even worse.

There also has been insufficient understanding of how each of the contending parties whose conflicts have prevented the establishment of stable democracy in many foreign countries may believe God is on *its* side and how severe a fault line religious identification can be in such lands. This deficiency is related to how religion in America has functioned more as an element in a shared national civil religion than as a distinction that divides subnational communities. The United States has experienced nothing like the religiously based warfare that plagues many places in Africa and Asia, that helped lead to the formation of the European state system, and that even has appeared in modern Europe in Northern Ireland and the former Yugoslavia. Americans thus have less basis than most others for anticipating and understanding such warfare when it arises in countries with which the United States has become involved. The leading recent example is the failure of the makers of the Iraq War to anticipate, despite expert advice on the subject, the severe and still ongoing strife between Sunnis and Shiites in Iraq.

THE JUDEO-CHRISTIAN NATION

The seamless and not always conscious weaving of generic religiosity into the American public philosophy has come to apply as well to some content associated with specific religions. It was not always so. The Founding Fathers were conscious of the hazards of religious sectarianism as well as of more secular forms of factionalism. George Washington said, "The United States is not a Christian nation, any more than it is a Jewish or Mohammedan nation."[31] When Thomas Jefferson and James Madison put a draft of the Virginia Statute for Religious Freedom (a precursor to the Establishment Clause of the U.S. Constitution) before the state's General Assembly in 1779, devout Christians such as Patrick Henry tried to insert a reference to "Jesus Christ" in the opening words but were voted down overwhelmingly. Jefferson approvingly interpreted the vote as a sign that the legislature wanted the law "to comprehend, within the mantle of its protection, the Jew and the Gentile, the Christian and Mahomedan, the Hindoo, and Infidel of every denomination."[32]

Subsequent surges in religious sentiment in America, however, beginning with the Second Great Awakening, were squarely in the Judeo-Christian tradition and led to a widely accepted view of the United States as a Christian nation.[33] Over time, the dominant influence has narrowed further to Protestantism and especially the evangelical forms of it, as demonstrated by such compromises of the Establishment Clause as proselytization at U.S. military academies.[34] The sectarian influence on American thinking is not always quite that narrow, however. Santorum, the Catholic who felt sickened by Kennedy's pledge not to insert his own Catholicism into government affairs, is a clear example of a Christianist politician, every bit as much as many political leaders in other countries are Islamist politicians.

The principal effect of the sectarian influence on American understanding of the world abroad concerns threat perceptions. Americans are quicker to see threats from outside the Judeo-Christian sphere than ones from inside it. In particular in recent times, the sectarian influence has contributed to Islamophobia. The crudest forms of it are found in some anti-Islamic expressions from American preachers, which, to the detriment of the American image abroad, get more noticed in majority Muslim countries than they do in the United States.[35] Islamophobia exists in western Europe, too, but there it stems more from immediate economic and social fears of people living near Muslim populations that are larger and less integrated than those in the United States. In America—with a population more religious than that of western Europe—the bias is more deeply rooted in religious identification itself.

The bias in threat perceptions extends to official business, especially business related to terrorism. A series of hearings of the House Homeland Security Committee in 2011 was supposed to be about domestic terrorist threats, but the focus was entirely on Islamic radicalism. Even more pertinent to perceptions of threats abroad was the statement *National Strategy for Counterterrorism*, which the Obama administration released in June 2011.[36] Despite the general title, nearly the entire document was about al-Qaʿida. In a nineteen-page paper, a single section of seven sentences titled "Other Terrorism Concerns Requiring Focus and Attention" was all the attention anything else got.

It is, of course, fact and not misperception that the terrorist problems the United States has most had to deal with and that have most touched American lives in recent years have been primarily Islamist. What has become the strong American tendency to equate terrorism with Islamist terrorism induces errors of understanding in two directions, however. One is to overlook terrorist threats of other types. A counterterrorist strategy document that dismisses everything non-Islamist in a few sentences will be prime fodder not only for the usual recriminations but perhaps for justified criticism after a major terrorist attack at the hands of any non-Islamist perpetrator. The other error is to see threats in Islamist movements where they do not necessarily exist, resulting in broader misunderstanding of political dynamics and lines of conflict in areas where such movements are significant players.

The latter problem has characterized much American discussion of political change in the Middle East, especially since the start of the Arab Spring. The habitual way of viewing such change has been to see Islamists pitted against secularists, with a disproportional wariness of the former and preference for the latter. This view ignores how political Islam is not a single ideology and does not represent a single point on any scale of extremism versus moderation. Instead, it is more of a political vocabulary that permeates discourse throughout the Middle East and through which a wide variety of aspirations are expressed and pursued.[37] Lumping Islamists together, as is so commonly done in American discourse about the region, obscures more than it illuminates. In particular, the practice overlooks the extent to which Islamist parties and movements are vehicles for the expression of grievances that are not inherently Islamist.

A particular focus of the wariness of Islamists is the fear expressed in the slogan "one man, one vote, one time"—the idea that even democratically elected Islamists will not surrender power once they have it. During the Cold War, the same idea had been applied to leftists such as Salvador Allende in Chile, who were believed to be following an undemocratic Communist script of never relinquishing any momentarily gained power. In one of its first post–Cold War manifestations, this fear motivated U.S. toleration of a military coup in Algeria in 1991 that aborted a free election that an Islamist group was expected to win; the coup ushered in a savage civil war in Algeria in which the death toll probably reached six figures. A similar outlook underlay the mild U.S. reaction to the military coup in Egypt in 2013 that overthrew the country's democratically elected president, Mohamed Morsi, who happened to be a leader of the Muslim Brotherhood. There is little reason to suppose that Islamists who have competed in democratic elections, such as the Islamic Salvation Front in Algeria and the Egyptian Muslim Brotherhood, are any more prone to clinging undemocratically to power than are military officers or many African big men, not to mention Communists. In Tunisia, the birthplace of the Arab Spring, the Islamist Ennahda Movement voluntarily stepped down and yielded power to a technocratic government in 2014 amid political deadlock and a loss of some of the popular support that had won it a plurality in a free election three years earlier. The sectarian dimension that is part of the typical American outlook, however, encourages the perception that Islamists are inherently more prone than others to undemocratic power grabs. That outlook has underlain policies that supposedly are protective of democracy but instead have tended to diminish it.

The American worldview's Judeo-Christian background also has significantly reinforced the tendencies in how Americans view the conflict between Israel and Palestinian Arabs, described in the previous chapter. The religious aspect has influenced thinking about the conflict for reasons that go beyond biblical literacy and sentiments about divine gifts of land. The ancient Hebrews were precursors to Christ, whereas Muslims follow a prophet who came later and whom Muslims consider to have received the definitive word of God. This theological sequence is bound to figure into the attitudes of American believers, the majority of whom are Christian, regarding a conflict that pits a primarily Jewish people against a primarily Muslim one.

The theology gets even more specifically applicable for evangelical Christians influenced by the doctrine of dispensationalism, according to which God has yet to fulfill His promises to the nation of Israel and must first do so before Christ can return. Again, the mental and emotional transition from the ancient Israelites to today's State of Israel is seamless in this way of thinking, without letting any historical, demographic, or genetic complications get in the way. Dispensationalism in the United States has a long history. A major Christian figure in the late nineteenth century promoting the idea of moving Jews to Palestine was the evangelist William Eugene Blackstone, who prepared a letter to President Benjamin Harrison on the subject that elicited signatures from such luminaries as the Speaker of the House, the chief justice of the Supreme Court, J. P. Morgan, and John D. Rockefeller.[38] The U.S. president at the time of the Balfour Declaration, Woodrow Wilson, was not an evangelical but a son and grandson of Presbyterian ministers and a daily Bible reader whose view of Zionism was influenced by his friend Louis Brandeis's description of it as a form of American progressivism.[39]

The role of specific Christian religious beliefs is reflected in polls that register American public opinion regarding the Israeli–Palestinian conflict. A poll in 2013 asked Americans, "Was Israel given to the Jewish people by God?" Among all respondents, 44 percent replied yes. Jewish respondents were *less* likely to say yes (40 percent, although 84 percent of Orthodox Jews agreed with the statement). Affirmative responses from all Christians totaled 55 percent, from Protestants 64 percent, and from white evangelicals 82 percent.[40]

The religious dimension of American attitudes toward the Israeli–Palestinian conflict amplifies the other reasons why Americans identify disproportionately with Israel and why their perceptions of the conflict are accordingly distorted. The conflation of religious faith and beliefs about the conflict also provides a ready mental and emotional channel for disposing of any evidence that may run contrary to the beliefs. Walter Russell Mead observes, "Criticism of Israel and of the United States for supporting it leaves evangelicals unmoved. If anything, it only strengthens their conviction that the world hates Israel because 'fallen man' naturally hates God and his 'chosen people.'"[41] This posture leads to rejection of evidence that Israeli and U.S. policies have much to do with the foreign criticism and that a major ingredient in anti-Americanism in parts of the world is what is seen as unfair U.S. support to Israel.[42]

THE LIBERAL DEMOCRATIC CONSENSUS

Whatever specific effects ethnicity, race, and religion have had on Americans' perceptions of the world beyond their borders, the overall success of liberal democracy in America has had a grander influence on those perceptions. Despite all of the imperfections and frictions this democracy exhibits, it still stands out among the universe of nation-states and not only because of its longevity. The United States was long the most populous democracy until India gained independence. It is still by far the most powerful democracy. Equally important as an influence on American attitudes is the very prominent role that the image of the United States as a successful democracy has played in Americans' national self-identity.

The sequence of historical events has much to do with this self-identity as well as with the success of the democracy itself. An exceptional aspect of the history of the United States is that other than Iceland it was the first new nation to transition from colony to independent state. Its very existence has been defined by its citizens from the beginning in terms of political principles rather than an ethnically based birthright. Apart from the decid-edly undemocratic, predominantly Russian, and ultimately ephemeral Soviet Union, the United States is unusual in having an ideological identity and raison d'être.[43] It is almost unique in how much its nationality is identi-fied with a particular political creed—which in this case is a creed of liberal democracy.[44] Either national identity or a political creed can strongly influ-ence the perceptions of a public and its leaders, but that in the United States identity and creed are so closely enmeshed to a degree unmatched by any other nation makes the combined influence on perceptions all the stron-ger.[45] The fusion of identity and creed is reflected as well in how Americans see what they are *not*; the United States may be the only country to have a legislative committee that incorporates the fusion in a name such as the "House Committee on Un-American Activities," which existed for three decades in the mid–twentieth century.

The success of American liberal democracy rests on the near unanimity among its citizens in believing in underlying principles of liberalism. Louis Hartz explained in the mid-1950s how historical circumstances account for this happy attribute and how it has made the United States different even from its sister modern democracies in Europe. The starting point was the feudal tradition that Europe had and America did not and that gave rise to competing ideologies. "European liberalism," wrote Hartz, "because it was cursed with feudalism, was forced to create the mentality of social-ism, and thus was twice cursed. American liberalism, freed of the one was freed of the other, and hence was twice blessed."[46] The historical sequence of industrialization and political and social development also made America less vulnerable than Europe to ideological division and associated politi-cal strife. Robert Heilbroner observed that in Europe industrial technology was injected into societies that already were stratified, with roles already parceled out. The technology thus was disruptive, engendering fear and resistance from the aristocracy and laboring classes alike. In the United States, where social patterns had not yet crystallized, the technology was less disruptive and instead seen more positively as an instrument of mobility and development.[47]

Hartz identified some of the extensive negative effects that America's domestically unchallenged tradition of liberalism has had on Americans' understanding of the rest of the world:

> It is the absence of the experience of social revolution which is at the heart of the whole American dilemma. . . . In a whole series of ways it enters into our difficulty of communication with the rest of the world. We find it hard to understand Europe's "social question" and hence tend to interpret even the democratic socialisms of Europe in terms of our own antiradical fetishism. We are not familiar with the deeper social struggles of Asia and hence tend to interpret even reactionary regimes as "democratic." We fail to appreciate nonpolitical definitions of "freedom" and hence are baffled by their use.[48]

In various other respects, understanding issues and fissures in foreign lands tends to come especially hard to Americans because of an absence of domestic counterparts or even analogies in the American national experience. Different usages of otherwise familiar terms are also involved, as Hartz mentioned regarding *freedom*. In many places, a predominant yearning is for freedom *from* hunger or other forms of want or *from* the physical dangers associated with disorder, but it is hard for an American to comprehend a willingness to sacrifice the positive political freedom at the center of the liberal democratic creed.

Justice is another concept whose use abroad can be opaque to most Americans, who tend to think of it in narrow procedural and legal terms and who would not see it taking precedence over political freedom. The usage elsewhere often gets into basic—or what Americans would consider constitutional—issues of distribution of power and even more often into questions of economic distribution. Non-American concepts of justice infuse much political conflict in the Middle East. Failure to understand its usage there is an additional ingredient in American wariness—or outright rejection—of some manifestations of political Islam, which is seen by adherents of Islamist movements as a vehicle for erecting a more just social order but by Americans as a vehicle for imposing alien and undemocratic strictures.

A common thread in such misunderstandings is that they involve social and political conflicts that do not resemble anything the United States has experienced, however common they may be elsewhere in the world. Americans thus have difficulty appreciating the bases and fundamental motivations for many conflicts, leading to one of two different but comparably uncomprehending responses. One is simply to reject any legitimacy of whichever side seems farthest removed from the political principles with which Americans are comfortable and thus to consider it the evil side of the Manichean divide. The other response, grounded in the American record of reconciling differing interests within the shared consensus of liberalism, is to believe that with enough persistence and negotiating skill—and sometimes with the help of pressures to change one side's calculations—differences can be bridged and conflict-resolving deals can be struck.

The latter response characterized American perceptions of the war in Vietnam. Failure to understand fully the lines of conflict in that country underlay U.S. frustrations beginning in the early 1960s, when internal divisions within South Vietnam, highlighted by Buddhist self-immolations in protest against the Diem regime, severely impeded the mounting of an effective effort against the Communist insurgency. As Frances FitzGerald observes in her chronicle of the war, "To American officials throughout the war it seemed absolutely unreasonable that the non-Communist sects and political factions could not come to some agreement, could not cooperate even in their opposition to the Communists."[49] There certainly was American understanding that the contest against the Communists themselves represented a significant ideological divide, but even there the differences were perceived as bridgeable through bargaining. Striking deals with Communists was done at other times during the Cold War—for example, regarding Indochina in 1954 and with Moscow at other times and on other topics. FitzGerald notes the domestic American roots of this perception: "Never having known a serious ideological struggle in their history, many Americans persisted in thinking of the Vietnamese conflict as . . . a battle between two fixed groups of people with different but conceivably negotiable interests."[50] The misperception was common both to the Johnson administration, which believed that a mutually acceptable solution could be reached with the help of motivation-changing firepower, and to dovish opponents of the administration who believed that a stable and genuinely neutralist settlement was possible.

The agreement that eventually was negotiated and got U.S. troops out of Vietnam marked the start of only a decent interval before Communist forces overran South Vietnam, completing the Viet Minh version of a nationalist, social revolution. Robert McNamara, in his later litany of U.S. failures regarding the Vietnam War, summarized well the basic perceptual shortcoming and the reason for it: "We viewed the people and leaders of South Vietnam in terms of our own experience. We saw in them a thirst for—and a determination to fight for—freedom and democracy. We totally misjudged the political forces in the country."[51] The shared American experience, with its political creed of freedom and democracy, was more influential in shaping policy makers' perceptions than were the judgments of the U.S. intelligence community, which had provided a succession of gloomy assessments about the prospects for South Vietnam being able to stand as a free and strong society.[52]

THE HIGHEST AND FINAL GOOD

The effects of a shared political creed and a closely related national identity are further accentuated by their being associated with ideas of morality and inevitability. A tenet of the liberalism that dominates American thought is that all good things go together.[53] What is seen as moral, what is seen as inevitable because it is being propelled by some sort of historical imperative, and what is distinctively American thus tend to get merged in American minds. The infusion of morality also reflects the greater tendency in the United States, as contrasted with European nations, to define many policy disagreements in moral terms rather than as straightforward conflicts of interests—the other type of response, different from the one that characterized attitudes toward Vietnam, that Americans may exhibit when facing a type of conflict with which they are not familiar.[54] The infusion of morality leads to the definition of the domestically shared creed of liberal democracy as morally superior to any alternatives the United States encounters abroad. This definition in turn bolsters the self-image of exceptional America as being exceptionally good, manifested in expressions such as Bush's "I know how good we are," and so an encounter with anyone overseas who does not perceive the United States the same way often brings surprise and consternation.[55]

The element of inevitability involves a sense that history is inexorably moving in the direction of liberal democracy. Description and prescription get mixed in this way of thinking. The United States is seen as appropriately leading this march of history, and it is considered good policy for it to grab the drum major's baton and to wave it proudly in doing the leading, but with an assurance that the world was already heading in the desired direction anyway. All of these elements were in the thinking of the first U.S. president to make expansion of democracy a major theme, Woodrow Wilson.[56] The modern and more muscular successor to this tradition of American thought, neoconservatism, also believes in a larger worldwide progression toward liberal democracy and in the ability of liberal democracy to take hold in many different places, although it places more emphasis on the United States bringing about this change.

These long-standing tendencies in American thinking underlay the big splash that Francis Fukuyama made in the United States with his "end of history" idea in 1989.[57] The splash was remarkably big for an article that was really about political philosophy and the outcome of some debates within the realm of ideas. The author did not claim that the real, material world was about to lapse into boring entropy and that editors would soon have trouble finding stories to fill the world news sections of their newspapers, but many people responded as if he had. Different meanings of the word *history* as well as euphoria associated with the end of the Cold War (Fukuyama's article was published in the same year the Berlin Wall came down) account for much of the response. Another reason for the reaction, however, was how well Fukuyama's theme fit with the idea, already deeply entrenched in American thinking, of a one-way historical progression in which

American-style liberal democracy is the highest, most moral, and final form of political organization.

INSTALLING DEMOCRACY OVERSEAS

One consequence of the American consensus about liberalism and the moral coloration Americans apply to it is a tendency to overstate the danger that nonliberal and nondemocratic forces pose to American interests.[58] Probably the biggest misunderstanding stemming from the consensus, however, involves underestimation of the difficulties in getting liberal democracy to take root in other countries. The misunderstanding begins with confidence in the malleability of political systems and the people (evildoers excepted) who are part of them. Tocqueville saw in democratic nations, unlike aristocratic ones, a belief in the indefinite perfectibility of man.[59] Add in the successful American experience of engineering a stable as well as liberal and democratic political order, and the result is a strongly held belief that once impediments (usually in the form of autocratic or foreign rule or both) are eliminated, people in other lands can enjoy the blessings of freedom, democracy, and stability as well.

The belief underlay the Wilsonian anticipation of a more democratic and peaceful Europe once the empires that had brought about World War I were no longer around. During the Cold War, a similar belief underlay the expectation that the blessings of liberty and democracy would come wherever the Communist menace was successfully beaten back—South Vietnam being the most conspicuous and costliest example of this expectation. The end of the Cold War was seen as not just a victory over the chief Communist protagonist but also an opening to what President George H. W. Bush called a "new world order" based on freedom and democracy. Again, this expected new order was grounded in America's own experience. "Never before," said the elder Bush, "has the world looked more to the American example."[60] The world order was seen as new, but the American idea of other countries following America's example in how they order their internal affairs is as old as John Winthrop's words in 1630 about a city upon a hill. Jeremi Suri has observed about the American attitude toward nation building, "Nothing could be more American than to pursue global peace through the spread of American-style institutions"—and to expect support for that process from, among others, the local populations involved.[61]

For many reasons, even after autocracy is overthrown or beaten back, stability and democracy often do not fall into place. And so since the end of the Cold War there have continued to be disappointing divergences between expectations for what would fall into place when America took a leading role in moving the march of history along, on the one hand, and a messier and less stable reality, on the other. The disappointments have included Afghanistan after the ouster of the Taliban and Libya after the ouster of Muammar Qadhafi.

The resulting pattern involves a complicated set of contrasts between American attitudes and the attitudes found in most other Western countries. Americans and American politicians are avowedly less favorably inclined than Western counterparts to get into nation building, especially as a declared mission for their armed forces. Americans see the overthrowing of tyrants who block the road to democracy as a more appropriate job for their military. Many other Western nations—Germany and Japan, the heirs to the rare examples of successful American-guided democracy building after World War II, are the best examples—are instead happier if their soldiers do *not* do the heavy combat necessary to overthrow a regime and so stick to less-violent nation-building tasks. But Americans, even though not favorably disposed in the abstract to getting immersed in nation building, have repeatedly gotten involved in it anyway, driven by an optimism that is based on America's own experience and that incorrectly anticipates quick and successful reconstruction after a regime-changing military operation. Until, that is, the optimism turns to disillusionment when reconstruction proves not to be quick and successful.[62]

The costliest and most glaring divergence between the expectations of those who tried to accelerate a movement toward liberal democracy and the actual results of their efforts was in the neoconservative experiment known as the Iraq War. The war makers' chief purpose, notwithstanding other issues they employed to muster public support for the war, was to use the overthrow of an Iraqi dictator as a hoped-for catalyst for political and economic change in the Middle East in the direction of American-style liberal democracy and free-market economics.[63] The confidence that historical inevitability was on their side and that the only thing needed was to kick out of the way a dictator who was impeding history's march led to the belief that a new Iraqi order would fall into place smoothly and inexpensively. The distinctive attribute of the neoconservatives' project was the launching of a war of aggression, which was not the case with U.S. involvement in the wars of the twentieth century. Despite this difference, in other respects neoconservatism is firmly embedded in the long-standing American outlook about how all peoples are capable of enjoying freedom and democracy and how America's leading role is to help remove the impediments to their doing so. In his war message to Congress in 1917, Wilson said that "the world must be made safe for democracy"; the neoconservatives thought that was what they were doing, too. And, as always, America's own unusually happy experience of the past shaped these thoughts. As Patrick Lang summarizes the perceptions leading to the Iraq War, "Americans invaded an imaginary Iraq that fit into our vision of the world. We invaded Iraq in the sure belief that inside every Iraqi there was an American trying to get out."[64]

The American misunderstanding about the ability of stable, liberal democracy to take hold in other countries is a matter not of absolutes but instead of degrees of difficulty and of the conditions that encourage or discourage the establishment of liberal democracy. It would be ethnocentric prejudice to contend that other people can *never* enjoy freedom and democracy. To a large extent, the relevant issue is one of timing—how long it takes to establish the habits, values, and patterns of thought that make it possible for liberal democracy to work and to work well. It takes a very long time. It has taken several centuries for Anglo-American people to get from Magna Carta to where they are now. Most of those centuries had already transpired when the United States came into being, and Americans thus tend to take that part of the process for granted. The Founding Fathers built upon habits, values, and patterns of thought they had inherited from Britain. With Americans being ahead—though only slightly ahead—of the mother country in taking the next couple of steps away from monarchical rule and toward popular sovereignty, and with U.S. independence being a breaking away from the mother country, this inheritance gets overlooked. Americans thus tend to think of the habits and values necessary for successful democracy to be either already in the hearts of humankind everywhere or as easily and quickly grown as grain on the North American prairie—hence the optimism about being able to establish democracy at a forced-draft pace in places such as Iraq.

The economic conditions for stable liberal democracy similarly get overlooked. Because Americans so often take for granted the abundance the United States has enjoyed, they do not sufficiently take into account its role in domestic politics and stability when trying to export the American political model elsewhere. "Thus our whole conception of our mission in the world," wrote David Potter, "was distorted by our failure to understand what the world regarded as most significant in our development"—that is, the economic abundance—"and what the essential conditions of democratic life in the American sense really are."[65]

The moral veneer that Americans place on liberal democracy and on their own adoption of it colors their perceptions of the choices other people have made among political forms and the degree to which they have had any choice at all. The common American conception is that people everywhere, or those who rule them, do indeed have a choice, that the basic choice is between civil and political liberties or the absence of them, that a choice in favor of liberty is the only morally right decision, and that the United States has been most clearly and strongly in front of the rest of the world in making that choice. This outlook on domestic political structures and their relation to international politics was especially strengthened during the Cold War, when the global political lineup was customarily divided into "freedom-loving nations" or "freedom-loving peoples" and those who did not love freedom.

The outlook exacerbates the Manichean way of perceiving the world, wherein differences among those on one side of the good–bad divide are underestimated and differences between nations assigned to opposite sides of the divide are overestimated. The outlook leads to overestimation of the extent to which people or even their rulers really do have a choice in designing systems of governance, bearing in mind the conditions that make some systems less feasible than others. It underlies insufficient appreciation of the reasons, other than a morally infused choice, why many other nations are not American-style liberal democracies.

The outlook skews explanations and inhibits understanding of radical and destructive behavior originating abroad. A moralistic view of loving or hating American-style freedom and democracy as an all-encompassing explanation for foreign behavior underlay why the president of the United States, in a speech to Congress in the aftermath of the 9/11 terrorist attacks, responded to the question "Why do they hate us?" with this answer: "They hate what we see right here in this chamber—a democratically elected government. Their leaders are self-appointed. They hate our freedoms—our freedom of religion, our freedom of speech, our freedom to vote and assemble and disagree with each other."[66] Such an answer overlooks and obscures more accurate explanations of the motives and attitudes underlying international terrorism, including grievances against the target country in addition to, as noted earlier, the political and economic conditions where the terrorism originates.

The same outlook also leads to a failure to anticipate resistance to the export of democracy or other American values. The overwhelming power of the United States, combined with broad support within the United States for promotion of those values overseas, can be disturbing even to other democracies. As Stephen Walt observes, "Even societies that admire certain U.S. values may not want to adopt all of them—and especially not at the point of a gun."[67] Insufficient American appreciation of such non-American concerns underlay the surprise and disappointment when most Iraqis did not greet U.S. troops with flowers and when other U.S. troops eventually wore out a welcome in Afghanistan.

VARIETIES OF REVOLUTION

The American view of why people take up arms to effect political change and why they *should* do so is heavily colored by the experience of America's own birth. That experience was a storybook tale even before the retelling of the story in ways that have tended to downplay both the role of European conflict in making it possible and the story's less-attractive aspects, such as profiteering by speculators who bought up debt generated by the Revolutionary War. The American Revolution was a mostly orderly affair with an orderly result, led by respectable and well-established citizens, conducted for moderate and admirable political objectives, avoiding chaos and widespread destruction, and fully concluded only after constructing a new constitution that would prevent unchecked use of power and protect individual rights.[68] George Kennan observed how Americans' outlook toward those who disturb the peace abroad stems "in part from the memory of the origin of our own political system—from the recollection that we were able, through acceptance of a common institutional and juridical framework, to reduce to harmless dimensions the conflicts of interest and aspiration among the original thirteen colonies and to bring them all into an ordered and peaceful relationship with one another."[69]

Against the backdrop of their own country's creation, Americans have difficulty appreciating the range of motivations that may move other people to revolt or to make war, the extent to which those motivations can differ from those found in the story of 1776, the frequency with which such motivations can drive or disrupt history, the extent to which the people involved consider those motivations just as much a justification for disruption as the goals that drove the makers of the American Revolution, and the extent to which disorder much greater than what the Americans' revolution entailed is often accepted as necessary. Kennan was referring primarily to international war when he noted, "To the American mind, it is implausible that people should have positive aspirations, and ones that they regard as legitimate, more important to them than the peacefulness and orderliness of international life."[70] The same disjunction between common American perceptions and revolutionary reality applies at least as much to internal upheavals in foreign countries as to interstate war.

Americans' resistance to appreciating and accepting revolutions unlike their own manifests itself in several ways. They are surprised when such revolutions occur because of an assumption that the world is or should be more orderly and predictable than that, but they also believe that they ought not to have been surprised. The belief leads to accusations that intelligence services or other bureaucracies failed to prevent surprise, as illustrated by reactions to the Iranian Revolution of 1979. Americans also mistakenly identify the impulses driving a revolution. Motivations less familiar to the American mind are replaced in that mind by the familiar and assumed yearning for freedom and democracy, as in American perceptions of the conflict in South Vietnam. Alternatively, the disruption is blamed on individual evildoers or on ideologies that are alluring but, in the American view, illegitimate.

The deficiencies in understanding foreign revolutions also lead to confusion, consternation, and sometimes recrimination when revolts that initially looked like a promising turn toward greater freedom and democracy take unpromising turns or fail altogether. Such a sequence has characterized much of the American view of the upheavals in the Middle East beginning in 2010 that became known as the Arab Spring. The unrest was initially viewed with optimism as a beneficial shake-up that would bring more democracy to the world's least-democratic region. Optimism turned to dismay as old power structures reasserted themselves (in Egypt), chaos followed revolt (in Libya), or both (in Syria). The calendar of seasonal metaphors was reversed as the Arab Spring appeared to turn into an Arab Winter. Underlying most of the dismay felt by American observers was insufficient appreciation of how much of the motivating energy for the revolts came not just from a yearning for liberal democracy but also from other aspects of social revolution or from animosities and ambitions with sectarian, ethnic, or even tribal origins. Probably also little appreciated was the extent to which apparent democratic success in the initial stages of upheaval in a country such as Egypt was due to the easily reversible sufferance of the country's military.

What distinguishes the American backdrop to such perceptions is not only a revolution that was clearly pointing toward liberal democracy but also a revolution that was *successful*. The world has had many unsuccessful revolutions; the United States has not. Before Russia got to 1917, it had the unsuccessful uprising of 1905. Much of Europe experienced the revolution of 1848—possibly the closest historical analogue to the Arab Spring as a region-wide upheaval—which fizzled out with little immediate political change to show for it except in France. The one big internal revolt in the United States, the Civil War, was a failure for the rebels but a success for the United States itself; the union was preserved, slavery was abolished, and the country became more of a liberal democracy than it had been before. The background of revolutionary success has encouraged "Who lost the Middle East?" recriminations about the course of the Arab Spring, which combine a presumption that democratic revolutions should succeed with a belief that if they do not succeed, then it must be because the United States did not do enough to make the world safe for democracy.[71]

Economic motivations have been prime drivers of foreign rebellions that do not have a counterpart in the American experience. Jefferson and some of the other landed Founding Fathers who made in America a political revolution unaccompanied by a social and economic one were initially admirers of the French Revolution, which they saw as a like-minded democratic overthrow of monarchical rule. Their experience did not prepare them for the later bloody turn the revolution in France took, propelled by other sources of discontent among a dispossessed underclass. A century later, Americans who saw the liberation of Cuba as part of their Manifest Destiny did not understand that Cubans were revolting at least as much against economic conditions that were related to, among other things, U.S. tariffs as they were against political misrule by Spain.[72] Today, Americans probably have comparably insufficient appreciation that events in Egypt, like events in France in the late eighteenth century, will depend at least as much on the price of bread as on political principles.

Political change overseas that Americans find both unattractive and unfamiliar encourages thoughts about malevolent individuals, nefarious ideologies, or other dark forces that are presumed to be responsible. The U.S. involvement in conflicts overseas during the past century has further encouraged such thoughts, as the next chapter will explore.

5

SEARCHING FOR MONSTERS TO DESTROY

AMERICANS DEFINE THEMSELVES, at least as much as other people do, in terms of who they are *not*—in terms of what America has rejected, what it stands in contrast to, and what it has fought against. Samuel Huntington observed almost twenty years ago, "From the start, Americans have constructed their creedal identity in contrast to an undesirable 'other.'"[1] Because Americans could not distinguish themselves culturally from the country against which they fought for independence, they had to distinguish themselves politically. Americans have continued to define their nation as the antithesis of and the leading challenger to all that was backward and unfree, including monarchical old Europe of the nineteenth century and totalitarian ogres of the twentieth century.

The process of self-definition intensifies whenever confrontation with undesirable others escalates to armed conflict. The Revolutionary War was only the first instance of American images of an adversary being shaped by the intellectual and psychological need that Huntington identified.[2] Wars are especially formative influences on national culture and attitudes for other reasons as well, not only for the United States but also for any nation that has ever gone to war. Wars are the exclamation points in a nation's history, when the most intense costs are sustained and the most prominent glory is won. They are the moments when history itself is most likely to take a turn, when territories may be gained or lost, and when generations may go missing. It is for these reasons that nations memorialize their wars in stone and in their lore.

The impact that America's wars have had on American consciousness extend not only to self-definition and self-image but also to perceptions of the world beyond America's borders. And the impact on perceptions extends not only to the immediate adversary in any one war but also to how Americans tend to see all other nations and other conflicts. The nature of past armed struggles shapes American perceptions of current struggles and their likely course and outcome.[3] The nature of enemies in past wars affects how Americans perceive current enemies and whether they should be thought of as enemies at all. The distinctive attributes of the U.S. experience in past wars accentuate some of the patterns described in earlier chapters and foster some additional tendencies.

THE ON-OFF SWITCH OF WARFARE

The physical isolation of the United States ensured that warfare against foreign enemies during the first half of the nation's history would be only an intermittent affair, interspersed with long periods of peace. The lack of European-style close quarters with untrusted neighbors meant a lack of European-style recurrent combat.

The pattern of intermittence and Americans' understanding and expectations of this pattern dated from the earliest days of independence. Four days after the signing of the Treaty of Paris in 1783, which formally ended the Revolutionary War, the Confederation Congress instructed George Washington to demobilize "such parts of the federal army now in service as he shall deem proper and expedient." Washington initially retained a force to confront the British in New York, but once the redcoats left New York, he discharged all but about six hundred men in a single infantry regiment and one artillery battalion, which were retained to guard supplies at West Point and a few other posts. Washington later suggested creation of a small regular army "to awe the Indians, protect our trade, prevent the encroachment of our neighbors of Canada and the Floridas, and guard us at least from surprises; also for security of our magazines." When Congress under the new constitution established a war department in 1789, however, the army it created numbered only about eight hundred men. Until the run-up to the War of 1812, the army never got larger than about four thousand. Financial limitations, difficulties in recruitment, and traditional suspicions of standing armies combined with the lack of significant proximate enemies to keep the American military small.[4]

U.S. wars against foreign adversaries in the nineteenth century were rare: the conflicts against Britain and Mexico in the first half and then after another five decades and right before the century's end the "splendid little war" (in the words of Secretary of State John Hay) against Spain. These conflicts' relatively low costs to the United States left relatively little lasting impression on American consciousness. Certainly any casualty-induced impression was far less than that of the Civil War, in which the death toll of about 625,000 was ten times the total American deaths in all wars against foreign enemies before World War I—from the Revolutionary War to the Spanish-American War.

America's wars against foreign enemies through the nineteenth century, although avoiding a deep negative imprint of high costs, left a positive conception of war as something that always would end with what could confidently be called both peace and victory. Even the conflict that actually ended as a draw—the War of 1812—would be thought of more as a win largely because the war's last battle, at New Orleans, was a smashing American victory (although negotiators on the other side of the Atlantic had already signed a peace treaty when the battle was fought). The wars of the first half of the nation's history also carried the positive accoutrements of glory and heroes. For two of those heroes—Washington, the Revolutionary War commander, and Andrew Jackson, the victor at New Orleans—wartime fame led to the U.S. presidency (as it would for the Civil War hero Ulysses S. Grant).

Alexis de Tocqueville, writing in the 1830s, stressed that the paucity of U.S. wars and of what he considered to be the negative effects of military glory contributed significantly to the strength of American democracy. He referred to the rarity of American wars in explaining the exception to his observation represented by Jackson, whom Tocqueville disdained as "a man of violent temper and mediocre talents." He wrote that Jackson rose to the presidency "solely by the recollection of a victory which he gained, twenty years ago, under the walls of New Orleans; a victory which was, however, a very ordinary achievement, and which could only be remembered in a country where battles are rare."[5]

The rarity of battles against foreign enemies through the end of the nineteenth century meant that U.S. military history during that period had only modest effects on later American perceptions. A mostly clean slate was left for what would be the greater effects of the wars of the twentieth century. The early history did, however, establish a pattern of American thinking about wars as exceptional digressions from peacetime normality and as episodes having distinct beginnings and clear and positive endings. Even the Indian Wars, although they collectively stretched out over centuries, were fought and thought of mostly as discrete conflicts, from the Pequot War to the Ghost Dance War, each of which was limited in time and place and ended with the defeat and subjugation of whatever tribe or band was the Indian protagonist, after which white settlers could resume their peaceful business. A strong and recurring strain in American thought about the U.S. relationship with the rest of the world is thus that the relationship can be one of either war or peace but not something in between. This form of black-and-white thinking has long affected Americans' perceptions not only of the adversaries against whom they have waged war but also of war itself.

Walter Russell Mead identifies this pattern of thinking with the school of thought he names after Jackson, although his description contains elements that Tocqueville also would have recognized as a broadly held American perspective. "Jacksonians," writes Mead, "see war as a switch that is either on or off. They don't like the idea of violence on a dimmer switch. Either the stakes are important enough to fight for, in which case you should fight with everything you have, or they aren't important enough to fight for, in which case you should mind your own business and stay home."[6] This aspect of the

Jacksonian outlook has dominated American thinking about war and peace in large part because of its roots in the history of America's actual wars.

SALLYING FORTH IN THE TWENTIETH CENTURY

The turn from the nineteenth to the twentieth century was a perceptual pivot in the history of U.S. foreign relations for multiple but related reasons. It was when the closing of the frontier made the exercise of Manifest Destiny a transoceanic phenomenon. It was also when the growth of U.S. power and the ability to project it at a distance in the age of steam began to bring into reach more sweeping objectives for the use of U.S. military power.[7] After the conflict in which these developments first came together, the Spanish-American War, the nation's foreign wars were seen primarily as exercises of the burden of world leadership. For these and other reasons, observers of diverse ideologies have regarded the 1890s as the inauguration of modern American foreign policy.[8]

Wars of the twentieth century have had a greater impact than earlier wars on current American perceptions about the outside world because some of the twentieth-century wars were far bigger, longer, and bloodier than the earlier conflicts; because they involved what were genuinely and justifiably regarded as serious foreign threats more than as opportunities for American expansion; and because they were more recent, some of them being within the memories and formative years of Americans living today.

Dramatic or traumatic experiences such as wars and revolutions are especially likely to be the basis for analogies used to interpret the present. Recent experiences are more likely to be used this way than distant ones.[9] America's wars in the twentieth century thus are major influences on American perceptions in the twenty-first century. The influence includes explicit analogizing by policy makers and more general molding of American public perceptions of wars, international conflict, and foreign states.

Although John Quincy Adams was speaking truthfully as secretary of state in 1821 when he said that "America does not go abroad in search of monsters to destroy,"[10] wars of the twentieth century did involve the United States going abroad to destroy monsters. World War I set the pattern of applying the on–off concept of the use of military force inherited from the nineteenth century to the vanquishing of more distant enemies. American involvement in the war followed a script that revolved around the idea of the New World having to rescue the Old World from messes the latter had made. Nearly three years of carnage had already taken place in Europe when the United States entered the war, and several more months would go by before the American Expeditionary Forces saw their first combat. The script was consistent with the American exceptionalist idea that Americans are peace-loving people who rise up and go to war only when necessary to deal with those who are of a less-peaceful, less-admirable disposition. Wartime American themes further burnished the pure self-image by identifying American patriotism with righteousness. President Woodrow Wilson said, "There is not a single selfish element so far as I can see, in the cause we are fighting for. We are fighting for what we believe and wish to be the rights of mankind and for the future peace and security of the world."[11]

Although World War I ended with an armistice rather than with a sur-render, the ending was close enough to the idealized American concept of wars ending with a clear and successful conclusion and giving way to pro-longed peacetime that the experience of this war bolstered that concept in American minds rather than undermining it. The notion of World War I as the "war to end war" was voiced in several Allied countries but later became more closely associated with Wilson and his similar-sounding slogan about making the world safe for democracy, even as among Europeans the idea became an object of cynicism. That cynicism increased during the tough bargaining at the postwar peace conference, about which the British officer (later field marshal and earl) Archibald Wavell remarked, "After the 'war to end war' they seem to have been pretty successful in Paris at making a "peace to end peace.'"[12] Wilson would have his own tough bargaining at home about the League of Nations, but the dominant American view at the time was that the New World had successfully accomplished its mission in the Old World and could retire back across the ocean and enjoy a pro-longed peace. Opinion in Congress and the American public rejected a War

Department proposal to maintain a regular army of a half-million men, and interest in funding even a smaller mobilization force quickly waned. Within a year of the armistice, the army demobilized nearly 3.25 million troops, leaving an active force of about 225,000.[13]

The same American perspective underlay Warren Harding's election to the presidency in 1920 with 60 percent of the vote after campaigning for "normalcy" and the strong American isolationist sentiment during the interwar years. The isolationism manifested the "off" part of the characteristically American on–off view of international conflict and the use of military force. It also illustrated how this view can involve significant misperception of events overseas. Germany was seen as having been defeated; the fighting may have ended with an armistice, but it was the Germans who sued for peace and the Western allies who imposed the peace terms. Americans at the time did not see defeated foes as continuing threats and problems, any more than they saw the British, Mexicans, and Native Americans that way after the United States had finished fighting them. What would happen in the Weimar Republic was thus not a focus of American attention. The United States was not alone in being slow to respond to the rise of the Axis, but it had shifted from a response mode to a peacetime mode more completely than Europeans did. It had packed up and gone home, and American opinion had significantly farther to go before it would engage once again in the Old World's security problems.

World War II was even bigger than World War I and bloodier for the United States, as well as being more recent. It also fit even better the monster-destroying American script for foreign wars. The foes, especially the Nazi dictator in Germany, were surely monstrous enough. America's direct involvement in the war began abruptly with a major, blatant act of aggression at Pearl Harbor, after which the U.S. Congress formally declared war—the last time it would unambiguously do so under Article I, section 8, of the U.S. Constitution, as distinct from later and more ambiguous authorizations of military force. Probably most important, the war ended with clear and undeniable victory in the form of unconditional surrender by Germany and Japan. All these attributes constitute what, to American eyes, is what war ought to look like. This is part of why World War II has occupied such a large place in American culture, including cinema and literature. The frustrations and ambiguities of some later conflicts, such as the Vietnam War, have only enhanced World War II as a model and archetype for Americans of how a war should go and how it should end.[14]

The bright line that Americans have drawn between wartime and peacetime points in a different direction from the ideas of the great strategic thinker Carl von Clausewitz, who taught that war is a continuation of policy by other means.[15] It is not insignificant that Clausewitz was a European rather than an American. The world wars of the twentieth century increased further the split between European and American conceptions of war and peace. For Europeans, the wars were catastrophes that destroyed any lingering ideas that one's nation was guided and protected by providence or that a war could be viewed positively as a temporarily costly but ultimately effective way to rid the world of an evil. The horrible experience of the wars motivated Europeans to embark on their great experiment in integration and to shift to a paradigm about the use of military force in world affairs that would be more different than ever from that of the Americans.[16] By contrast, the world wars and especially World War II were for Americans, despite the costs, positive reaffirmations of much of what they had already believed regarding the relationship of their nation to providence and how evil exists but can, with forceful U.S. leadership, be destroyed.[17] Victory in World War II was the greatest accomplishment of the Greatest Generation.[18] It not only seemed consistent with American exceptionalist thinking but also developed further what exceptionalism meant in terms of how Americans perceived the nature of the nation's foes and the nature of struggles to defeat those foes.

THE COLD WAR

The Cold War followed World War II too closely for post–World War I normalcy and isolationism to repeat themselves, and the Cold War itself would seem well designed to dispel rigid distinctions between time of war and time of peace. The Cold War was, after all, a prolonged period of heightened tension that did not involve direct combat between the two superpowers but did have multiple military dimensions, including other applications of U.S. and Soviet military forces, proxy wars, and an arms race. It was a long-term confrontation in which, given military technology in the missile age, Americans finally were getting a taste of what Europeans had long had to live with: continuing physical danger. If anything should have taught Americans a Clausewitzian lesson in how the lines between peace and war are actually quite blurred, the Cold War was it. For the most part, however, the lesson was not absorbed; the Cold War itself was viewed like hot wars as a discrete episode with a beginning and an end. This perspective was reflected in the very term *Cold War*—a usage popularized in particular by the American journalist Walter Lippmann right after World War II.[19]

Early Cold Warriors amplified this perspective in the course of selling to the American public and the political class the need for the extensive U.S. global involvement that the Cold War would entail. Their task of salesmanship would have been harder if they had tried to refute the widely held view—what Mead calls the "myth of virtuous isolation"—that most of U.S. history had consisted of aloofness from world affairs, interrupted only by the necessary periodic forays to slay monsters. So the Cold Warriors accepted the myth and argued instead that although aloofness had been the right approach for an earlier time, circumstances and the challenges they present had changed.[20] This approach helped to confirm the American notion of a black-and-white dichotomy between wartime and peacetime, even though isolation was an inaccurate perception of much nineteenth-century U.S. foreign policy—as a few writers in the 1940s, including Lippmann, tried to explain.[21] Besides further entrenching the on–off view of war and peace and how it characterized past U.S. foreign policy, this method of rationalizing Cold War activism also exacerbated the American tendency to overestimate the newness of threats and challenges and impaired the ability to perceive continuity in them. It precluded a longer-term view (pertinent to some later issues involving terrorism, as discussed later) of the Cold War as the final four decades of a two-hundred-year period, from the fall of the Bastille in 1789 to the fall of the Berlin Wall in 1989, in which various manifestations of the revolutionary Left and responses to it formed a continuous thread in international conflict.

The perceived beginning of the Cold War involved a set of mostly European developments compressed into the first couple of years after World War II. The strong American consensus that Stalin's Soviet Union was to blame for "starting" the Cold War would later be challenged by New Left historians.[22] The very fact there could be a debate over assigning blame for initiating this conflict assumed that there was such a start in the same way that a hot war could be said to have been started by one side firing the first shot or being the first to roll tanks across an international border. This was not necessarily the best way to understand the foreign-policy challenges of the late 1940s. At least as insightful would have been a perspective that was not confined to the idea of a new "war" starting then but instead perceived the confrontation as being much longer in the making (although temporarily overshadowed by the war against the Axis), based on older ideological conflict and the way that rising powers change geopolitical realities. In this respect, both sides of the "who started the Cold War" debate offered truncated views of the challenge represented by the Soviet Union.[23]

Besides an identifiable beginning, the war imagery required a comparably identifiable ending. Here events seemed to conform readily to the image, given the rapidity with which Communist regimes in eastern Europe collapsed. Moreover, the events conformed to the American conception of wars as having endings that are not only clear but successful; the West "won" the Cold War. Misunderstanding began to set in, however, with a focus on the one other event, besides the fall of the Berlin Wall, that is most often seen as marking the exact end of the Cold War: the break-up of the Soviet Union into its constituent republics. This focus was natural and understandable. What better indication could there be of the defeat of the main Cold War adversary than that the adversary itself had dissolved?

The application of the classic American mental model of wars, in which a war ends clearly with peace and victory, to the Cold War encouraged Americans to overlook some important continuing realities, just as they had overlooked certain realities regarding a defeated Germany after World War I. The subjugation of the non-Russian republics in the Soviet Union to

Moscow's rule had never been the principal ingredient in the Cold War confrontation, especially as far as the ideological competition was concerned. Russia without the other Soviet republics, although weaker than the Soviet Union had been, was still a significant nuclear-armed power with many of the same national interests and objectives that had been in evidence during the Cold War and with significant capacity to frustrate the aims of the United States and the West. But American awareness of and sensitivity to these realities sank amid postvictory exuberance—which began even before the break-up of the Soviet Union—about what the United States could accomplish during its "unipolar moment,"[24] as if Russia could be shoved aside to near irrelevance the way some of America's previous wartime foes had been.

One of the most significant results of this post–Cold War outlook was the eastward expansion of the North Atlantic Treaty Organization (NATO). Much of the expansion took place during the 1990s while a Democrat was in the White House. Then later, under a Republican U.S. president, the United States pushed its European allies to make a commitment to extend future NATO membership right into the former Soviet Union, specifically to Georgia and Ukraine. This move reflected inattention to continuing Russian interests and likely Russian reactions, which would eventually include invading and occupying chunks of Georgia and, after an internal political crisis in Ukraine, seizing Crimea and fostering a separatist insurgency in eastern Ukraine.[25] If U.S. policy makers had not been under the influence of the long-standing American concept of war, victory, and peace and had not applied that concept to the Cold War, they would have been less likely to make such mistakes.

TERRORISM FILLS THE POST–COLD WAR VACUUM

A tension between mindset and reality immediately became apparent once the Cold War was declared to be over. After four decades in which the Cold War had provided a framework and a foe, what would serve as a framework now? Americans had to face more squarely than ever before an inconsistency between the light-switch view of war and peace—molded in earlier eras in which war was seen to be followed by demobilization and disengagement—and a modern reality of extensive and continuous American engagement overseas. A non-Clausewitzian perspective had to come to terms with a Clausewitzian world.

Besides the question of what would serve as a new framework, there was the further question of who would serve as a foe. Arthur Schlesinger Jr., writing when the Cold War was almost but not quite over, correctly perceived the national yearning involved: "There was in 1940 a very real monster to destroy and after 1945 another very real monster to contain. But the growth of American power also confirmed the messianism of those who believed in America's divine anointment. That there were a couple of real monsters roaming the world encouraged a fearful tendency to look everywhere for new monsters to destroy."[26]

The fumbling for new enemies and new ways of organizing thinking about America's role in the world continued for a decade. It was reflected in part in overstatements of the newness of challenges that really were not so new, such as weapons proliferation and the economic dislocations caused by globalization. It also was reflected in pundits' struggles to come up with an era-defining label more distinctive than merely the "post–Cold War era."

Then ten years after the Soviet Union broke up came the 9/11 terrorist attacks. The foe, the framework, and the label all appeared suddenly to fall into place. And they fell into a place shaped by America's previous experience with foreign wars and by the habit of defining America's encounter with the world in terms of those wars. A new metaphorical war was declared: the "war on terror."

"War on terror" never was a logical concept. Terrorism is a tactic, not an enemy. As Zbigniew Brzezinski observed, to speak of waging a war on terror makes as much sense as calling World War II a war on blitzkrieg.[27] The war metaphor served parochial purposes for the administration of President George W. Bush: it imparted a previously lacking sense of purpose by making Bush a "war president," and it set the stage for selling the neoconservative project of invading Iraq. But Americans immediately warmed to the concept for more deeply rooted reasons, as indicated by how much of a life the phrase "war on terror" acquired independent of any labeling or promotion by the Bush administration. This "war" would be in the minds of Americans the latest chapter in their nation's history of periodic monster-slaying forays overseas. Considering themselves to be at war reduced the cognitive dissonance that would have come from being extensively and expensively engaged overseas during what was supposed to be peacetime.

This conceptual framework was distinctively American, for reasons that went beyond the fact that the 9/11 attacks targeted the United States. Many foreign governments went along with the "war on terror" idea for their own reasons—because of the importance of their relationship with the United States, because they wanted U.S. material support, and in some cases because it was a handy cover for cracking down on dissidents or restive minorities in their own countries. But foreign governments, including western Europeans who had been working longer and more continuously against international terrorism than Americans had been, did not view concentrated counterterrorism as something that started when a switch was flicked in September 2001.

The conceptual framework of a war has engendered American misunderstanding that in turn has entailed several problems for U.S. counterterrorist policy. The war metaphor automatically imparted more of a military tinge to the whole business, both threat and response, than it warranted. It nurtured the idea that international terrorism presents many good military targets when it fact it does not, certainly as far as terrorist operations against the United States are concerned. The 9/11 operation itself, prepared chiefly in European apartments and U.S. flight schools, imparted that lesson, but Americans were not paying attention. The war metaphor also led to a broader overemphasis on military force in many American minds and to insufficient awareness of the limitations to military force as a counterterrorist tool.[28]

The conception of a war as having a definite beginning and end has encouraged other misperceptions. Viewing 9/11 as a beginning omits a long history of both threats and responses. Besides reducing awareness of how terrorism is a tactic that has been used for millennia—and thus encouraging unwarranted expectations about the ability to eliminate it—this truncated historical perspective has limited understanding of how even the religious variety of terrorism that has become the principal concern of today has a long pedigree and is not nearly as new a threat as is often postulated. Some of the very terrorism-associated terminology in use today actually originated with religious fanatics centuries ago.[29] The two hundred years of left–right conflict from the French Revolution through the end of the Cold War obscured how religion has more often been the basis of motivations and rationales for political violence, including terrorism. Also largely overlooked was the substantial pre-9/11 experience with counterterrorism not only in Europe but also in the United States. The widespread American public perception that serious counterterrorism did not begin until the start of a "war" in 2001 has led to the reinventing of wheels (such as governmental reorganizations duplicating earlier reorganizations[30]) and the forgetting of previously learned lessons (such as the hazards of publicity given to hostage incidents[31]).

The notion that a "war on terror" has a discernible end involves at least as many problems as the idea that it had a clear beginning. Despite some cautions that U.S. leaders issued about this notion—George W. Bush's secretary of defense, Donald Rumsfeld, noted that defeating terrorism would not have a "terminal event" comparable to Japan's surrender on the USS *Missouri*[32]—the tendency to think of the "war on terror" as one more war that America would someday win and consign to history as the nation returned to peace was too strong to overcome. Certain policies and practices were adopted that could make sense only if seen as temporary wartime expedients. Chief among them was the incarceration of individuals vacuumed up in areas of conflict from Afghanistan to Bosnia. The war framework underlay strong political resistance, especially in the Republican Party, to trying prosecutable individuals in civilian courts, but a newly devised system of military tribunals proved to be a creaky and less-effective alternative. In a regular hot war, prisoners of war would be paroled or exchanged once the conflict was over. But in a "war on terror" the detainees' status is uncertain, with their detention of uncertain duration. The most visible and embarrassing manifestation of this state of affairs is the controversial U.S.

detention facility at Guantanamo, Cuba, which President Barack Obama promised to close in his first year in office but was unable to do so.

MISTAKEN GAUGING OF THE THREAT

Besides the problems of war imagery that were specific to counterterrorism, the issue of terrorism illustrates another chronic misperception associated with on–off conceptions of war and peace: the public underestimates foreign threats when the switch is off and overestimates them once it is turned on. These miscalculations are in part the natural psychological response of any people, not just Americans. Governments also tend to exacerbate this tendency because they have an interest in exaggerating a threat as they try to muster support for vigorous efforts to counter it. But the non-Clausewitzian outlook that prevails in the United States makes the misperception of threat levels even more marked there than elsewhere.

The American public underestimated the danger from terrorism in the years before September 11, 2001 (in a way that did not correspond to the tragedy that would materialize on that day), and then suddenly began overestimating it (in a way that did not correspond to dangers that materialized—or, rather, failed to materialize—in the years after 9/11). When the Chicago Council on Global Affairs asked Americans in its regular biennial survey in 2002 to name the two or three biggest problems, either foreign or domestic, facing the United States, terrorism easily topped the list with a 36 percent response. When the same question had been asked four years earlier, terrorism did not make it onto the list at all.[33] Queries by the Pew Research Center about whether Americans were worried about another terrorist attack showed that significant post-9/11 fear had lowered only slowly at first and then more rapidly a dozen years later.[34] The sudden change in the public's fears and beliefs from before 9/11 to after 9/11 did not correspond to any change in the reality of which terrorist groups existed and what they were doing. The 9/11 attacks, notwithstanding the drama and trauma they involved, did not provide much new information about the overall level of terrorist threat. The U.S. intelligence community's assessments of world-wide threats to U.S. interests, prepared and made public prior to 9/11, had already placed international terrorism, specifically terrorism from Osama bin Laden's group, at the top of the list of dangers.[35]

The American public's perception of the degree of threat from terrorism has failed to correspond not only with available information and warnings but also with actual terrorism against American interests. In the mid-1970s, for example, a wave of terrorist attacks in the United States perpetrated by foreign as well as domestic terrorists included bombs going off in the U.S. Capitol and LaGuardia Airport, a car bomb detonated on the streets of Washington, D.C., and much else. In a post-9/11 context, such a wave of violence would have been seen as a horrifying breakdown of security and a losing of the "war on terror." Probably a major reason why it was not seen this way in the 1970s was that the security agencies relied upon to respond were themselves the subject of public controversy regarding alleged excesses and abuses.[36] Moreover, having just extricated themselves from Vietnam, Americans were in no mood to embark on another war, whether against terror or against anything else. Whatever were the specific contributions to public attitudes, the war–peace switch did not get switched to war in the 1970s, and there was not an elevated public perception of threat from terrorism comparable to the elevated occurrence of actual terrorism.

BLAMING BAD GUYS WITH BAD IDEAS

Another attribute of Americans' past experiences with foreign wars, closely related to the concept of definite beginnings and endings, is that the enemy could be identified as a particularly malevolent regime or organization driven by a particularly malevolent ideology. Eliminate the regime and the ideology, according to the image that this experience left in American minds, and the problem that caused the war would go away—and with it the prospect of more wars with the same cause. The focus, in other words, has been on what Americans have regarded as temporary, eradicable problems rather than on continuing ambitions or conflicts of interest.

World War II has again served as the archetype. Look at stolid, peaceful Germans today, and one can reasonably conclude that the horrors culminating in World War II in Europe were due to Germans having gotten temporarily infected with the disease of Nazism. For Americans, the war in Europe was a war to eradicate that disease, somewhat like eradicating smallpox or polio. A look at the Japanese—who are now, like the Germans, allies of the United States—and their postwar turn toward pacifism leads to a similar conclusion about the Pacific war to eradicate Japanese militarism. The Cold War, as a contest against a regime whose legitimacy rested on an ideology hostile to that of America and with the contest perceived as ending once that regime collapsed, seemed to fit a similar pattern and thus reinforced American thinking based on that pattern.

In his "why do they hate us" speech after 9/11, George W. Bush defined the task at hand as being squarely in this same framework, notwithstanding the abstract "war on terror" reference to a tactic. The enemy was seen as a finite number of malevolent individuals who would later repeatedly get referred to simply as "the terrorists." Bush explicitly linked them to the malevolent ideologues of past wars. "They are the heirs of all the murderous ideologies of the 20th century," he said. "By sacrificing human life to serve their radical visions—by abandoning every value except the will to power—they follow in the path of fascism, and Nazism, and totalitarianism."[37]

The favorable American exceptionalist self-image, in which the United States is seen as a benevolent and well-intentioned actor in world affairs, contributes to the tendency to view anyone who even opposes or resists the United States, let alone attacks it, as a malevolent ideologue. If the United States is, according to this self-image, consistently a force for good in the world, then anyone who does not go along with it is perceived as a force for what is bad. "When others do not offer us the gratitude we think we deserve," writes Stephen Walt, "we conclude that they are either innately hostile or inspired by some sort of anti-American ideology, alien culture, or religious fanaticism."[38]

The habit of attributing untoward happenings overseas to a few identifiable bad actors who fit neatly into a familiar tradition of malicious ideologies leads in several respects to serious misunderstanding of those happenings—of what causes them and what is required to respond to them. To begin with, even when a specific and important bunch of bad guys can accurately be identified, to equate them, as Bush did in his speech, to other bad guys whom the United States encountered in the past is to misperceive what drives these new actors and where they derive their support. The perpetrators of the 9/11 attacks were quite different from the twentieth-century totalitarians the United States had dealt with in past wars. Bush's assertion to the contrary evolved into widespread use in the United States of the misleading and unhelpful term *Islamofascism*. Although the values according to which the makers of the 9/11 attacks operated were at least as different from liberal democratic values as were those of twentieth-century fascism, they could not all be reduced, as Bush asserted, to a will to power.

The American perspective of attributing bad happenings entirely to bad actors also overlooks all the other ingredients that help to produce violent or aggressive behavior. The perspective is a Pied Piper theory of misbehavior— the idea of people being led astray by some malevolent but alluring influence. This perspective disregards the important role that conditions, grievances, and fears among larger populations play in determining the propensity of those populations to be led astray. It impedes understanding of how, even though Germans are not inherently bad people, millions of them willingly supported the Nazis amid an economic crisis as well as the resentment-nurturing legacy of World War I and the postwar peace settlement. The perspective also impedes understanding of how aggressive Russian behavior in Ukraine or Georgia is not just a matter of Vladimir Putin's ambitions and machinations but also of support for his actions among many Russians whose nationalist sensibilities have been engaged. As for international terrorism, the perspective results in heavy emphasis on killing leading terrorists and destroying their groups but far less and probably insufficient attention to how political and economic circumstances affect people's propensity to become terrorists in the first place or to lend sympathy and support to those who do.[39]

SEARCHING FOR MONSTERS TO DESTROY

The bias toward interpreting problems overseas more in terms of specific malevolent perpetrators and less in terms of surrounding circumstances applies not only to entire campaigns of aggression or terrorism
but also to the explanation of individual events. One example concerns
the attack on a U.S. facility in Benghazi, Libya, in 2012 that resulted in
the death of four Americans, including the U.S. ambassador, and was followed by endless recriminations in the United States. The recriminations
came largely from Republican opponents of the Obama administration
as they seized on the incident to try to discredit the administration and
Democratic presidential aspirant Hillary Clinton, who had been secretary
of state at the time. The accusation was that the administration had for
some reason tried to deny or downplay that the incident was an act of
terrorism. The logic of the accusation and why a lethal incident on the
administration's watch would be any more or less embarrassing to it if
the incident were labeled terrorism or something else were never entirely
clear. Nevertheless, whether any accusation with a political motivation
gains traction depends in large part on whether it has resonance with
the public's predisposition to see things in certain ways. Americans are
predisposed to interpret a lethal attack on their fellow citizens overseas
as the act of a terrorist group, especially one connected with the terrorist
group they have most heard of, al-Qaʿida. To think of an attack as growing out of disorder stemming from regime change in which the United
States participated does not fit nearly as well in the American mindset.
The idea of an attack being grounded in broader anti-Americanism in the
country in question is even less compatible with American exceptionalist thinking. So the notion of the Benghazi incident as a terrorist attack
rather than as an epiphenomenon of broader things going on in Libya—
although it actually could have been both—caught on with much of the
American public, even though the disorder and anti-Americanism had at
least as much explanatory power as anything else in understanding what
happened in Benghazi.[40]

The influence of America's own actions in stimulating untoward happenings abroad—by fostering either general anti-Americanism or more
focused resentment of particular policies—is especially likely to escape the

American public's notice. This blindness is primarily a direct consequence of the positive exceptionalist self-image. But the added tendency to see an ill-intentioned "other," whether an unfriendly regime or a terrorist group, as responsible for bad happenings magnifies this deficit in understanding. The related belief that the ideological allure of malevolent Pied Pipers is a major cause of ill will toward the United States magnifies the tendency to look first for better ways to wage ideological debate, which has led to the perennial hand-wringing about the apparent ineffectiveness of U.S. public diplomacy, rather than to reconsider U.S. policies that engender the ill will.

THE MONOLITHIC VIEW OF TERRORISM

The view of problems overseas as being embodied in specific organizational entities, similar to how the Axis regimes were the problems to be overcome in World War II, entails misunderstanding of problems that are not actually so embodied. This sort of misunderstanding has afflicted the mainstream American view of international terrorism. After 9/11, Americans quickly came to view the enemy as the group that perpetrated that attack, al-Qaʿida. This perspective had the advantage of reducing some of the abstraction in the newly expanded counterterrorist campaign; a war on al-Qaʿida would make more sense than a "war on terror." But many Americans perceived this specific, named group as the embodiment of international terrorism in general and as *the* enemy in the "war on terror." That was a misperception. Not only did al-Qaʿida *not* represent all of international terrorism, but it also did not even represent all of the radical, Sunni, jihadist variety of it. Osama bin Laden's strategy of attacking the "far enemy" as a way of weakening support for his near enemies was only one of several viewpoints in the radical jihadist world and not necessarily the most popular one.[41] Subsequent organizational diffusion and metastasis, with new jihadist groups appearing that would take their own operational initiative even though some adopted the al-Qaʿida name and some did not, further complicated the picture.[42] The tendency to refer to this entire mélange of groups and individuals as "al-Qaᶜida" reified an entity that did not exist. The actual al-Qaᶜida—the group that perpetrated the 9/11 attacks—is still around but is only a part of this larger picture. Failure to understand this picture means a failure to understand the motivations and objectives of many of the groups in it.

The equating of al-Qaᶜida with terrorism in general entailed other problems. One concerns the limits of the military portion of the war being waged. The authorization for the use of military force that the U.S. Congress passed after 9/11 referred specifically to groups that had been involved in those attacks. This specific reference led to uncertainty and controversy regarding the use of force against groups that did not fit that description but may pose a current threat—a problem that remained unresolved more than a decade later. Another problem inherent in applying the war metaphor to counterterrorism is the hazard of lending stature to a terrorist group and thus enhancing it in the eyes of its constituency and potential recruits by equating it with states that were previous wartime foes, such as the Axis powers. Yet another difficulty and source of further misunderstanding is a skewing of threat perceptions according to the organizational scheme in the public's mind. One of the first questions habitually raised about any terrorist-related arrest or incident has been whether it has any "links" to al-Qaᶜida—as if the public should be worried if there are such links but relaxed if there aren't.

A further difficulty is exemplified by the equating of terrorist threats with al-Qaᶜida in the Obama administration's *National Strategy for Counterterrorism* statement, with its meager attention to "other terrorist concerns requiring focus and attention."[43] Such asymmetry makes it likely that other terrorist concerns will *not* receive adequate focus and attention. Modern international terrorism has come in different waves with markedly varied ideologies.[44] Avoiding a future big terrorist-related national surprise requires being attuned to whatever the next wave will be, however different it may be from the current one that has been preoccupying Americans. Such awareness is unlikely, however, amid a narrow national focus on whoever is the enemy in the current "war."

FAITH IN TOTAL SOLUTIONS

The equating of problems abroad with identifiable entities that can be combated and destroyed encourages the often mistaken belief that the problems themselves can be eliminated altogether. This belief has been a persistent strain in American thinking about terrorism—a strain also nurtured by the war metaphor and the expectation that a "war on terror" can be won with as much finality as World War II was won, whether there is a surrender ceremony on the deck of a battleship or not. In this regard, American attitudes toward terrorism have differed significantly from attitudes in, for example, Britain. The British, conditioned especially by their prolonged experience with the Irish Republican Army and related splinter groups, see terrorism as a problem to be dealt with, managed, and ameliorated. Americans, in contrast, see it as an enemy to be defeated and a danger to be exterminated.[45] Especially during the early years of the "war on terror," any analysis in the United States that sounded as if it were talking more about management than about extermination was shouted down as being a timid lack of commitment to victory in the "war."[46]

The faith in victory through extermination of a foe has led to mistaken beliefs regarding the ability to eliminate not only a broad problem such as terrorism but also even the specific foe. This pattern became especially apparent when, thirteen years after 9/11, events in Iraq and Syria finally led another group to eclipse al-Qaʿida as the most frightening embodiment of terrorism. This group began as al-Qaʿida in Iraq during the U.S. military occupation of that country and later, after a break with al-Qaʿida itself and successive name changes, called itself the Islamic State, but it was best known by the acronym ISIS, for "Islamic State in Iraq and Syria." A major reason ISIS seized American attention was its dramatic territorial gains in western and northern Iraq to go along with ground it had come to control in Syria amid that country's civil war. People could follow this development through maps in their newspapers, just like they could follow the movement of front lines in previous wars. Long-standing mental habits born among those previous wars quickly became engaged. This meant that the problem of ISIS was addressed in American political discourse mostly in terms of what sort of military force should be brought to bear to defeat the group and much less in terms of political developments in Iraq and Syria and the associated disaffection of those countries' Sunni citizens, which had at least as much to do with the gains made by ISIS as anything else. It also meant that the goal had to be the complete elimination of ISIS. President Obama said the objective of U.S. efforts against the group was "to degrade and ultimately destroy" the group.[47] The president's statement accurately noted the diffusion and metamorphosis of terrorist groups but left unaddressed the question of why, after thirteen years in which al-Qaʿida had been degraded but not destroyed, the prospect for the destruction of ISIS should be any different. But complete elimination was a politically necessary goal.

Also probably politically necessary for the same reasons was the expansion of U.S. military operations into Syria in the form of airstrikes. Another unanswered question was who would fill whatever vacuum would be left if ISIS could be exterminated, given the weakness of what passed for a moderate Syria opposition and the continued U.S. policy goal of also ending the regime of Bashar al-Assad. This uncertainty involved another recurring consequence of the American tendency to equate solving a problem with eliminating a malevolent foe: failure to plan for what comes afterward. That failure also was in evidence when the United States joined in the external intervention to oust Libyan dictator Muammar Qadhafi in 2011, after which interminable chaos ensued in Libya.

An even clearer case—both because it was more of an American than a European project and because it was a war of choice rather intervention in an ongoing civil war—was the extraordinary failure to plan adequately for dealing with the mess in Iraq after Saddam Hussein's regime was ousted in 2003, notwithstanding the anticipation of this very mess by the intelligence community and some other parts of the bureaucracy.[48] Although hubris and carelessness among the war makers can fairly be blamed, the failure was in part rooted in the American experience with previous wars and especially the wonderfully positive postwar stories of West Germany and Japan. One of the chief promoters of the Iraq War, Paul Wolfowitz, repeatedly likened what the United States was doing in Iraq to what a previous generation of

Americans had done with Germany and Japan.[49] The insufficient appreciation of the difference political culture makes was an outgrowth not only, as discussed in chapter 4, of taking America's own political culture for granted but also of the World War II experience.

PERSONALIZING THE ENEMY

Americans' propensity to reduce their conception of a problem or challenge overseas to a single, extinguishable entity often goes even further by reducing it to a single person. The habit of doing so dates to the beginning of the republic. The Declaration of Independence, after its initial affirmation of self-evident truths, turns to "the present King of Great-Britain." About half of the entire document is a bill of particulars expressed in the third-person singular in which each sentence begins with "He," meaning the king. These particulars lead to the conclusion that "A Prince, whose Character is thus marked by every act which may define a Tyrant, is unfit to be the Ruler of a free People." Before the culminating assertion of independence, there is only a relatively short paragraph about the unresponsiveness of the rest of "our British Brethren" to American grievances.

The wars of the twentieth century also provided personal foes, especially German: first Kaiser Wilhelm II—whom Americans blamed for the war more than Europeans did—and then Adolf Hitler, with Hitler being the biggest single influence on subsequent thinking about America's adversaries. And during World War II, Hitler really was a powerful dictator—unlike King George III, who tried to reassert powers that under his predecessors had already shifted in large part to a council of ministers and whose powers were reduced further by the loss of the American colonies.

Narrow focus on an individual leader frequently involves underestimation of the extent to which even most dictators face constraints determined by interests within their own regimes, by opinion among their publics, and by fixed interests of their nations. The focus tends to involve overestimation of the extent to which the person at the top is running the whole show. In counterterrorism, the intense American focus on Osama bin Laden as the personification not only of al-Qaʿida but of international terrorism overstated the role he had come to play by the time he was tracked down and killed in 2011. Material captured during the raid that dispatched him indicated that during the preceding few years he had been doing much exhorting but very little commanding or organizing of operations. Bin Laden also was the best example of how intense focus on one person can help enhance the stature of that person in the eyes of his or her would-be followers, with Americans not always realizing that their personalizing of a threat has this counterproductive effect.

Heavy emphasis on an individual leader can lead to underestimation of how much even a dictator—or any other leader Americans prefer to view as a disagreeable and illegitimate usurper—can have genuine popular support. This was probably the case with former Iranian president Mahmoud Ahmadinejad, who for Americans became the disagreeable face of Iran for his eight years in office even though in the Iranian system the president is not even the top leader. It became widely assumed among American commentators that Ahmadinejad stole the election in 2009 that gave him a second four-year term, even though there is considerable evidence that he had enough popular support to win even without any election irregularities.[50] Underestimation of a leader's popular support exacerbates the failure to understand how much improving a bilateral relationship requires coming to terms with broadly shared and deeply rooted interests and concerns on the other side (which is certainly the case with Iran) and not just defeating or replacing a disliked regime.

Undue emphasis on a single leader leads to exaggerated expectations of political change once the leader departs. Such expectations almost certainly have been central to the frame of mind that has underlain U.S. policy toward Cuba, which Barack Obama finally and partially reversed in 2014. The policy has included an economic embargo that has lasted for decades but has been both ineffective and out of step with thinking in the rest of the world (as reflected in annual United Nations General Assembly resolutions calling for an end to the embargo by overwhelming votes). At some point, the embargo became a matter of waiting for Fidel Castro to depart. But when Castro, in old age and ill health, stepped down as president in 2008 and as party leader in 2011, there was no sign of the regime crumbling. The transfer of power to Castro's younger brother Raúl appears to have been the first step in change that will be only evolutionary rather than counterrevolutionary.

A BIFURCATED VIEW OF THE WORLD

In America's past big wars, the lineups of friends and foes were fairly clear-cut. When the United States entered World War I, it was the Allied and Associated Powers against the Central Powers; in World War II, it was the Allies against the Axis. There even was the same principal European enemy—Germany—in both world wars. Americans were not bothered much that nice people such as the Finns were on the German side in World War II because that alignment involved an extraneous issue with the Soviet Union that was of little concern to the United States. Given America's sporadic and episodic involvement in the Old World's contests, the lineups seemed all the more fixed and clear-cut. The United States had not had the experience of ever-shifting coalitions, which had little or nothing to do with political or moral values, that Europeans acquired during their many years of balance-of-power politics and monarchical war making.[51]

Even the anomaly of being allied with a regime as foreign to American values as Stalin's Soviet Union did not destroy the mental framework Americans applied to the war. The alliance existed because of the immediate and overwhelming priority placed on defeating the Axis, of course, but a particular American perspective was also in play, as reflected in the different views that Franklin Roosevelt and Winston Churchill brought to dealing with the Soviets. Churchill was willing to make deals with Satan to win the war, but he never doubted that the Soviet Union had malign expansionist intentions in Europe and represented a major strategic problem. Roosevelt instead believed that in the course of working with the Soviets they could be civilized into accepting something closer to an American vision for postwar Europe. The difference was not just a matter of softness on the part of a president who was frail by the time of the Yalta conference in 1945. Two years earlier, in response to Churchill's concern, Roosevelt had commented to the U.S. ambassador to the Soviet Union, "I just have a hunch that Stalin is not that kind of a man . . . and I think that if I give him everything I possibly can and ask for nothing from him in return, *noblesse oblige*, he won't try to annex anything and will work with me for a world of democracy and peace."[52]

Roosevelt's mention of democracy and peace in the same breath reflected the type of liberalism that has dominated American thought for a long time. One tenet of that liberalism is that all good things go together, with economic development and prosperity as well as peace and democracy usually being among the good things.[53] This type of perceived consistency also has even deeper roots in a common human need for cognitive balance, a need that has surfaced in international politics in other ways.[54] Americans exhibit this tendency more strongly than most—so strongly that even a leader as smart as Roosevelt believed that a wartime ally who was a ruthless tyrant with the blood of millions on his hands could be a positive force for democracy and peace. Americans are especially prone to perceive lineups of friends and foes that are not only internally consistent but morally consistent with their own values. This perception is another instance of the habit of seeing the world in simplified Manichean terms of good guys versus bad guys. Much of U.S. history has reinforced rather than challenged this habit and the associated sense that America's political values are consistent with how it has participated in world politics and in warfare. It is a history that began with a war that was not only for independence but also to replace monarchical rule with a republic. The history later included overseas wars that supposedly were fought to end wars and to make the world safe for democracy. It included a "war on terror" in which President George W. Bush declared, "Either you are with us, or you are with the terrorists."[55]

When there arise serious challenges to the habit of viewing the world in rigidly bifurcated terms, Americans tend to blur or erase the challenges with cognitive-balancing misperceptions. One type of misperception is exemplified by Roosevelt's mistake about Stalin: the belief that the enemy of one's enemy is a friend not only in a temporary tactical sense but also in the broader sense of sharing objectives and values. A more recent example is the extensive backing in the United States for the Iranian opposition group Mujahedin-e Khalq (MEK). The group received endorsements from large proportions of the U.S. Congress and other notables in a campaign that culminated with the Obama administration removing the group from the official U.S. list of foreign terrorist organizations in 2012. Such support is extraordinary given that MEK has a long and violent record of behavior antithetical to American interests and values, including terrorist operations that killed U.S. personnel in pre-revolutionary Iran, support for the taking of U.S. hostages at the embassy in Tehran, and later functioning as an arm of Saddam Hussein's security forces in Iraq.[56] It currently has the nature of a cult. Its success in garnering American support evidently is due in part to ample funding that has allowed it in effect to buy endorsements, but it is unlikely to have enjoyed such success if Americans did not believe that any group opposed to the current regime in Tehran is worth supporting and did not tend to overlook the dark side of any such enemy-of-my-enemy.

A valid empirical basis exists for one particular instance, related to war and peace, of good things going together. Political scientists have exhaustively studied this correlation and call it the "democratic peace theory": the concept that democracies do not wage war against each other.[57] It probably is no accident that American scholars in particular have dwelled on this concept, which has become the leading example of explaining war and peace in terms of states' internal structure.[58] Misunderstanding begins, however, when American liberalism tries to stretch the idea beyond the core concept about the absence of wars between established democracies. The theory says nothing about democracies not making war against nondemocracies, and political scientists have observed that fragile or emergent democracies are among the most warlike states of all.[59] Insufficient understanding of these other, more complicated ways in which external warfare relates to internal political forms has fostered misplaced hopes for what can be accomplished through democratization or wars designed to make some part of the word safe for democracy. Such misplaced hopes for the Middle East were part of what underlay the use of an offensive war to overthrow the Iraqi regime in 2003; the hopes were misplaced even though Saddam Hussein's record as a serial aggressor had provided some basis for believing that a different regime in Baghdad would mean a less-aggressive Iraq.

Transferring the image of wartime coalitions, along the lines of what the United States knew in the world wars of the twentieth century, to other situations has led to overestimation of the unity and even the feasibility of friendly coalitions as well as overestimation of the unity and common purpose of hostile ones. The wartime experience has accentuated a more general human tendency toward cognitive simplification by seeing less complexity and more unity than actually exists.[60] Overestimation of unity among friendlies has been involved in efforts to address the Middle East through coalitions of "moderates" to confront "extremists" or "militants," even though Middle Easterners themselves do not view their region as organized that way and even though the image lumps into the moderate camp such vastly different actors as Israel and the monarchies of the Arabian Peninsula, which have many conflicting objectives. This particular conceptual lumping also is another example of Americans overlooking the gap between their own nation's values and their presumed allies' values. The gap involves the absence of democracy in some of the Arab monarchies and the differentiation of political rights according to religion and ethnicity in Israel (and in the territories it controls), even though Israel nonetheless routinely gets described in the United States as sharing America's democratic values. The bifurcated view of the Middle East leaves little room for understanding the role of an actor such as Turkey, which does not fit neatly into either camp and whose policy is dedicated in large part to blurring the line between the two. That view also overlooks how much any apparent unity in the supposed militant camp is based on what its members perceive as a threat from the United States and Israel.[61]

During the Cold War, the American view of the world as clearly split into two camps underlay persistent difficulty in U.S. relations with those who pointedly refused to join either camp. This was especially true in U.S. relations with India, the most prominent leader of a posture known as neutralism and later more commonly referred to as nonalignment. *Neutralism* became as dirty a word to many American ears as *Finlandization*. John Foster Dulles, the secretary of state for most of the Eisenhower administration, annoyed the Indians by referring to their brand of neutral-ism as "immoral."[62] In 1956, Dulles declared, "These neutral governments do not seem to realize that the Communist intentions are so diabolical and so hostile to their freedom and independence." He said that "they would eventually succumb unless they could develop a crusading spirit against the evil forces of Communism."[63] Such an attitude provides most of the explanation for why relations between the world's two largest democracies were so sour for so long.

Overestimation of the unity and common purpose of a worldwide Communist coalition was repeatedly exhibited in American thinking throughout the Cold War. The U.S. decision to intervene in the first big hot war during the Cold War—the one in Korea—was based on an American image of the world as divided into two contending camps: one was a Soviet-led international, revolutionary political movement; the other was a U.S.-led coalition opposing Communist expansion.[64]

The image of two contending worldwide camps still prevailed as Americans reacted to the insurgency in South Vietnam in the 1960s. The U.S. secretary of defense at the time, Robert McNamara, later described the outlook that he shared with his countrymen: "My thinking about Southeast Asia in 1961 differed little from that of many Americans of my generation who had served in World War II and followed foreign affairs by reading the newspapers but lacked expertise in geopolitics and Asian affairs. . . . Like most Americans, I saw Communism as monolithic. I believed the Soviets and Chinese were cooperating in trying to extend their hegemony."[65]

President Lyndon Johnson, who made the decisions to escalate U.S. involvement in Vietnam into a major war, confirmed that he shared this image as well. "It became increasingly clear," he wrote in his memoir, "that Ho Chi Minh's military campaign against South Vietnam was part of a larger, much more ambitious strategy being conducted by the Communists."[66]

The image of a monolithic Communist bloc with a single grand strategy was a grand misperception. The Axis powers, notwithstanding how much they differed from each other in other respects, shared the overriding objective of winning World War II; in contrast, no single global Communist objective was shared that much. Ho Chi Minh's campaign had different goals from those of his Communist comrades in China, as later evolution of the relationship between their two countries would make plain. Americans were slow to perceive that difference, just as they had been slow to see the divide between China and the Soviet Union.[67]

The consequences of perceiving a monolith where there isn't one include but are not limited to overestimation of the global stakes of any one conflict and a resultant commitment of resources that is out of proportion to the real stakes. Failure to understand divisions in the opposing camp also may mean missing signals of adversaries' intentions and misjudging their degree of commitment. During the Korean War, distrust and disagreement within the Communist camp led to delayed and disjointed responses, especially by China, to the northward advance of U.S.-led United Nations forces after Douglas MacArthur's successful Inchon landing in September 1950. This delay led to an American misjudgment that China would not intervene in the war at all. A more accurate American perception of the interplay among China, the Soviet Union, and North Korea might have avoided that misjudgment and enabled both a halt of the United Nations advance and an armistice a couple of years earlier than the one that was finally reached.[68] During the Vietnam War, the Soviets favored a negotiated settlement as of the mid-1960s but had to give up on that approach when the Chinese pressed the North Vietnamese to reject advice from the "revisionist" Soviets and provided substantial military aid to Hanoi that Moscow felt obliged to match.[69] American failure to understand fully the competition among the Communist states fostered both overestimation of how much the outcome on the ground in Vietnam would count on the global Cold War scorecard and underestimation of how that same competition encouraged arms flows that helped to keep the North Vietnamese war effort going.

The presumption of a grand global Communist objective later led to American misinterpretation of some other Soviet actions. Soviet policies that were primarily responses to local problems or opportunities were instead seen as aggressive and part of a global expansionist agenda. This view was in a sense the opposite of the misperception that had characterized Roosevelt's view of Stalin—opposite because the same Soviet Union that had been an ally in World War II was now the chief adversary in the Cold

War. During a crisis in South Asia in 1971 (involving an Indo-Pakistani war and the secession of what became Bangladesh), Richard Nixon and Henry Kissinger acted on their assumption that the crisis was a Cold War proxy conflict in which Moscow had instigated Indian moves to crush the U.S. ally Pakistan—even though this assumption clashed with the conclusions reached by the professional bureaucracy based on its examination of the evidence, and it would have been more accurate to interpret both Soviet and Indian motives as more modest and reactive.[70] Several years later Jimmy Carter and Zbigniew Brzezinski responded to the Soviet intervention in Afghanistan on the assumption (which was never critically examined) that the intervention was part of a larger strategy by Moscow to expand its empire southward to the Persian Gulf, even though Moscow's action was more likely a defensive effort to prevent the fall of a neighboring Communist state by an insurgency that could cause trouble within the Central Asian portion of the Soviet Union itself.[71]

DEMONIZATION

From a presumption that an adversary is always up to no good, it is a short step to believing that the adversary is downright evil. The religiously infused American proclivity, as described in the previous chapter, to moralize about foreign policy provides strong roots for the tendency to demonize adversaries of America. The previous century's experience with foreign wars has strengthened that tendency. In some parts of that experience, the distorting effects of demonization were already apparent; in other parts, the perception of the enemy of the moment was fairly accurate but provided lasting images that, when applied to other adversaries, were not.

Demonization of a wartime adversary can serve the purpose of rallying popular support and enthusiasm for prosecuting the war. In this respect, the phenomenon is not unique to the United States. American exceptionalism makes the phenomenon more pronounced in the United States, however, in part because even in peacetime the self-image of America as innately good sets up the counterpoint view of adversaries who must be innately bad. The element of that self-image, as shaped originally by the Puritans, that portrays America as on a sacred errand sets up as an antithesis an image of adversaries to America as being not just bad but evil.[72] The effect is accentuated further once war begins to be consistent with the self-image of peace-loving Americans who go to war only when the odiousness of an adversary makes it necessary to do so.

The initial U.S. foray as a great power sallying forth overseas with military power—the one against Spain in 1898—did not set much of a pattern in this regard because Spain was a weak and overmatched adversary that did not fit well the role of an alien monster. The story was different regarding the German enemy in World War I. There quickly arose in the United States a hatred of all things German, extending even to literature, music, and the teaching of the German language.[73] The United States certainly was not alone in dissociating itself from anything that sounded German. The British royal family renamed itself from the House of Saxe-Coburg and Gotha to the House of Windsor, and the city of Berlin, Ontario, in Canada renamed itself after the British officer Field Marshal Kitchener. But these moves did not come until well into the war; Americans did not need years of carnage to embrace an image of German evil as an element of American wartime patriotism.

Demonization of the European enemy in World War II did not require any boost from American exceptionalist bias because Hitler and the Nazis really *were* innately bad. The Nazis' actions warrant placing them at or near the top of any list of movements that have embodied evil, and the same thing can be said about Hitler as an individual leader. Moreover, Americans did not have to look back later at their portrayal of the Nazis and apologize for wartime excesses in the nature of the portrayal. During the 1930s, Americans had a rather complex debate about the nature of Nazism. There was a lack of consensus in the United States on the subject, with Charles Lindbergh being the most prominent figure representing a less than uniformly negative view of the Nazis. Against the background of this tempered and searching debate, what came to be mainstream governmental and media views of Nazi Germany during the war were rather accurate.[74] When Allied armies came upon the death camps, the camps only confirmed the darker elements of those views. In short, the Nazi enemy in World War II gave Americans the best possible example of a demonic adversary while giving them no reason to become aware of their own tendency to demonize excessively or indiscriminately.

The good-versus-evil contrast of World War II combined with the sheer scale and generation-shaping impact of the war to make it the single biggest influence, among all U.S. foreign wars, on how Americans have perceived later adversaries. Hitler and the Nazis have been the preeminent references for analogies applied ever since to a wide variety of foreign-policy problems. The application was readily apparent with some of the major conflicts during the Cold War, perhaps in part because American leadership at the time had come of age during the Nazi rise prior to World War II.[75] When Harry Truman was contemplating his response to North Korea's invasion of South Korea in June 1950, he immediately thought of comparisons with earlier actions by Hitler and the Axis.[76] A decade and a half later the same analogy figured prominently in the Vietnam War decision makers' thinking.[77] Thoughts about the Nazis entered the thinking of Cold Warriors in the Reagan administration. Assistant Secretary of Defense Richard Perle said at the time that when he was uncertain about the next Soviet move, he would ask himself, "What would Hitler have done?"[78] The Nazi analogies have continued beyond the Cold War into a generation that had not yet been born when Hitler rose to power—references to Hitler and the Nazis became a staple of those who promoted the invasion of Iraq in 2003.[79]

The single biggest element in the analogies to Hitler has been the notion that any coming to terms with rather than militantly confronting such an adversary is appeasement (as at Munich) and that appeasement will only lead to worse things (as with World War II). The American analogizing, however, is not just a critique of past diplomatic mistakes but instead an attribution of profound evilness to the adversary. Since World War II, U.S. leaders and broader American discourse have repeatedly spoken of foreign-policy challenges in terms of evil lurking on the other side of the issue. Harry Truman, a month before the invasion in Korea, spoke publicly of

Soviet communism as "a compound of evils."[80] Dulles's castigation of the neutralists was based on what he described as their failure to recognize the "evil" of communism. Ronald Reagan famously labeled the Soviet Union an "evil empire." In the speech delivered to a group of Christian evangelicals in which Reagan used that term, he said, "If history teaches anything, it teaches that single-minded appeasement or wishful thinking about our adversaries is folly."[81]

Destined for as much prominence as the term *evil empire* was George W. Bush's term *axis of evil*.[82] In this case, there was an especially strong need to demonize the targeted adversary because the war that this rhetoric was intended to justify departed conspicuously from an American tradition of nonaggression—the war in Iraq being the first major offensive war the United States had launched in more than a century. Depicting Saddam Hussein as especially vile was thus a major part of the sales campaign to justify the war. Vice President Richard Cheney said of the Iraqi regime, "We are dealing here with evil people." National Security Adviser Condoleezza Rice said seven months before the war that "there is a very powerful moral case for regime change" because Saddam is "an evil man."[83]

The American proclivity for demonization, rooted originally in religiously infused moralizing at home and confirmed and accentuated by wars abroad, led George Kennan to observe, "There seems to be a curious American tendency to search, at all times, for a single external center of evil, to which all our troubles can be attributed, rather than to recognize that there might be multiple sources of resistance to our purposes and undertakings, and that these sources might be relatively independent of each other."[84] Kennan was writing during the Vietnam War and referring specifically to the mistake of regarding North Vietnam as a Soviet puppet, a mistake that exemplified how the demonizing habit can exacerbate the war-bred tendency to see adversaries as united in an opposing coalition. The failure to perceive or comprehend multiple sources of resistance to U.S. undertakings has arisen repeatedly since the Cold War, especially the failure to understand that resistance to U.S. military operations overseas can be as diffuse and nonevil as ordinary people becoming upset over damage those operations cause to their lives.

Most of the other misperceptions that flow from the habit of demoniza-tion revolve around the fact that not every adversary of the United States is a Hitler (or even close to being one) and not every international dispute is equivalent to a parley at Munich about the Sudetenland. Demonizing the adversary impedes the ability to understand whatever reasonable bases there may be for the adversary's actions and policies. Demonization fosters perceptions of an adversary's intentions as being farther reaching and more threatening than they really are. The habit also encourages the perception that the adversary is unwilling to compromise or at least—and here lies the chief respect in which the memory of Munich is a scourge—to compromise on terms consistent with U.S. interests.

THE DEMONIZATION OF IRAN

The United States does not have Saddam Hussein to kick around anymore, and in the eyes of most Americans the role of chief demon in that part of the world is now filled by the Islamic Republic of Iran.[85] The reasons why Iran holds this position are multiple. It is hard to imagine a relationship with a new regime getting off to a worse start than its holding fifty Ameri-can officials hostage for more than a year in 1979–1981, when the Islamic Republic was just getting organized. President Mahmoud Ahmadinejad's later rabble-rousing rhetoric invited the most negative interpretations of Iranian intentions. The unrelenting campaign by Israel's rightist govern-ment to paint Iran as the "real problem" underlying troubles in the Middle East rather than any cause involving Israel itself unquestionably has been a major influence on American attitudes, given the Israeli government's extraordinary political clout in Washington. All these influences have found fertile ground in the mental habits of an American populace predisposed to attribute the troubles in that most troublesome of regions to a regime that is Islamist, that has in the past done some genuinely hostile and illegal things, and that runs a country significant enough to be perceived as the leader of a hostile bloc of extremists.

In American perceptions, Iran has come to play the role, in Kennan's phrase, of "a single external center of evil." The theme of evil pervades much American discourse on Iran. In a book by a prominent neoconservative titled *Accomplice to Evil: Iran and the War Against the West*, more than half the chapter headings contain the word *evil*.[86] When conservative Republican senator James Inhofe introduced legislation to designate certain federally owned lands for increased oil production, he justified it as a way to reduce Iranian oil revenues and thereby to deny financial resources "to an evil regime intent on harming America and our allies."[87]

The demonization of Iran has fostered several persistent misperceptions. Chief among them is the image of Iranian leaders as irrational rogues whose minds operate in a fundamentally different way from our own and who cannot be deterred. That image is inconsistent with the behavior Iranian leaders have displayed during the three and a half decades of the Islamic Republic's existence. The Iranians have repeatedly demonstrated that they respond to foreign challenges and opportunities the same way other leaders do with the same considerations of costs and benefits to their regime. This pattern of response is illustrated by Iran's ending of an earlier campaign of assassinating dissident Iranian exiles in Europe when it became apparent that the assassinations were significantly damaging Tehran's relations with European governments. The pattern also was demonstrated by Ayatollah Ruhollah Khomeini's calculated decision to accept an armistice to end the extremely costly Iran–Iraq War of the 1980s.

Related to the image of Iranian leaders as crazed fanatics is the belief that they are constantly engaged in region-wide destabilization and troublemaking. This part of the common American perception of Iran is repeatedly and automatically invoked without reference to the actual record of Iranian behavior. The belief overlooks how the Islamic Republic has never started a war and has never invaded another country's territory, except for counterattacking into Iraq in the war that Saddam Hussein started. It also overlooks how, except in the first few years after the Iranian Revolution, when Iranians were looking for like-minded revolutions elsewhere (most visibly in Lebanon) in the interest of sustaining their own, Iran has been predominantly a status quo power (except for opposing, as does most of the rest of the region, continued Israeli occupation of Palestinian-inhabited territory). The popular American image of Iran also impedes understanding of how much Iranian and U.S. interests in the United States and South Asia run parallel, especially in opposing radical Sunni groups such as ISIS.

The predominant American perception has impeded understanding of the bases for Iranian distrust of and even hostility toward the United States. The bases include the constantly evident American hostility toward Iran, accompanied by implicit and even explicit threats of military attack against Iran made credible by the U.S. military presence in Iran's immediate neighborhood. They also include historical baggage that is the counterpart to Americans' memory of the takeover of the embassy in Tehran and the ensuing hostage crisis. For Iranians, the salient historical events include the U.S.-supported coup to overthrow the Iranian prime minister in 1953 and the shooting down of an Iranian civilian airliner by a U.S. warship in 1988, which most Iranians believe—mistakenly—to have been intentional rather than accidental. There are misperceptions in each direction here, and they are due in part to the general psychological mechanism of attributing someone else's negative behavior to that person's innately negative qualities rather than to the provocations of our own behavior.[88] The American exceptionalist self-image and proclivity for demonization of adversaries accentuates this pattern in the case of perceptions of Iran.

Alarm over Iran's nuclear program, which became the most prominent Iran-related issue for Americans, has demonstrated some of the same tendencies for making worst-case assumptions about Iranian intentions. It also has demonstrated that the effects extend to factual misperceptions. A poll in 2012 asked Americans, in a multiple choice question, what the U.S. intelligence services' assessment about Iran's nuclear program was. Only 25 percent got the correct answer: "Iran is producing some of the technical ability to build nuclear weapons, but has not decided to produce them or not." A mere 4 percent erred in the benign direction by picking "Iran is producing nuclear energy strictly for its energy needs." A plurality, 48 percent, incorrectly chose "Iran has decided to produce nuclear weapons and is actively working to do so, but does not yet have nuclear weapons." An additional 18 percent chose "Iran now has nuclear weapons."[89]

Such widespread misperception among Americans has made the task of moving toward better U.S.–Iranian relations, specifically the conclusion and implementation of an agreement to restrict Iran's nuclear program in return for relief from economic sanctions, far harder than it should be and than it otherwise would have been. The vigorous efforts by international elements, most conspicuously the Israeli government, to oppose any agreement with Iran have had much to do with making the task hard. But the opponents of U.S.–Iranian rapprochement have been aided by the public misunderstanding that has flowed from Iran's status in the public mind as demon of the day.

PERPETUAL WAR

The combination of extensive U.S. engagement overseas, including ways that involve the U.S. military, and the association in American minds of such engagement with the notion of monster slaying implies a need for monsters. More precisely, it implies a need to see monsters threatening America whether they exist or not. No such need is felt by Americans who reject most U.S. overseas involvement, but these people represent a relatively small slice of American politics, confined mostly to the noninterventionist Left and the libertarian Right. The need to perceive foreign monsters is a culmination of Americans' tendency, which as Huntington noted extends back to the founding of the republic, to define their nation as the counterpoint to some nefarious "other."

No Americans would explicitly say that they want to have monsters challenging them or that once engaged in a conflict they would not want to win the conflict and be finished with it. Nonetheless, one can find during the post–World War II era of continuous global engagement indications among the American public and American policy makers that they are more comfortable with waging unending conflict against identifiable adversaries than with having to step into a brave new world bereft of the reference point and sense of purpose that an adversary provides. This phenomenon resembles what arises among some members of insurgent movements who have engaged in a struggle for so long that they know no other life and have no way of directing and imparting meaning to their lives other than the struggle itself.

During Ronald Reagan's administration, the president himself had a clear idea of how he wanted the Cold War to end and a clear belief that the end was fairly near. His secretary of state, George Shultz, was in tune with his thinking in this respect. But other prominent Cold Warriors in the administration, such as Secretary of Defense Caspar Weinberger and intelligence chief William Casey, opposed conciliatory moves toward the Soviets that would anticipate or prepare for a resolution of the conflict.[90] For some, the Cold War had become an addiction, and it appeared they would have been most comfortable waging it forever.[91] The Cold War ended nonetheless, but remnants of a perspective based on waging it forever lived on, especially in the U.S.-led perpetuation and expansion of the preeminent Cold War alliance, NATO.

Terrorism is well suited to fill a perpetual need for monstrous adversaries because terrorism will never end, even though the "war on terror" concept implies that it will. Historian of religion Ira Chernus suggests that the main goal of the "war on terror" has been "to give Americans a global arena where they can show their moral strength, their allegiance to permanent values, and their ability to hold back the whirlwind of change. To prove all that, Americans need to be fighting against sin, evil, and moral weakness; they need monsters to destroy. So the point of the war is not to win. It is, on the contrary, to keep on fighting monsters forever."[92] This analysis understates any American political leader's likely willingness to seize an opportunity to claim victory in such a "war" as well as the genuine physical requirement to protect U.S. citizens from terrorism. It does capture correctly, though, how a concentrated American focus on combating terrorism responds to a more deeply engrained American need.

Servicing that need leads Americans to view some ordinary competitors in international politics as grander and more nefarious than just competitors and to view some genuinely monstrous actors as more of a threat to the United States than they really are. An example of the latter perception is the alarm in the United States over the rise of the extremist group ISIS in the Middle East. Although the group's methods from the beginning clearly were barbaric and its ideology thoroughly alien to American values, it was focused on seizing and holding territory in its area of operations in Iraq and Syria. It considered the United States an adversary only in a more distant future and only if events in the interim went the group's way—that is, unless direct U.S. action against it made the United States a target for revenge. In the meantime, the group's barbarity and narrow sectarian orientation contained the seeds of its own decline.[93] The extent of public and political American alarm about ISIS, including baseless warnings that it was about to sneak fighters into the United States across the U.S.–Mexico border, went well beyond the actual problem that it posed, which was a problem chiefly of disorder and instability in parts of the Middle East. ISIS was moving into the role of chief terrorist devil in American minds that al-Qaʿida had been filling for more than a decade, even though ISIS's plans were markedly different from al-Qaʿida's strategy of hitting the American "far enemy" as a way to get to its near enemies.

American attitudes toward Russia as relations with Moscow worsened amid crisis and insurrection in Ukraine in 2014 exemplified how a competitor can come to be seen as representing a more nefarious danger than it really is. After the triumphalist, post–Cold War posture of viewing Russia as a loser and increasingly irrelevant has-been, the Ukraine crisis and the Russian assertiveness that went with it suddenly stimulated much talk in the United States about a "new Cold War."[94] Use of this term—another indication of persistence of the addiction to the original Cold War—masked the major differences between old and new. This time there was no global ideological contest, no nuclear arms race, and no tests of strength between contending superpowers in a bipolar world.

The events associated with the crisis over Ukraine were much more akin to the tussles of old-style European balance-of-power politics, although with an extra dollop of nationalism. Vladimir Putin's snatching of Crimea from a weakened and distracted Ukraine was like the Prussian Frederick the Great's seizing Silesia from Austria in 1740, and the issue of whether the internal politics of Ukraine would lead it to look eastward or westward in its international affiliations was somewhat similar to the issues that underlay the War of the Spanish Succession in the early eighteenth century. Concerns that Europeans, especially eastern Europeans, have had about Russia amid the newest crisis are very old concerns and follow in this same tradition. The greater American tendency to think instead in Cold War terms has represented a less-insightful understanding of what is going on. Viewing differences over Ukraine less in terms of competing nationalisms and demarcation of spheres of influence in Russian borderlands and more in terms of a global contest of wills has probably impeded the search for solutions to the conflict.

In addition to such impediments in dealing with individual issues, American habits of thinking about war and peace have a more general effect that can be described most succinctly as a bias toward war. The persistence of forms of overseas engagement that Americans have associated with the war switch being on is leading to the switch being stuck in the on position—with everything else that assumption implies on matters ranging from the disposition of prisoners and the role of military force to domestic issues of privacy and civil liberties. An irony of U.S. history is that a scarcity of wars in the nineteenth century helped to shape mental habits that, combined with requirements of America's global involvement in the twenty-first century, has brought Americans close to seeing themselves in perpetual war.

Of course, the American public periodically expresses revulsion when wars get too hot and the cost of them gets too high. There was a "Vietnam syndrome" after the very costly Vietnam War—a syndrome that many considered to have been dissipated by the decisive and relatively inexpensive expulsion of Iraqi forces from Kuwait in 1991—and some have observed a similar "Iraq syndrome" setting in after the costly and frustrating Iraq War.[95] In 2013, amid heightened concern about an escalating civil war in Syria and possible use of chemical weapons there, the U.S. Congress and president read American public opinion as being strongly against involvement in another Middle Eastern war. But revulsion against high-cost forms of waging war has not diminished the propensity for perceiving monsters that need destroying with lower-cost forms of warfare—or what are hoped to be lower-cost forms.[96] The end of conscription in 1973 and the reliance on an all-volunteer military since then have made it easier for the American public to make such distinctions and have precluded a reaction as strong as the Vietnam syndrome.

U.S. military involvement in Afghanistan became as of a few years ago the longest-ever U.S. involvement in a hot war. The U.S. war in Iraq has come and gone, but some U.S. troops have been put back into Iraq in response to the fear of ISIS. The same fear led, only a year after U.S. political leaders backed off from intervening against the Syrian regime, to U.S. airstrikes against extremist groups in Syria. And U.S. officials advise the public that the United States is in for the long haul in its campaign against ISIS. The search for monsters has brought Americans as close as ever not just to believing themselves to be in but to actually being in perpetual war. That may be the most important consequence of the distorting effects of the American prism.

6

UNENDING MISPERCEPTION

I T WOULD BE infeasible to construct a scorecard that tallies correct and incorrect images that Americans hold of the outside world. Americans see many things correctly, but correct perceptions are not what require study and explanation. Correct perceptions are what should flow, naturally and unsurprisingly, from directly facing reality without distorting influences. It is the incorrect perceptions that require explanations. Incorrect perceptions also have been more consequential in contributing to bad policies, including costly and unsuccessful wars. Even without attempting to compile a comprehensive scorecard on American public understanding of the world, it is clear that many significant misperceptions have had substantial policy consequences and have been closely related to aspects of America and the American experience that set it apart from other nations.

DEMOCRACY, BUREAUCRACIES, AND LEADERS

To some extent, distortions found in American thinking have been found in other democracies as well. It was in such terms that Walter Lippmann explained the poor performance of Western democracies between the world wars of the twentieth century. They compiled this record, wrote Lippmann, because "the prevailing public opinion has been destructively wrong at the critical junctures. The people have imposed a veto upon the judgment of informed and responsible officials. They have compelled the governments, which usually know what would have been wiser, or was necessary, or was more expedient, to be too late with too little, or too long with too much, too pacifist in peace and too bellicose in war, too neutralist or appeasing in negotiation or too intransigent."[1] The interwar years, when a British prime minister came to personify appeasement of the Nazis, was probably the period when on any scorecard of public perceptions Americans would look no worse than their counterparts in other democracies. But it was Americans who would later apply analogies based on Munich and the 1930s to all sorts of situations more indiscriminately and misleadingly than almost anyone else. Some of the other misdirections in public opinion to which Lippmann referred have been most marked among Americans. Exaggerated swings of the perceptual pendulum between peacetime and wartime, for example, are exemplified most clearly by the Jacksonian, and thus American, concept of war and peace.

A veto on the judgment of informed and responsible officials is one way in which public perceptions have influenced policy and public misperceptions have led to bad policies. In other instances, the impact has not been definitive enough to warrant the term *veto*. Informed officials have instead had to struggle more and to use more of their political capital to act according to their best judgment. Relations with Iran during the Obama administration are a recent example. In some instances, the result has been, although not an outright veto, policies that exhibit in Lippmann's terms action that is either "too late with too little" or "too long with too much." Much U.S. counterterrorist policy has exemplified this result. All of these mechanisms are in addition to the influence that the public philosophy has exerted through policy makers' internalization of that same philosophy.

Lippmann's relatively favorable portrayal of the perspicacity of officialdom clashes with the American habit of blaming bureaucracies for inaccurately appraising what is going on overseas—a habit that also has roots in the American national experience and in the culture and attitudes this experience has bred.[2] Lippmann's perspective has a sound basis in that some of these same bureaucracies, including U.S. intelligence agencies that were in their youth when he was writing in the mid-1950s, place heavy emphasis on training and techniques expressly designed to overcome mind-sets and biases, including the ones that are common to all humanity as well as the ones that are more peculiarly American.[3]

Then there is the record of bureaucratic judgments on important policy-relevant questions. Notwithstanding the perpetual public and political hand-wringing over intelligence failures, at some critical junctures in modern U.S. history the intelligence bureaucracy has rendered sound judgments that were overridden by broadly shared popular perceptions, with costly consequences. One such sound judgment was the assessment prior to the U.S. military intervention in Vietnam that South Vietnam was unlikely ever to be able to stand on its own feet, a judgment outweighed by popular perceptions about the need to stop Communists from knocking over dominoes. Another was the assessment that Iraq after Saddam Hussein was gone would be a contentious and violent mess, a judgment outweighed by neoconservative-stimulated popular perceptions about how Saddam was a dangerous Hitlerian ogre who needed to be removed and how once he was removed, Iraq would slide smoothly into democracy.[4]

The overriding of such bureaucratic judgments is especially likely in America because bureaucracies, including intelligence bureaucracies, tend to be held in lower popular esteem there than in other advanced democracies. The contrast is especially marked with parts of East Asia, such as Singapore, where professional civil servants enjoy status (and compensation) that would be unheard of in the United States. In Japan, the permanent bureaucracy has been so powerful that ministers who supposedly lead ministries instead sometimes defer to the bureaucracy's wishes. In France, where the lines between government bureaucracy and the upper reaches of politics and society are more blurred than in the United States, the educational ticket that more top French political leaders have punched than any other is a school for civil servants, the École Nationale d'Administration.

LEADERS' MANAGEMENT
OF POPULAR PERCEPTIONS

Top political leaders in the United States, being opinion makers themselves, are better positioned than U.S. bureaucracies to contain, correct, or otherwise deal with widespread beliefs of the American public that are rooted in the American experience. The American lawyer Elihu Root, who served as secretary of war and secretary of state under Theodore Roosevelt, addressed this topic in the inaugural issue of the journal *Foreign Affairs* in 1922. Root wrote that when foreign offices are ruled by autocracies or oligarchies, the danger of war lies in "sinister purpose." By contrast, "when foreign affairs are ruled by democracies the danger of war will be in mistaken beliefs." That danger, Root stated, can be corrected by leaders providing the people with correct information.[5]

Root's optimism about this method of correction was perhaps influenced by his having worked for a president who coined the term *bully pulpit* and was an especially enthusiastic and proficient user of that pulpit. The larger pattern of American leaders having to deal with widespread, entrenched, and mistaken beliefs among their citizenry is more complex and gives fewer grounds for optimism. The most significant American public misperceptions have not been simple factual errors susceptible to correction with good data coming from a national leader or some other authoritative source. They have instead been whole ways of looking at foreign actors and foreign situations. Entire mindsets are more resistant to correction from above than the individual mistaken beliefs those mindsets generate. Although American leaders' management of popular beliefs about foreign affairs has varied widely from president to president and from problem to problem, it is hard to find examples of leaders explicitly correcting specific mistaken beliefs widely held by the populace.

In some happy circumstances, the public already holds a generally correct view of a problem that mirrors the leadership view, in which case public
sentiment assists in what the leadership wants to accomplish. Such a coin-
cidence of leadership and public perceptions existed to some extent during the 1980s, when President Reagan's view of the U.S.–Soviet arms race
and larger competition as well as the prospects for winning that competition were basically correct and had substantial resonance with most of the
American public. Reagan's view was arrived at less through analysis than
through instinct and intuition, a method that at different times and in different circumstances was liable to yield woefully inaccurate beliefs. But in
this particular instance the result was more right than wrong, and the very
fact that the president arrived at this thinking through a simple faith in
American free enterprise that he shared with most of the American public
accounted for the popular resonance that his views enjoyed. Reagan's worldview, nurtured not in academic study or in a foreign-policy establishment
but instead in mainstream America, is one of the leading examples of how a
leader's internalization of a popular perception serves as a transmission belt
between that perception and the making of policy.

However, public beliefs have more often presented complications and
impediments rather than reinforcement for an American leader who has
accurate perceptions about an overseas relationship and an agenda to go
with them. And most often in such instances the leader has not been able to
overcome the impediments simply by dispensing correct information in the
manner Root suggested. Rather, the response usually has been a combination of work-arounds and gradual attempts to create new facts with new
policies. A successful example of this pattern was Richard Nixon's historic
opening to China in the early 1970s. Although most American foreign-
policy elites had by this time come to accept the need for a better relationship with China, public opinion lagged behind. High public skepticism
about China was reflected in pluralities still opposing diplomatic relations
with China or its membership in the United Nations.[6] Nixon's management
of this situation involved gradual and tentative acclimation to contacts with
China through ping-pong diplomacy and, in a final work-around, extreme
secrecy in arranging his trip to China.

LEADERS' EXPLOITATION
OF POPULAR PERCEPTIONS

Inaccurate images of the world abroad, bent and colored by the American prism, can affect U.S. policy unfavorably not only through the erection of impediments to action being undertaken by more enlightened leaders but also through internalization of the inaccurate images by leaders themselves. Another possibility is that mistaken perceptions held by the public can provide a ready audience for leaders' deliberate manipulation of images—and outright purveying of false images—to muster public support for their initiatives. In this instance, public perceptions are not the original drivers of misguided policies but are an important accessory to them. The prevailing patterns of thought that dominate public discourse make it harder for anyone to rebut or expose the manipulation.

The American tendencies to demonize adversaries and to overestimate some types of threats are among the patterns most relevant to such manipulation. So is the tendency to believe that once a threat is eliminated, American-style democratic order will easily fall into place. Both tendencies provide grist for any administration trying to grind out support for assertive policies that it pitches as being necessary for defeating a threat. A result is a long-standing American pattern of enlisting support for foreign policies by overselling both threats and remedies.[7] The tendency to overestimate the unity of America's adversaries also has figured into leaders' manipulation of images, including notably in the selling of several initiatives taken during the Cold War in the name of containing a supposedly united global Communist menace.

With such manipulation, there is no correction of popular misperceptions, at least not until and unless ill consequences of policies based on such misperceptions become fully apparent. Policy makers' exploitation of a misperception may instead imbed that misperception ever more deeply into the public's thinking. It remains there to infect discourse on other topics in the future.

The American tendencies to demonize and to presume that adversaries are unified as well as the tendency to be overly optimistic about the establishment of democratic order were significant accessories to one of the biggest manipulations of public perceptions in modern U.S. foreign policy: the selling of the offensive war against Iraq in 2003. It does not take anything away from the energy and skill of the sales campaign to note that the campaign's success depended heavily on certain preconceptions and distinctively American tendencies. To get two-thirds of Americans to believe, as the campaigners did by August 2003, that Saddam Hussein had been personally involved in the 9/11 attacks[8]—notwithstanding publicly known facts about the attacks, about al-Qaʿida and about Saddam's regime that indicated otherwise and notwithstanding the contrary findings by U.S. intelligence agencies—was extraordinary in any case. To have induced that result without exploiting the American people's preexisting tendencies and preconceptions would have been almost impossible.

UNHELPFUL RESPONSES TO MANIPULATION

Sometimes much of the American public can see through leaders' efforts to manipulate their perceptions, at least after the fact. Sometimes this ability leads to healthy skepticism about any future manipulation, as it did in a sense after World War I when a majority of Americans, as reflected in opinion polls, came to doubt the most incendiary propaganda about alleged German atrocities during the war.[9] At least as often, however, the longer-term responses to manipulation have involved overreactions or unconstructive disillusionment.

Americans exhibited significant disillusionment with World War I even though they suffered far fewer costs than the European participants had. Because the Wilson administration—appealing to the American willingness to believe that the United States sallies forth into overseas engagements only for righteous and altruistic reasons—portrayed the war in idealistic terms as making the world safe for democracy, a broader disillusionment set in amid a postwar world that was far from being completely democratic or safe and that discredited progressive action of any kind, including on domestic issues.[10] Regarding foreign affairs, the disillusionment was an ingredient in isolationist sentiment and rejection of the League of Nations. Meanwhile, the healthily skeptical attitude toward anti-German propaganda in the previous war had a downside in possibly slowing American recognition of the rise of a German movement that really was highly aggressive and capable of the worst sort of atrocities.

A different type of public reaction occurred after World War II. During the war, U.S. leaders had to acclimate the American people to being in alliance with the Stalinist tyranny in the Soviet Union. The acclimation, aided by the American tendency to believe that all good things go together and thus that allies have congruent interests, was successful enough that during the war even American conservatives supported lend–lease assistance to the Soviets and made some friendly references to "Uncle Joe." But this success set the stage for an anti-Soviet reaction after the war that was even stronger than it might otherwise have been because of resentment over what was seen as Soviet ingratitude.[11] This reaction probably hastened and intensified the escalation of U.S.–Soviet tensions in the early years of the Cold War.

Sometimes the public never sees through some of the manipulation of their perceptions during a conflict, which sets the stage in a different way for future conflict. After Saddam Hussein's Iraq invaded and swallowed Kuwait in 1990, the George H. W. Bush administration faced an uphill battle in getting sufficient support from the American public for the military expedition to liberate Kuwait.[12] Patient explanation of limited U.S. objectives in securing oil resources and preserving a balance of power in the Middle East would not do it. Operation Desert Storm the following year instead had to be justified as an idealistic campaign to stop aggression. Saddam Hussein was portrayed as evil incarnate, and the administration resorted to invoking the familiar Hitler analogy.[13] A by-product of this method of mustering support for the war was a lingering sense of lack of fulfillment when, although Kuwait was liberated, the supposed latter-day Hitler was left in power.[14] This lack of fulfillment provided a base of sentiment on which the makers of the war of choice against Iraq twelve years later could build.

AXES TO GRIND

Incumbent leaders are not the only ones to exploit the American public's proclivities to misperceive and misunderstand overseas situations in certain ways. Anyone with a policy agenda can do it. Or, more accurately, it can be done by anyone with a policy agenda that happens to run in a direction that parallels the direction of the American people's principal perceptual proclivities. And just as when leaders do it, others' exploitation of popular misperceptions also reinforces those misperceptions. An insalubrious circle results, in which the historical roots of common American thinking interact with the interests of present-day agenda pushers to carve certain mistaken views about the outside world ever more deeply into the American mind.

The most pertinent proclivities in this regard are the ones that involve seeing threats as more grave and more demonic than they really are, supplemented by the views that conceive of protecting American interests abroad in terms of wars. There have always been interest groups that would like Americans to think of U.S. foreign policy in such terms. President Dwight D. Eisenhower was referring to such interest groups when he warned in his farewell address about the "acquisition of unwarranted influence" by the "military-industrial complex."[15] To the extent such groups need enemies and need to conjure up enemies where they do not really exist, they find a susceptible audience among a monster-seeking American populace.

Interest groups doing the exploitation do not need to be armament-manufacturing merchants of death or military forces looking for a mission—the sorts of specific, material groups evoked by Eisenhower's phrase. Very often today they can be better described as ideological interest groups. Present-day American neoconservatism is the prime ideological interest that feasts on the American people's proclivities to see the outside world in certain ways, although the ideology sometimes labeled as liberal interventionism has been sustained in the same way. Some neoconservative interests may be material and parochial, such as think tanks' interest in getting financial support or pundits and politicians' interest to achieve prominence and further their careers. But for the most part such interests are purely ideological. In the case of neoconservatism, the view of foreign affairs is one in which the advance of U.S. interests is defined chiefly as confrontation with an endless series of demons and includes a heavy emphasis on war and the military instrument, a unilateralist bent and little patience for foreign opinions, and a strong faith in the universal applicability of what neoconservatives consider to be American values.

The congruence of that view with many of the principal perceptual tendencies described in earlier chapters is obvious. In fact, neoconservatism can be described as growing directly out of those tendencies and as having become the strongest and purest expression of them. This is why neoconservatism is specifically an American ideology; it is the most extreme form of American exceptionalism. With neoconservatism's solidification as a distinct ideology, however, and not just a synonym for American thinking generally, the same vicious circle of exploitation and reinforcement of mistaken perceptions takes place as it can with other special interests.

The demonization of Iran is probably the most salient recent example of this circle in action. On this issue, neoconservatives have been joined by another special interest, Israel's rightist government, which has made demonization of Iran a major part of its strategy to ascribe all problems of the Middle East to an actor other than itself and to keep a regional enemy prominently in American minds as a basis for U.S.–Israeli strategic cooperation. Although the Israeli government does not enjoy as much congruence with mainstream American thinking as the neoconservatives do, it benefits from the parallels, described in chapter 3, that many Americans see between Israel's experience and their own.

The ability to ride Americans' mistaken perceptions of the outside world helps to explain why neoconservatives have continued to dominate the Republican Party's foreign-policy direction despite the different views contending for influence within that party. The main contender is the Tea Party movement, which has enjoyed much influence on domestic issues and whose adherents would favor a less-assertive and less-militarist foreign posture than the neoconservatives. Anatol Lieven attributes the Tea Party's failure to make any significant inroads against neoconservative dominance of Republican Party foreign policy to "sheer ignorance of the world outside the United States" coupled with "basic chauvinist prejudices."[16]

Given the glaring and still recent blunder that is most closely associated with neoconservatives—the Iraq War—a conspicuous fact about current American discourse on foreign policy that cries out for explanation is that the neoconservatives are still a big part of that discourse rather than being dismissed as a discredited remnant. That some of the main strands of neoconservative thinking have roots in the American national experience provides much of the explanation.

INTERACTION WITH FOREIGN PERCEPTIONS OF THE UNITED STATES

The influence of ideologically defined interests that both grow out of and in turn exploit and exacerbate popular American misperceptions is not the only vicious circle that is at work here. Another involves how certain American perceptions about foreigners produce U.S. statements and policies that lead the foreigners to speak and act in ways that start to make the perception true, even if it wasn't originally. Perceive someone as an enemy and treat him as such, and you have gone a long way toward making a real enemy. "Ideology," noted Arthur Schlesinger Jr., "offers a field day for self-fulfilling prophecies. If you shape policy to what you regard as a predestined result, chances are that you will get the result you predestine." Schlesinger pointed to an example from the 1980s: "Having decided *a priori* that the Nicaraguan revolution was a Soviet–Cuban conspiracy, Washington gave the Sandinistas no alternative but the Cubans and Russians."[17]

The American perceptual tendencies most at play in this sort of interaction are the ones that see enemies even where they may not exist and that see ordinary competitors or adversaries as more demonic than they really are. The vicious circle is made all the more intense by the foreigners' own misperceptions, so that their and the Americans' misperceptions reinforce each other. Many in the Muslim world, for example, are prepared to believe the worst about American intentions, including that an American objective is to kill Muslims. One might argue endlessly in a chicken-and-egg manner about how this or any other spiral of malign mutual distrust got started, but the ongoing dynamic is less arguable. American perceptions of enemies in the Muslim world promote American statements and actions that strengthen Muslim beliefs about malign American intentions, which promote statements and sometimes actions by Muslim foreigners and their governments that in turn strengthen Americans' beliefs that their perception of Muslim enemies was right in the first place. And so on.

The American tendencies to see the world in Manichean terms as divided between good guys and bad guys and to overestimate unity among the bad guys lead similarly to self-reinforcing cycles. This was true of numerous situations during the Cold War, including Nicaragua. More recently, the tendency to perceive the Middle East as divided into moderate and extremist camps leads to American attitudes, statements, and policies that have given the "extremists" all the more reason to work together even if they otherwise have much that divides them. As a result, the United States has done more to unite its foes than to develop cohesion among its friends, especially but not solely in the Middle East.[18]

Americans have difficulty in doing their part to break this kind of damaging attitudinal reciprocation, not just because the specific misperceptions involved have deep roots. Americans are strong nationalists, but they don't recognize that their sentiments are a type of nationalism that is akin in important ways to nationalism found in many other nations.[19] Americans eschew the very term *nationalism* as applied to themselves, using *exceptionalism* as a kind of euphemism that by its very nature underscores differences from rather than similarities to nationalisms elsewhere. This outlook makes it harder for Americans to see their own attitudes as one side of a perceptual loop that is reinforcing misbelief on both sides. Added to this blindness is general American incuriosity about views held by people overseas, an incuriosity that became all the greater during the triumphalist years following the end of the Cold War. Only after the 9/11 terrorist attacks did the "why do they hate us" question become a significant part of American discourse.[20] Even then, as noted earlier, the prevailing answer to that question was mostly blind to the ways in which the American posture toward the rest of the world has significantly contributed to other countries' attitudes toward America.

IMPEDIMENTS TO SELF-AWARENESS

Prospects for ameliorating or overcoming the distorting effects of the American prism are dim. They are dim in part for the same reasons that any well-rooted set of perceptual biases is hard to overcome. Recognition of a bias is the first step in overcoming it, but the very meaning of bias implies blindness or resistance to such recognition. Experience-based bias is also a heuristic of the sort needed to provide the mental shortcuts that make life manageable. Thus, even an earnest effort by policy makers to correct for the biases can go only so far.[21]

Americans have additional reasons more peculiar to their own nation's experience and circumstances that make it hard for them to recognize the prism and the distortions it causes. The very strength and success of the United States have made Americans, despite periodic foreign-policy failures, less inclined toward sustained introspection about national inadequacies, including inadequacies of perception and understanding, than people of other nations whose failures have been more sustained and unmistakable. American habits in this regard are the opposite, for example, of the habit in the Muslim world to reflect on a millennium-long decline of the Muslim Middle East relative to the West, a decline that was made undeniable by the weakening of the Ottoman Empire in the eighteenth and early nineteenth centuries and that led to the recurring question that Middle Eastern Muslims ask among themselves, "What went wrong?"[22]

The large amount of unspoken and thus unrecognized ideological consensus in American social and political thought further discourages introspective thought about one's own thinking and how it may have distinctive distortions rooted in a shared national experience.[23] Also discouraging such introspection is an American outlook, related to the view of the United States as embodying a New World that was created by breaking away from the Old, that rejects what Robert Heilbroner called a "historic future." He observed, "We [Americans] are naturally sympathetic to ideas which stress the plasticity and promise, the openness of the future, and impatient with views which emphasize the 'fated' aspect of human affairs." He described this sympathy as a distinctively American trait: "Unlike its mother-nations, America has never experienced the dragging weight of a changeless past."[24] America's past has imposed its own dragging weight, but because that past has not been changeless and because of an American faith in the ability to change further, the weight goes largely unrecognized.

Overcoming the weight of the past and of whatever misperceptions and misunderstandings are dragged along with it is primarily a matter of leadership. This means, first of all, that national political leaders must exercise enough care about their own thought processes to avoid internalizing popular misperceptions, and then to resist caving in to those misperceptions. Both tasks are harder to do than to say—the first for all the reasons already given that discourage the necessary critical introspection and the second because resisting widely held conventional wisdom is politically risky.

Leaders can also try to use the bully pulpit, along the lines that Elihu Root had in mind, to change the conventional wisdom. But trying to alter prevailing popular perceptions is also politically risky. Most of the political incentives are in the direction of bowing to rather than bumping up against those perceptions. It is not feasible to treat the American public as if they were intelligence analysts being trained in a classroom to acknowledge and overcome their mindsets. Probably no one has ever won an election in the United States by telling citizens how ignorant or biased they are.

LIMITS TO LEARNING FROM FAILURE

Besides inspired and courageous political leadership, other possible influences conceivably might change the American public philosophy. One is reality. When preconception collides with the world as it really is, some-thing has to give. Usually what gives is a clear view of reality, with the pre-conception being preserved as the mind uses its subconscious techniques of bending and selectively excluding information to keep the perception con-sistent with the reality. But when the discrepancy with reality becomes glar-ing enough, these cognitive mechanisms are insufficient, and the precon-ception finally changes. This is how advances in scientific understanding of the natural world sometimes operate,[25] and it is reasonable to suppose that broader American public understanding of the political, social, and security world outside the United States might operate this way as well. Failure can be the catalyst for perceptual change. America has not had the sort of sus-tained failure that led Middle Eastern Muslims to ask what went wrong, but there have been intermittent failures, most notably wars that did not go well. Popular reactions to some of those failures, such as the attitudes that came to be labeled the "Vietnam War syndrome," have involved revision of what previously had been broadly held perceptions of the world abroad.

Substantial caveats and limitations apply, however, to this avenue for possible change in the American public mindset. A revision to prevailing perceptions of particular situations or adversaries of the day—revisions that take place within a broader framework of how Americans habitually look at overseas problems—is different from alterations in the framework itself. The Vietnam War syndrome involved changes of the former type, not the latter. It marked one more cycle in the flicking of the on–off war switch, not an instance in which the habit of thinking of war and peace in terms of such a switch was abandoned. And although the Vietnam War syndrome was part of a national realization that world communism was not really as monolithic as Americans had commonly supposed, the habit of overesti-mating adversaries' unity did not end. It returned a generation later amid talk of "Islamofascism" and "World War IV" in a tendency to lump all vari-eties of militant political Islamism into one undifferentiated enemy.[26]

Many mistakes and misperceptions do not have sufficiently direct and traumatic effect on the public or even on the political fortunes of their leaders to force a change in American ways of thinking about the outside world. The mistaken perceptions may have costly consequences, but these consequences are not immediate enough and the connections with the misperceptions not obvious enough for the necessary lessons to be drawn. Insensitivity to the security concerns of foreigners who do not enjoy the protection of ocean moats, for example, underlies the ineffectiveness or negative side effects of some U.S. policies, but the connection between this insensitivity and the ultimate ineffectiveness of the policy and costs to the United States is usually too subtle for Americans to register.

Wars tend to be preeminent national learning experiences because the costly consequences are not only major but also in many cases glaring, direct, and immediate. Even the instructional potential of wars, however, may have diminishing returns for many Americans. The end of conscription four decades ago and the shrinking proportion of the American population that has served in the military have made fewer citizens feel the costs of war in a sufficiently direct and traumatic way to force changes in mindsets. The effect is seen in opinion surveys that distinguish those who have worn the uniform from those who have not. Among American elites, civilian non-veterans are more in favor of interventionist policies than either military officers or veteran civilians.[27] These survey results directly record preferences rather than perceptions, but they are associated with different perceptions of the efficacy of force applied to overseas problems, a difference that in turn is related to the differential learning experiences of those who have directly borne the costs of war and those who have not.

Whatever potential the Iraq War and the failures it represents may have as a learning experience are diminished because the war was not only fought with an all-volunteer military force but also financed with borrowed money. The administration that launched the war lowered taxes rather than raising them. Most Americans made almost no immediate sacrifices on behalf of the war. The follow-on costs of what turned out to be a very expensive conflict are substantial,[28] but few members of the next generation that will feel the effects of the costs will make any connection between those costs and the mistaken beliefs their fathers and mothers had about how nasty regimes and terrorist groups always go together or about how removing a dictator opens the way to liberal democracy.

Americans' habitually poor use of history and their tendency to over-estimate the newness of things exacerbate the problem of not learning lessons. Americans have a weak sense not only of a historic future but of a historic present. Conscious drawing of lessons from history tends to consist of simplistic selections of a few salient events and their application with little regard to how present circumstances differ from as well as resemble earlier circumstances, as in the endless analogies to Munich and Hitler.

Even recent history is especially likely to be ignored when that history contradicts Americans' benign exceptionalist self-image as a people who right wrongs but do not commit wrongs themselves. An example arose in 2014 with a furor over the use of torture several years earlier to try to extract information from suspected terrorists in detention. The principal vehicle for national catharsis was a mammoth report, five years in the making and cost-ing $40 million to prepare, from the Democratic staff of the Senate Select Committee on Intelligence.[29] The report made no recommendations and appeared to serve little purpose other than to achieve a cathartic effect by focusing all blame for this ugly episode on a single government bureaucracy, the Central Intelligence Agency, thereby keeping the public self-image pure. Receiving less attention than the cascade of details about the tech-niques that had been used on detainees was the fact that this interrogation program had been approved at the highest levels of the executive branch and briefed to the appropriate overseers in Congress, who at that time had the opportunity to object but did not do so. The committee's report received enormous attention, but other sources telling this larger story received little.[30] Largely missed among the raucous public discourse was the biggest story of all, which was how much the mood and priorities of the American public and thus of their elected representatives had changed between the early days after the 9/11 terrorist attacks and the time the report was released. A lesson that thus went unlearned was what led to the use of torture—not a government agency running amok but instead public fear and militancy that had become so intense that such methods were condoned and even expected even if few called them torture at the time. Also unlearned was the broader lesson that the American public habitually reacts to events in the oscillating manner Lippmann described, sometimes in such an extreme way that it leads to violation of what are considered at other times to be core American values.

The lessons that Americans do draw from failures or other disturbing episodes tend to be heavily colored by their existing worldview rather than to force a revision of the worldview itself. George Kennan saw something like this happening with repeated references to the United States having "lost China" following the Chinese Communist Party's ascent to power. Such references, wrote Kennan, "seriously distorted the understanding of a great many Americans about foreign policy, implying as they did that our policy was always the decisive mover of events everywhere in the world; that in any country of the world, including China, we had it in our power to prevent the rise to positions of authority of people professing Marxist sympathies."[31] The distortion was consistent with the American tendencies to overestimate the efficacy of American power applied overseas and to underestimate the appeal of systems of social and political organization other than American-style liberal democracy.

Similar distortions sometimes lead to resistance to recognizing a failure as a failure at all. This was true of a widely held belief that the Iraq War had been "won" or almost won as of 2009 after a surge and subsequent de-escalation of the U.S. presence in the country. The belief entailed turning a blind eye to a continued high level of violence in a sustained civil war and the failure of the enhanced U.S. military efforts to achieve its purpose of making possible reconciliation among the warring Iraqi political factions.[32]

The continuous application of U.S. military force in Afghanistan, Iraq, Syria, and elsewhere after the turn of the twenty-first century might be expected at least to put a dent in the Jacksonian on–off view of war and peace. But the framing in American minds of how American power is being applied lags well behind the reality. The framing of the application of U.S. military force as sallying forth to vanquish the enemy of the moment and then retreating to the North American redoubt lives on. President Barack Obama continued to frame counterterrorism as a "war on terror" in a speech in 2013, and he did so in a way that related it to American democracy and to Americans' view of history. "Our systematic effort to dismantle terrorist organizations must continue," Mr. Obama said, "but this war, like all wars, must end. That's what history advises. That's what our democracy demands."[33] The president may have been wise to speak of needed retrenchment from the military commitments the United States had been undertaking in the name of counterterrorism, but he did so in terms that sustained a popular misconception—in this case the misconception of terrorists as one more set of evildoers to be vanquished in a foray overseas, after which the problem will be over and done with.

DIVIDED VIEWS WITHIN AMERICA

American opinion and views of the outside world are not monolithic, just as the Communist bloc during the Cold War wasn't either. A further potential corrective to distortions imparted by the American prism is thus the give and take of discourse among Americans themselves. Walter Russell Mead, in his analysis of different American traditions of U.S. foreign-policy thought, sees grounds for optimism in this regard, suggesting that interplay among the different traditions has been a source of strength for U.S. foreign policy through most of U.S. history. He also sees glimmers of hope regarding the more specific task of acquiring better understanding of the outside world. He writes that adherents to what he labels the Jeffersonian school—which is especially concerned with protecting fragile American institutions from the damaging effects of foreign entanglements—"are interested in understanding foreign cultures and peoples on their own terms."[34]

Mead's overall argument about the positive value of competition among the different traditions is surely valid, but as a corrective to misconceptions rooted in the shared American experience it still has significant limitations. The Jacksonian outlook, which has provided the main propulsive force for the U.S. military expeditions of recent years, has come to dominate (along with a generous dose of values-promoting Wilsonianism) much of the American way of looking at the world abroad. And Jacksonianism, as Mead explains, "is less an intellectual or political movement than it is an expression of the social, cultural, and religious values of a large portion of the American public."[35] Insofar as it is an expression of values rather than an intellectual effort, it is more resistant to learning through experience. Mead's own view of the imbalances in strands of U.S. foreign-policy thinking is suggested by his comment that the particular type of thinking that the United States needs more of these days is Jeffersonian.[36]

The most salient fault line in discourse in the United States today, however—on foreign policy as well as on other aspects of public policy and even values—is between the Democratic Party and the Republican Party. For several reasons, such as the perfection of gerrymandering techniques and an associated decline in competitive congressional districts, the partisan divide in the United States has become deeper and wider over the past couple of decades. An accompanying divide in American public views also has become sharper on many matters. That divide extends not only to prescriptive preferences of what *ought* to be done but also to descriptive perceptions of what *is*. Most relevant to our present purposes, differences based on party affiliation extend to some perceptions of situations abroad.

A survey in 2012 by the Chicago Council on Global Affairs, for example, gauged public perceptions regarding one of the tenets of Samuel Huntington's thesis about a clash of civilizations. Respondents were asked which of two statements they agreed with more: "Because most Muslims are like people everywhere, we can find common ground and violent conflict between the civilizations is not inevitable" or "Because Muslim religious, social, and political traditions are incompatible with Western ways, violent conflict between the two civilizations is inevitable." The responses correlated markedly with party affiliation. Those choosing the first statement included 42 percent of the surveyed Republicans, 58 percent of the Democrats, and 58 percent of the independents; choosing the second statement were 56 percent of the surveyed Republicans, 38 percent of the Democrats, and 40 percent of the independents.[37] One might hope that dialogue among Republicans, Democrats, and independents on such a question would lead in a dialectical way to better understanding of the interaction between the Muslim world and the West. But *dialogue* is too positive a term to apply to much interparty communication in the United States today, which is more a matter of opposing camps shouting at each other. It is far from being a collective search for truth.

Moreover, many Americans' perceptions of what is fact and what is not and that exhibit party differences do not even derive from or have any logical and substantive connection to party ideologies. These beliefs are more a matter of tribal affiliation, with Republicans believing certain things because other Republicans say they are so, and Democrats similarly sharing beliefs within their own tribe. A trivial example that illustrates the point arose in 2008 during congressional hearings on the use of performance-enhancing drugs in professional baseball. The principal witnesses were the star pitcher Roger Clemens and his former trainer. A factual question for the committee members was whether to believe the trainer, who said he had injected a drug into Clemens, or Clemens, who denied the accusation. Republicans predominantly sided with Clemens, and Democrats with the trainer. Perhaps there was in this divide a story of a rich hero being pitted against a little guy. Probably even a bigger factor was that it was a Democrat, former senator George Mitchell, who had fingered Clemens in a report on drug use he had prepared for the commissioner of baseball.[38] If party affiliation can shape—in the crude sense of tribal loyalty—beliefs regarding as narrow a factual question as whether a drug was or was not injected into a professional athlete, then it surely affects in the same crude way beliefs on many broader and more important factual questions, such as those involving relations between the Muslim world and the West.

Diversity of party views is clearly not an effective corrective to broadly shared American misunderstandings about the outside world. It is more likely to be an impediment to correction, given how party affinity so often trumps dispassionate searches for truth.

Partisan competition often worsens misunderstandings through recriminations that appeal to American tendencies to believe certain things about the outside world. The fact that a recrimination appeals to such tendencies is what makes it plausible and gives it the potential to score partisan points. The recrimination cements the misunderstanding more firmly in the public mind through repetition and, for a portion of the public, simply because party leaders with whom these people identify say they are true. The recriminations directed against the Truman administration over "losing China" appealed to a preexisting American tendency to believe that the United States really is the prime mover of events everywhere in the world; the recriminations themselves, as Kennan noted, then exacerbated this misbelief. A similar process occurred with the endless Republican-promoted recriminations over the fatal incident at Benghazi, Libya, which both exploited and worsened popular misunderstandings about what determines the frequency and severity of international terrorism. A similar process took place with the misbelief that the Iraq War was "won" after the troop surge ordered by the Bush administration and before the successor Obama administration supposedly snatched defeat from the jaws of victory by withdrawing the remaining U.S. troops from Iraq. The need for promoters of the war to relieve their cognitive dissonance and preserve their reputations was obviously a major driver of this myth, but the myth was also a recrimination directed at an Obama administration being painted as weak and irresolute. As a result, American public misbeliefs both about the troop surge and the supposedly peaceful status of Iraq afterward when in fact a civil war was still being fought at a substantial clip[39] and about the general nation-building efficacy of U.S. military force were exacerbated.

The intensely bitter conflict that party competition in the United States has become can also exacerbate some American misunderstandings about the outside world in another manner. Mental habits applied in one arena, specifically the arena of daily political combat at home, get naturally applied to another arena, foreign affairs. The American perceptual tendency toward a Manichean view as well as the related penchant for demonizing adversaries have come to characterize the mindset that some participants in U.S. politics, particularly on the right, bring with them to the domestic political battle, constituting another reinforcement for bringing them to perceptions of foreign relations. "Externally directed chauvinist hatred," writes Anatol Lieven, "must therefore be seen as a by-product of the same hatred displayed by the American Right at home, notably in their pathological loathing of Presidents Bill Clinton and Barack Obama."[40]

THE DOWNSIDE OF DEMOCRATIC GREATNESS

One conclusion to be drawn here is that the patterns described in this book are likely to continue—a discouraging conclusion insofar as those patterns involve significant and sometimes damaging misunderstanding of events outside the United States. There will be no shortage of circumstances in which the relevant types of damage are likely to materialize. After Iran, other adversaries will be demonized, just as Iran replaced the Soviet Union as demon after the Cold War ended. There will be additional situations to which inflated hopes for expanding democracy and free enterprise will be applied. And there will be further wars, whether hot or cold, literal or metaphorical, to wage and to which characteristically American attitudes about war will be applied.

Underlying the continuity of these patterns is the largely unchallenged, even if mostly unrecognized and unacknowledged, power of whatever happens to be prevailing American public opinion, a power that Alexis de Tocqueville observed in the first half of the nineteenth century. The American republic, founded with a dedication to free thought and expression that would quickly be codified in the Bill of Rights, had been in existence for half a century when the perceptive French traveler wrote, "I know no country in which there is so little true independence of mind and freedom of discussion as in America." In the Europe that he knew, he explained, there was no single authority that controlled everything, and dissenters could always find sources of support. "But in a nation where democratic institutions exist, organized like those in the United States, there is but one sole authority, one single element of strength and of success, with nothing beyond it": the majority opinion of the American public. "In America, the majority raises very formidable barriers to the liberty of opinion; within those barriers an author may write whatever he pleases, but he will repent if he ever step beyond them."[41]

The very freedom to speak and to write and to argue vociferously about many things leads most Americans to lose sight of all the other things regarding which the heavy hand of prevailing perceptions has the stifling effect that Tocqueville described. Today the divide between political parties and the cultural and ideological fissures associated with that divide are at least as large as they were in Tocqueville's time even without the issue of slavery, which was the great divider in America until after the Civil War. Americans vigorously voice genuine disagreements over taxes, abortion, and much else. The sharpness of their divisions on such issues only diminishes further their awareness of the barriers to genuinely unfettered consideration of other issues, many of which involve foreign relations.

A relevant test of unfettered discussion and of openness to challenging well-entrenched ways of looking at the outside world is not just what a court would protect under the First Amendment but instead what is politically feasible. The question, in other words, is how much an American politician can get away with saying and still get elected (or reelected). Iconoclastic public intellectuals do say and write things that challenge prevailing perceptions of the world abroad, and they do not necessarily repent what they wrote, but they would repent if they ever decide to run for office. For a leader to question openly the prevailing tenets about, for example, how Israel is a firm friend and ally or how terrorism can and must be vanquished would be political poison. So would any serious challenging of the assumption that the United States is powerful enough to accomplish almost anything it wants to accomplish overseas if it applies enough resources and determination to the task.[42] The barriers to free discussion of such things are demonstrated whenever a politician appears to breach a barrier, after which the reactions are vehement and the politician rapidly backpedals in explaining that is not what he really said or meant. This book could not have been written by anyone who aspires to public office that is elective or subject to senatorial confirmation.

National greatness inevitably has downsides, and in the case of the United States those downsides are not limited to carrying the burdens of world leadership. One downside is Americans' difficulty in understanding some things about the world that are understood more easily by those living in nations that are less free, less secure, less prosperous, and less great. The

American nation would be all the greater if it could erase that difficulty, but erasure is too much to expect.

The United States has benefited from having some leaders with good insight into how the world works and enough courage and savvy to get useful things done even when most of their countrymen lacked similar insight. In the course of getting things done through well-informed foreign policy, they have sometimes made it possible to budge, though usually only slowly and in small increments, the American people away from some of their preconceptions. The United States will need more leaders like that in the future.

NOTES

PREFACE

1. Paul R. Pillar, *Intelligence and U.S. Foreign Policy: Iraq, 9/11, and Misguided Reform* (New York: Columbia University Press, 2011).

1. THE AMERICAN PRISM

1. Paul R. Pillar, "The Errors of Exceptionalism," *National Interest*, November 30, 2010, http://nationalinterest.org/node/4497.
2. Gabriel A. Almond, *The American People and Foreign Policy* (New York: Harcourt Brace, 1950), 47.
3. Fabian Hilfrich, *Debating American Exceptionalism: Empire and Democracy in the Wake of the Spanish-American War* (New York: Palgrave Macmillan, 2012), 3.
4. Clyde Kluckhohn and Henry A. Murray, "Personality Formation: The Determinants," in Clyde Kluckhohn and Henry A. Murray, eds., *Personality in Nature, Society, and Culture*, 2nd ed. (New York: Knopf, 1961), 59.
5. Daniel Kahneman, *Thinking, Fast and Slow* (New York: Farrar, Straus and Giroux, 2011).
6. George F. Kennan, *American Diplomacy*, exp. ed. (Chicago: University of Chicago Press, 1984), 135.
7. Grant and Jim Crawley, *Transference and Projection: Mirrors to the Self* (Buckingham, U.K.: Open University Press, 2002), 18.
8. Louis Hartz, *The Liberal Tradition in America* (New York: Harcourt, Brace & World, 1955), 302.

9. Robert Jervis, *Perception and Misperception in International Politics* (Princeton: Princeton University Press, 1976), 324.

10. Paul R. Pillar, *Intelligence and U.S. Foreign Policy: Iraq, 9/11, and Misguided Reform* (New York: Columbia University Press, 2011), chap. 5; Richard H. Immerman, "Intelligence and Strategy: Historicizing Psychology, Policy, and Politics," *Diplomatic History* 32, no. 1 (2008): 7.

11. Almond, *The American People and Foreign Policy*, 56; Joseph Frankel, *The Making of Foreign Policy: An Analysis of Decision Making* (London: Oxford University Press, 1963), 107.

12. Walter Lippmann, *The Public Philosophy* (New York: New American Library, 1956), 28.

13. Kennan, *American Diplomacy*, 176–77.

14. Raymond L. Garthoff, *Détente and Confrontation: American–Soviet Relations from Nixon to Reagan*, rev. ed. (Washington, D.C.: Brookings Institution Press, 1994), 22.

15. Leslie H. Gelb and Richard K. Betts, *The Irony of Vietnam: The System Worked* (Washington, D.C.: Brookings Institution Press, 1979), 241.

16. Irving L. Janis, *Groupthink: Psychological Studies of Policy Decisions and Fiascoes*, 2nd rev. ed. (Boston: Houghton Mifflin, 1983).

17. Pillar, *Intelligence and U.S. Foreign Policy*, 13.

18. Ibid., 322–25.

19. Graham Allison and Peter Szanton, *Remaking Foreign Policy: The Organizational Connection* (New York: Basic Books, 1976), 89–90.

20. Norman A. Graebner, "Public Opinion and Foreign Policy: A Pragmatic View," in Don C. Piper and Ronald J. Terchek, eds., *Interaction: Foreign Policy and Public Policy* (Washington, D.C.: American Enterprise Institute for Public Policy Research, 1983), 15–16.

21. Melvin Small, "Public Opinion," in Michael J. Hogan and Thomas G. Paterson, eds., *Explaining the History of American Foreign Relations* (Cambridge: Cambridge University Press, 1991), 165.

22. Bernard C. Cohen, *The Public's Impact on Foreign Policy* (Boston: Little, Brown, 1973), 208.

23. Arnold Wolfers, *Discord and Collaboration: Essays on International Politics* (Baltimore: Johns Hopkins University Press, 1962), 42.

24. John Allman, *Evolving Brains* (New York: Scientific American Library, 2000).

25. Walter Russell Mead, *Special Providence: American Foreign Policy and How It Changed the World* (New York: Routledge, 2002), 6.

26. Richard E. Neustadt and Ernest R. May, *Thinking in Time: The Uses of History for Decision-Makers* (New York: Free Press, 1986), 245.

27. Ibid., 257–258; Michael H. Hunt, *Ideology and U.S. Foreign Policy* (New Haven: Yale University Press, 1987), xii.

28. Cecil V. Crabb Jr., *American Diplomacy and the Pragmatic Tradition* (Baton Rouge: Louisiana State University Press, 1989), 8–16.

29. Hunt, *Ideology and U.S. Foreign Policy*, 13.

30. Richard T. Hughes, *Myths America Lives By* (Urbana: University of Illinois Press, 2003), 8.

31. Alexis de Tocqueville, *Democracy in America*, 2 vols., trans. Henry Reeve (New York: Schocken, 1961), 2:15–16.

32. See, for example, John J. Mearsheimer, *The Tragedy of Great Power Politics* (New York: Norton, 2001).

33. Neustadt and May, *Thinking in Time*, 161–64.

34. See, for example, Alexander L. George and Juliette L. George, *Woodrow Wilson and Colonel House: A Personality Study* (New York: Dover, 1964).

35. Jervis, *Perception and Misperception in International Politics*, 113.

36. Philip E. Tetlock, *Expert Political Judgment: How Good Is It? How Can We Know?* (Princeton: Princeton University Press, 2005), 123.

37. Stephen Peter Rosen, *War and Human Nature* (Princeton: Princeton University Press, 2005), 28–31.

38. Stephen Brooks, *As Others See Us: The Causes and Consequences of Foreign Perceptions of America* (Peterborough, Canada: Broadview Press, 2006), 15.

39. U.S. Department of Education, "Teaching Language for National Security and American Competitiveness," January 2006, http://www2.ed.gov/teachers/how/academic/foreign-language/teaching-language.html.

40. Chris McComb, "About One in Four Americans Can Hold a Conversation in a Second Language," Gallup News Service, April 6, 2001, http://www.gallup.com/poll/1825/about-one-fourth-americans-can-hold-conversation-second-language.aspx.

41. Quoted in Thomas Hargrove and Guido H. Stempel III, "Americans Wistful for Foreign Language in High School," Scripps Howard News Service, June 20, 2007, http://www.newspolls.org/articles/19614.

42. European Commission, *Europeans and Their Languages*, Special Eurobarometer Report no. 386 (Brussels: European Commission, June 2012), 12, http://ec.europa.eu/public_opinion/archives/ebs/ebs_386_en.pdf.

43. U.S. Census Bureau, "Table 1268: International Travel, 1990 to 2010," in *The 2012 Statistical Abstract* (Washington, D.C.: U.S. Census Bureau, 2012), 777, http://www.census.gov/compendia/statab/2012/tables/12s1268.pdf.

44. William D. Chalmers, "The Great American Passport Myth," *Huffington Post*, September 29, 2012, http://www.huffingtonpost.com/william-d-chalmers/the-great-american-passpo_b_1920287.html.

45. IPK International, *World Travel Trends Report* (Munich: IPK International, 2008), 14–16, http://www.kongres-magazine.eu/data/pdf/Dokumenti_in_porocila/WORLD_TRAVEL_TRENDS_REPORT_2008.pdf.

46. Program on International Policy Attitudes, "World Public Opinion," poll, http://www.worldpublicopinion.org/pipa/pdf/nov10/ForeignAid_Nov10_quaire.pdf.

47. Colligan Market Research, "World Savvy: Global Competency Research Results," July 26, 2012, http://worldsavvy.org/assets/documents/uploads/Final_WS_Market_Research_Study_Aug_2012.pdf.

48. "Study: Geography Greek to Young Americans," CNN, May 4, 2006, http://www.cnn.com/2006/EDUCATION/05/02/geog.test/index.html, reporting on the National Geographic–Roper Public Affairs 2006 Geographic Literacy Study.

49. "Survey Results: U.S. Young Adults Are Lagging," in *National Geographic–Roper 2002 Global Geographic Literacy Survey*, *National Geographic*, n.d., http://www.nationalgeographic.com/geosurvey/highlights.html (accessed May 16, 2015).

50. Mead, *Special Providence*, 162–63, 240.

51. Richard Hofstadter, *The Paranoid Style in American Politics and Other Essays* (New York: Knopf, 1965), 6–7.

52. Anatol Lieven, *America Right or Wrong: An Anatomy of American Nationalism*, 2nd ed. (New York: Oxford University Press, 2012), 2.

53. Quoted in Ron Suskind, "Faith, Certainty, and the Presidency of George W. Bush," *New York Times Magazine*, October 17, 2004, http://www.nytimes.com/2004/10/17/magazine/17BUSH.html.

54. Hartz, *The Liberal Tradition in America*, 286.

2. BEHIND THE OCEAN MOATS

1. Alexis de Tocqueville, *Democracy in America*, 2 vols., trans. Henry Reeve (New York: Schocken, 1961), 1:341.

2. C. Vann Woodward, "The Age of Reinterpretation," *American Historical Review* 66 (October 1960): 2–8.

3. Otis A. Singletary, *The Mexican War* (Chicago: University of Chicago Press, 1960), 14–15.

4. Simon Romero, "Prosecutor in Argentina Sees Iran Plot," *New York Times*, May 30, 2013, A12.

5. An example of such alarmism is Deroy Murdock, "The Southern Border: Our Welcome Mat for Terrorists," *National Review*, April 25, 2013, http://www.nationalreview.com/article/346591/southern-border-our-welcome-mat-terrorists.

6. Alicia A. Caldwell, "Mexican Drug Violence Spills Over Into US," *Huffington Post*, February 9, 2009, http://www.huffingtonpost.com/2009/02/09/mexican-drug-violence-spi_n_165422.html; Ted Galen Carpenter, *The Fire Next Door: Mexico's Drug Violence and the Danger to America* (Washington, D.C.: Cato Institute, 2012).

7. Harry L. Coles, *The War of 1812* (Chicago: University of Chicago Press, 1965), 34–36.

8. Federation of American Scientists, "Status of World Nuclear Forces," n.d., http://www.fas.org/programs/ssp/nukes/nuclearweapons/nukestatus.html (accessed May 16, 2015).

9. Kennette Benedict, interview in Matthew Smith, "A Nuclear World with Nuclear Problems," *Chicago Policy Review*, August 29, 2013, http://chicagopolicyreview.org/2013/08/29/a-nuclear-world-with-nuclear-problems/.

10. Bruce Russett, Jonathan Cowden, David Kinsella, and Shoon Murray, "Did Americans' Expectations of Nuclear War Reduce Their Savings?" *International Studies Quarterly* 38, no. 4 (1994): 587–603.

11. Chicago Council on Global Affairs, *American Public Opinion and U.S. Foreign Policy 1983* (Chicago: Chicago Council on Global Affairs, 1983), 9, and *American Public Opinion and U.S. Foreign Policy 1995* (Chicago: Chicago Council on Global Affairs, 1995), 14.

12. Steven A. Hildreth, *Iran's Ballistic Missile and Space Launch Programs* (Washington, D.C.: Congressional Research Service, 2012), 35–38.

13. Duyeon Kim, "Fact Sheet: North Korea's Nuclear and Ballistic Missile Programs," Center for Arms Control and Non-Proliferation, August 2012, http://armscontrolcenter.org/publications/factsheets/fact_sheet_north_korea_nuclear_and_missile_programs/.

14. Philip Jenkins, *Images of Terror: What We Can and Can't Know About Terrorism* (New York: Aldine de Gruyter, 2003).

15. Thomas Jefferson, first Inaugural Address, in *The Papers of Thomas Jefferson*, vol. 33 (Princeton: Princeton University Press, 2006), 148–52, given at http://jeffersonpapers.princeton.edu/selected-documents/first-inaugural-address-0.

16. A critique of the general American tendency to overestimate the threat from terrorism is given in John Mueller, *Overblown: How Politicians and the Terrorism Industry Inflate National Security Threats, and Why We Believe Them* (New York: Free Press, 2006), esp. chap. 1.

17. Frank Newport, "In U.S., 46% Hold Creationist View of Human Origins," *Gallup Politics*, June 1, 2012, http://www.gallup.com/poll/155003/hold-creationist-view-human-origins.aspx.

18. Robert L. Heilbroner, *The Future as History* (New York: Grove Press, 1961), 50.

19. George F. Kennan, *American Diplomacy*, exp. ed. (Chicago: University of Chicago Press, 1984), 5.

20. Mary N. Hampton, *A Thorn in Transatlantic Relations: American and European Perceptions of Threat and Security* (New York: Palgrave Macmillan, 2013), 17.

21. David Gilmour, *The Long Recessional: The Imperial Life of Rudyard Kipling* (New York: Farrar, Straus and Giroux, 2002), 119.

22. Fabian Hilfrich, *Debating American Exceptionalism: Empire and Democracy in the Wake of the Spanish-American War* (New York: Palgrave Macmillan, 2012), 153.

23. Quoted in Frank Ninkovich, *The United States and Imperialism* (Malden, Mass.: Blackwell, 2001), 32.

24. Nadia Schadlow, "Root's Rules," *American Interest*, January 1, 2007, http://www.the-american-interest.com/articles/2007/01/01/roots-rules/.

25. Robert J. McMahon, *Colonialism and Cold War: The United States and the Struggle for Indonesian Independence, 1945–49* (Ithaca: Cornell University Press, 1981), 63–73.

26. Mark Philip Bradley, "Franklin D. Roosevelt, Trusteeship, and U.S. Exceptionalism," in Marc Frey, Ronald W. Pruessen, and Tan Tai Yong, eds., *The Transformation of Southeast Asia: International Perspectives on Decolonisation* (London: M. E. Sharpe, 2003), 199.

27. Quoted in David Halberstam, *The Best and the Brightest* (New York: Random House, 1972), 512, 564.

28. Hampton, *A Thorn in Transatlantic Relations*, 117, 127.

29. Jenkins, *Images of Terror*, 42–43, 49.

30. A summary of al-Qaʿida's motivations in this regard is in Daniel Byman, *The Five Front War: The Better Way to Fight Global Jihad* (Hoboken, N.J.: Wiley, 2007), 9–13.

31. The relationship between scholarship and the making of foreign policy is discussed in Alexander L. George, *Bridging the Gap: Theory and Practice in Foreign Policy* (Washington, D.C.: U.S. Institute of Peace Press, 1993).

32. Robert Jervis, *Perception and Misperception in International Politics* (Princeton: Princeton University Press, 1976), 136–37.

33. Robert Kagan, *Of Paradise and Power: America and Europe in the New World Order* (New York: Vintage, 2004), 63.

34. "President Woodrow Wilson's Fourteen Points," January 8, 1918, http://avalon.law.yale.edu/20th_century/wilson14.asp.

35. Manfred F. Boemeke, "Woodrow Wilson's Image of Germany, the War-Guilt Question, and the Treaty of Versailles," in Manfred F. Boemeke, Gerald D. Feldman, and Elisabeth Glaser, eds., *The Treaty of Versailles: A Reassessment After 75 Years* (Cambridge: Cambridge University Press, 1998), 610–11.

36. Jussi M. Hanhimäki, *Containing Coexistence: America, Russia, and the "Finnish Solution"* (Kent, Ohio: Kent State University Press, 1997), xv, 203; Anatol Lieven, *America Right or Wrong: An Anatomy of American Nationalism*, 2nd ed. (New York: Oxford University Press, 2012), 166.

37. Ross Colvin, "'Cut Off Head of Snake,' Saudis Told U.S. on Iran," Reuters, November 29, 2010, http://www.reuters.com/article/2010/11/29/us-wikileaks-iran-saudis-idUSTRE6AS02B20101129.

38. Prince Turki al-Faisal, interview by Lally Weymouth, *Washington Post*, November 4, 2013, http://www.washingtonpost.com/opinions/saudi-arabias-prince-turki-american-policy-has-been-wrong/2013/11/04/4f4a04d0-4576-11e3-a196-3544a03c235l_story.html.

39. Thomas Erdbrink, "Iran Takes Charm Offensive to the Persian Gulf," *New York Times*, December 5, 2013, A15.

40. See, for example, David J. Kramer, "U.S. Foreign Policy Comes Home to Roost with Russia's Actions in Ukraine," *Washington Post*, March 1, 2014, http://www.washingtonpost.com/opinions/us-foreign-comes-home-to-roost-with-russias-action-in-ukraine/2014/03/01/10be38bc-a18d-11e3-b8d8-94577ff66b28_story.html.

41. Zbigniew Brzezinski, "Russia Needs a 'Finland Option' for Ukraine," *Financial Times*, February 23, 2014, http://www.ft.com/intl/cms/s/0/7f722496-9c86-11e3-b535-00144feab7de.html#axzz2vDoo9l7t; Henry A. Kissinger, "How the Ukraine Crisis Ends," *Washington Post*, March 5, 2014, http://www.washingtonpost.com/opinions/henry-kissinger-to-settle-the-ukraine-crisis-start-at-the-end/2014/03/05/46dad868-a496-11e3-8466-d34c45176ob9_story.html.

42. Stephen W. Walt, *Taming American Power: The Global Response to U.S. Primacy* (New York: Norton, 2005), 101.

43. Ibid., 71–77.

44. Pew Research Center Global Attitudes Project, *America's Global Image Remains More Positive Than China's* (Washington, D.C.: Pew Research Center, July 18, 2013), http://www.pewglobal.org/files/2013/07/Pew-Research-Global-Attitudes-Project-Balance-of-Power-Report-FINAL-July-18-2013.pdf.

45. Results cited in Walt, *Taming American Power*, 67.

46. Pew Research Center Global Attitudes Project, *Confidence in Obama Lifts U.S. Image Around the World* (Washington, D.C.: Pew Research Center, July 23, 2009), 26, http://www.pewglobal.org/files/2009/07/Pew-Global-Attitudes-Spring-2009-Report-1-July-23-11am.pdf.

47. Pew Research Center Global Attitudes Project, *Arab Spring Fails to Improve U.S. Image* (Washington, D.C.: Pew Research Center, May 17, 2011), 9, http://www.pewglobal.org/files/2011/05/Pew-Global-Attitudes-Arab-Spring-FINAL-May-17-2011.pdf.

48. President George W. Bush, news conference, October 11, 2001, transcript at http://georgewbush-whitehouse.archives.gov/news/releases/2001/10/20011011-7.html.

49. Walt, *Taming American Power*, 62.

50. Samuel P. Huntington, "Why International Primacy Matters," *International Security* 17, no. 1 (1993): 68–83.

51. Walt, *Taming American Power*, 68.

52. One of the most extensive official examinations of public diplomacy, completed in the wake of the events of September 11, 2001, is the report by the Advisory Group on Public Diplomacy for the Arab and Muslim World, *Changing Minds, Winning Peace: A New Strategic Direction for U.S. Public Diplomacy in the Arab and Muslim World* (Washington, D.C.: Advisory Group on Public Diplomacy for the Arab and Muslim World, October 1, 2003), http://www.state.gov/documents/organization/24882.pdf.

53. Pew Research Center for the People and the Press, *Mistrust of America in Europe Ever High, Muslim Anger Persists* (Washington, D.C.: Pew Research Center, March 16, 2004), 18, http://www.people-press.org/files/legacy-pdf/206.pdf.

54. Ibid., 19.

55. Pew Research Center for the People and the Press, *Foreign Policy Attitudes Now Driven by 9/11 and Iraq* (Washington, D.C.: Pew Research Center, August 18, 2004), 29, http://www.people-press.org/files/legacy-pdf/222.pdf.

56. James J. F. Forest, "Terrorism as a Product of Choices and Perceptions," in Benjamin H. Friedman, Jim Harper, and Christopher A. Preble, eds., *Terrorizing Ourselves: Why U.S. Counterterrorism Policy Is Failing and How to Fix It* (Washington, D.C.: Cato Institute, 2010), 23–43; Paul R. Pillar, "Superpower Foreign Policies: A Source for Global Resentment," in James J. F. Forest, ed., *Root Causes*, vol. 3 of *The Making of a Terrorist: Recruitment, Training, and Root Causes* (Westport, Conn.: Praeger, 2005), 31–44.

57. Vice President Dick Cheney, interview, *Meet the Press*, NBC, March 16, 2003, transcript available at http://www.mtholyoke.edu/acad/intrel/bush/cheney meetthepress.htm.

58. Paul R. Pillar, *Intelligence and U.S. Foreign Policy: Iraq, 9/11, and Misguided Reform* (New York: Columbia University Press, 2011), chap. 3.

59. David D. Kirkpatrick, "Benghazi and Arab Spring Rear Up in U.S. Campaign," *New York Times*, October 22, 2012, A1.

60. Richard T. Hughes, *Myths America Lives By* (Urbana: University of Illinois Press, 2003), 91.

61. Lieven, *America Right or Wrong*, 19.

62. Richard A. Posner, *Countering Terrorism: Blurred Focus, Halting Steps* (Lanham, Md.: Rowman & Littlefield, 2007), 5.

3. ABUNDANCE AND POWER

1. Dean R. Snow, "Microchronology and Demographic Evidence Relating to the Size of Pre-Columbian North American Indian Populations," *Science* 268, no. 5217 (1995): 1601–4; Herbert S. Klein, *A Population History of the United States* (Cambridge: Cambridge University Press, 2004), 20.

2. Merle Curti, *The Roots of American Loyalty* (New York: Columbia University Press, 1946), 41.

3. Alexis de Tocqueville, *Democracy in America*, 2 vols., trans. Henry Reeve (New York: Schocken, 1961), 2: 343–44.

4. Frederick Jackson Turner, *The Frontier in American History* (1893; reprint, New York: Holt, Rinehart and Winston, 1962), 3, 32, 37.

5. Frederick J. Turner, "Social Forces in American History," *American Historical Review* 16, no. 2 (1911): 222.

6. David M. Potter, *People of Plenty: Economic Abundance and the American Character* (Chicago: University of Chicago Press, 1958), 94, 158–60, 164–65.

7. Ray Allen Billington, foreword to Turner, *The Frontier in American History*, ix–xvii.

8. Robert L. Heilbroner, *The Future as History* (New York: Grove Press, 1961), 17–18. On Americans' comparative optimism, see also Seymour Martin Lipset, *American Exceptionalism: A Double-Edged Sword* (New York: Norton, 1995), 51, and Gabriel A. Almond, *The American People and Foreign Policy* (New York: Harcourt, Brace, 1950), 50.

9. Robert Jervis, *Perception and Misperception in International Politics* (Princeton: Princeton University Press, 1976), 136.

10. Richard T. Hughes, *Myths America Lives By* (Urbana: University of Illinois Press, 2003), 100.

11. Anatol Lieven, *America Right or Wrong: An Anatomy of American Nationalism*, 2nd ed. (New York: Oxford University Press, 2012), 3.

12. "American Exceptionalism," Gallup poll, December 22, 2010, http://www.gallup.com/poll/145355/american-exceptionalism-pdf.aspx.

13. "Poll Results: American Exceptionalism," *YouGov Economist* poll, *YouGov*, September 2013, emphasis added, http://today.yougov.com/news/2013/09/19/poll-results-american-exceptionalism/.

14. James D. Rice, *Tales from a Revolution: Bacon's Rebellion and the Transformation of Early America* (New York: Oxford University Press, 2012), 212–15.

15. Val Percival and Thomas Homer-Dixon, "Environmental Scarcity and Violent Conflict: The Case of Rwanda," *Journal of Environment and Development* 5, no. 3 (1996): 270–91.

16. Quoted in Mary N. Hampton, *A Thorn in Transatlantic Relations: American and European Perceptions of Threat and Security* (New York: Palgrave Macmillan, 2013), 43.

17. *The Pentagon Papers*, 4 vols., Senator Gravel ed. (Boston: Beacon Press, 1971), 3:112–13.

18. Robert S. McNamara, *In Retrospect: The Tragedy and Lessons of Vietnam* (New York: Times Books, 1995), 322.

19. John J. Mearsheimer and Stephen M. Walt, *The Israel Lobby and U.S. Foreign Policy* (New York: Farrar, Straus and Giroux, 2007).

20. Quoted in Tom Segev, *One Palestine, Complete: Jews and Arabs Under the British Mandate*, trans. Haim Watzman (New York: Henry Holt, 2000), 150.

21. Lieven, *America Right or Wrong*, 195.

22. Lawrence Davidson, "Christian Zionism as a Representation of American Manifest Destiny," *Critique: Critical Middle Eastern Studies* 14, no. 2 (2005): 159; Sacvan Bercovitch, *The American Jeremiad* (Madison: University of Wisconsin Press, 1978), 7–8, 128.

23. Peter Grose, *Israel in the Mind of America* (New York: Knopf, 1983), 5.

24. Herman Melville, *White-Jacket: or, The World in a Man-of-War* (1850; reprint, New York: Modern Library, 2002), 151.

25. Lipset, *American Exceptionalism*, 64.

26. Davidson, "Christian Zionism," 158.

27. Leon Festinger, *A Theory of Cognitive Dissonance* (Evanston, Ill.: Row, Peterson, 1957).

28. John B. Judis, "John Kerry's First Peace Effort in Israel and Palestine Failed, but Now He Needs to Try Again," *New Republic*, July 9, 2014, http://www .newrepublic.com/article/118630/israel-palestine-murders-cause-criss-will -john-kerry-step; Paul R. Pillar, "Asymmetric Warfare in Gaza," *National Interest*, July 12, 2014, http://nationalinterest.org/blog/paul-pillar/asymmetric -warfare-gaza-10869.

29. Ker Than, "Massive Population Drop Found for Native Americans, DNA Shows," *National Geographic Daily News*, December 5, 2011, http://news.nation algeographic.com/news/2011/12/111205-native-americans-europeans-population -dna-genetics-science/.

30. Karen R. Humes, Nicholas A. Jones, and Roberto R. Ramirez, *Overview of Race and Hispanic Origin, 2010* (Washington, D.C.: U.S. Census Bureau, March 2011), 7, http://www.census.gov/prod/cen2010/briefs/c2010br-02.pdf.

31. For an official statement by British authorities of somewhat similar population numbers four years later, see *An Interim Report on the Civil Administration of Palestine*, July 30, 1921, http://unispal.un.org/UNISPAL.NSF/0/349B02280A93 0813052565E90048ED1C.

32. United Nations Special Committee on Palestine, *Report to the General Assembly*, Supplement no. 11, September 3, 1947, http://domino.un.org/unispal.nsf/9a798ad bf322aff38525617b006d88d7/07175de9fa2de563852568d3006e10f3?OpenDocument.

33. James Inhofe, "Israel's Right to the Land," *Aish.com*, March 4, 2002, http://www .aish.com/h/iid/48891682.html.

34. Doug Mataconis, "Newt Gingrich Calls Palestinians an 'Invented People,'" *Outside the Beltway*, December 10, 2011, http://www.outsidethebeltway.com /newt-gingrich-calls-palestinians-an-invented-people/.

35. Eli Clifton, "Santorum: 'All The People Who Live in the West Bank Are Israelis,'" *Think Progress*, November 21, 2011, http://thinkprogress.org/security /2011/11/21/373985/santorum-west-bank-israelis/?mobile=nc.

36. Quoted in Peter Theroux, *Sandstorms: Days and Nights in Arabia* (New York: Norton, 1990), 23.

37. Quoted in Neil Caplan, "Zionist–Arab Diplomacy: Patterns and Ambiguities on the Eve of Statehood," in Laurence Jay Silberstein, ed., *New Perspectives in Israeli History: The Early Years of the State* (New York: New York University Press, 1991), 250.

38. Kathleen Christison, *Perceptions of Palestine: Their Influence on U.S. Middle East Policy* (Berkeley: University of California Press, 1999), 4–5.

39. Natasha Gill, "The Original 'No': Why the Arabs Rejected Zionism, and Why

It Matters," Middle East Policy Council, June 19, 2013, http://www.mepc.org/articles-commentary/commentary/original-no-why-arabs-rejected-zionism-and-why-it-matters.

40. Jeremy Pressman, "Visions in Collision: What Happened at Camp David and Taba?" *International Security* 28, no. 2 (2003): 6.

41. Saree Makdisi, "Pro-settler Santorum Claims Mexico and the West Bank," *Slate*, January 6, 2012, http://www.salon.com/2012/01/06/from_texas_to_israel_santorums_twisted_history/.

42. Noga Kadman, *Acting the Landlord: Israel's Policy in Area C, the West Bank* (Jerusalem: B'Tselem, June 2013), http://www.btselem.org/sites/default/files2/201306_area_c_report_eng.pdf.

43. Edward L. Morse, "Welcome to the Revolution: Why Shale Is the Next Shale," *Foreign Affairs* 93, no. 3 (2014): 6.

44. Scott D. Sagan, "The Origins of the Pacific War," *Journal of Interdisciplinary History* 18, no. 4 (1988): 893–922; Edward S. Miller, *Bankrupting the Enemy: The U.S. Financial Siege of Japan Before Pearl Harbor* (Annapolis, Md.: Naval Institute Press, 2007), 123, 167.

45. Dean Acheson, *Present at the Creation: My Years in the State Department* (New York: Norton, 1969), 36.

46. Potter, *People of Plenty*, 93.

47. Quoted in Ashley Parker and Richard A. Oppel Jr., "Romney Trip Raises Sparks at a 2nd Stop," *New York Times*, July 31, 2012, A1.

48. Lyndon Johnson, speech to the AFL-CIO, March 22, 1966, quoted in Doris Kearns, *Lyndon Johnson and the American Dream* (New York: Harper and Row, 1976), 267.

49. Colin H. Kahl, Melissa G. Dalton, and Matthew Irvine, *Atomic Kingdom: If Iran Builds the Bomb, Will Saudi Arabia Be Next?* (Washington, D.C.: Center for New American Security, February 2013), http://www.cnas.org/sites/default/files/publications-pdf/CNAS_AtomicKingdom_Kahl.pdf.

50. Paul R. Pillar, *Terrorism and U.S. Foreign Policy* (Washington, D.C.: Brookings Institution Press, 2001), 4–5.

51. A review of the principal technical challenges is given in Richard A. Falkenrath, Robert D. Newman, and Bradley A. Thayer, *America's Achilles Heel: Nuclear, Biological, and Chemical Terrorism and Covert Attack* (Cambridge, Mass.: MIT Press, 1998), chap. 2.

52. Barry R. Posen, "Command of the Commons: The Military Foundation of U.S. Hegemony," *International Security* 28, no. 1 (2003): 5–46.

53. Stephen M. Walt, *Taming American Power: The Global Response to U.S. Primacy* (New York: Norton, 2005), chap. 3.

54. Micah Zenko, *Reforming U.S. Drone Strike Policies*, Council on Foreign Relations Special Report no. 65 (Washington, D.C.: Council on Foreign Relations, January 2013), 10–11.

55. Peter Beinart, *The Icarus Syndrome: A History of American Hubris* (New York: Harper, 2010), 381.
56. Paul R. Pillar, *Intelligence and U.S. Foreign Policy: Iraq, 9/11, and Misguided Reform* (New York: Columbia University Press, 2011), 13–14, 51–55.
57. Ken Adelman, "Cakewalk in Iraq," *Washington Post*, February 13, 2002, A27.
58. Thomas E. Ricks, *Fiasco: The American Military Adventure in Iraq* (New York: Penguin Press, 2006), 97.
59. Quotations of Wolfowitz's comments are given in Pillar, *Intelligence and U.S. Foreign Policy*, 319–20.
60. Paul Wolfowitz, statement to the U.S. House of Representatives, *Department of Defense Budget Priorities for Fiscal Year 2004*, hearings, 108th Cong., 1st sess., February 27, 2003.
61. Quoted in Michael Isikoff and David Corn, *Hubris: The Inside Story of Spin, Scandal, and the Selling of the Iraq War* (New York: Crown, 2006), 98.
62. McNamara, *In Retrospect*, 323.

4. THE SUCCESSFUL SOCIETY

1. Louis Hartz, *The Liberal Tradition in America* (New York: Harcourt, Brace & World, 1955).
2. James D. Rice, *Tales from a Revolution: Bacon's Rebellion and the Transformation of Early America* (New York: Oxford University Press, 2012), 215.
3. Andrew Jackson, fifth Annual Message to Congress, December 3, 1833, http://www.synaptic.bc.ca/ejournal/JacksonFifthAnnualMessage.htm.
4. Robert Jervis, *Perception and Misperception in International Politics* (Princeton: Princeton University Press, 1976), 284.
5. J. Hector St. John de Crèvecoeur, *Letters from an American Farmer and Sketches of Eighteenth-Century America* (1782; reprint, New York: Penguin, 1981), 68.
6. J. Allen Williams Jr. and Suzanne T. Ortega, "Dimensions of Ethnic Assimilation: An Empirical Appraisal of Gordon's Typology," *Social Science Quarterly* 71, no. 4 (December 1990): 697–710.
7. John Higham, *Strangers in the Land: Patterns of American Nativism, 1860–1925* (New York: Atheneum, 1963).
8. Jerry Z. Muller, "Us and Them: The Enduring Power of Ethnic Nationalism," *Foreign Affairs* 87, no. 2 (2008): 18.
9. Paul R. Pillar, "The Age of Nationalism," *National Interest*, no. 127 (September–October 2013): 9–19.
10. Office of the President, *The National Security Strategy of the United States of America* (Washington, D.C.: U.S. Government Printing Office, September 2002), http://georgewbush-whitehouse.archives.gov/nsc/nss/2002/.

11. Paul R. Pillar, *Intelligence and U.S. Foreign Policy: Iraq, 9/11, and Misguided Reform* (New York: Columbia University Press, 2011), 57.

12. Seymour Martin Lipset, *American Exceptionalism: A Double-Edged Sword* (New York: Norton, 1995), 113.

13. Michael H. Hunt, *Ideology and U.S. Foreign Policy* (New Haven: Yale University Press, 1987), 91.

14. Quoted in Henry F. Graff, *The Tuesday Cabinet: Deliberation and Decision on Peace and War Under Lyndon B. Johnson* (Englewood Cliffs, N.J.: Prentice-Hall, 1970), 99.

15. Scott Straus, "Darfur and the Genocide Debate," *Foreign Affairs* 84, no. 1 (2005): 126.

16. Caroline Kennedy, "The Manichean Temptation: Moralising Rhetoric and the Invocation of Evil in US Foreign Policy," *International Politics* 50, no. 5 (September 2013): 623–24.

17. Mary N. Hampton, *A Thorn in Transatlantic Relations: American and European Perceptions of Threat and Security* (New York: Palgrave Macmillan, 2013), 3.

18. Richard T. Hughes, *Myths America Lives By* (Urbana: University of Illinois Press, 2003), 171; Anatol Lieven, *America Right or Wrong: An Anatomy of American Nationalism*, 2nd ed. (New York: Oxford University Press, 2012), 54.

19. See, for instance, *Burwell v. Hobby Lobby Stores Inc.*, 573 U.S. (2014), http://www.supremecourt.gov/opinions/13pdf/13-354_olp1.pdf.

20. Lee-Ann Goodman, "Santorum Says He Doesn't Believe in Separation of Church and State," Associated Press, February 26, 2012, http://news.yahoo.com/santorum-says-doesnt-believe-separation-church-state-164307440.html.

21. Steve Crabtree and Brett Pelham, "What Alabamians and Iranians Have in Common," *Gallup World*, February 9, 2009, http://www.gallup.com/poll/114211/Alabamians-Iranians-Common.aspx.

22. Quoted in Paul Kengor, *God and George W. Bush: A Spiritual Life* (New York: Regan, 2004), 132.

23. Arthur M. Schlesinger Jr., *The Cycles of American History* (Boston: Houghton Mifflin, 1986), 54, 70, 74.

24. Lipset, *American Exceptionalism*, 63.

25. Daniel Bell, *The End of Ideology: On the Exhaustion of Political Ideas in the Fifties*, rev. ed. (New York: Free Press, 1962), 120.

26. Lieven, *America Right or Wrong*, 132.

27. Quoted in Ira Chernus, *Monsters to Destroy: The Neoconservative War on Terror and Sin* (Boulder: Paradigm, 2006), 124.

28. Katie Jagel, "Poll Results: Exorcism," *YouGov*, September 17, 2013, https://today.yougov.com/news/2013/09/17/poll-results-exorcism/.

29. James J. F. Forest, ed., *Root Causes*, vol. 3 of *The Making of a Terrorist: Recruitment, Training, and Root Causes* (Westport, Conn.: Praeger, 2006).

30. Third presidential candidates' debate, Tempe, Ariz., October 13, 2004, http://www.debates.org/index.php?page=october-13-2004-debate-transcript.

31. Quoted in Carey McWilliams, *A Mask for Privilege* (Boston: Little, Brown, 1948), 51.

32. Quoted in Christopher Hitchens, "Jefferson's Quran: What the Founder Really Thought About Islam," *Slate*, January 9, 2007, http://www.slate.com/articles/news_and_politics/fighting_words/2007/01/jeffersons_quran.html.

33. Hughes, *Myths America Lives By*, chap. 3.

34. D. Michael Lindsay, "Evangelical Elites in the U.S. Military," *Journal of Political and Military Sociology* 35, no. 2 (2007): 161–76.

35. Some representative statements are quoted in Lieven, *America Right or Wrong*, 148.

36. Office of the President, *National Strategy for Counterterrorism* (Washington, D.C.: U.S. Government Printing Office, June 2011), http://www.whitehouse.gov/sites/default/files/counterterrorism_strategy.pdf.

37. Graham E. Fuller, *The Future of Political Islam* (New York: Palgrave Macmillan, 2004), 25.

38. Lawrence Davidson, "Christian Zionism as a Representation of American Manifest Destiny," *Critique: Critical Middle Eastern Studies* 14, no. 2 (2005): 160.

39. Ibid., 163.

40. Michael Lipka, "More White Evangelicals Than American Jews Say God Gave Israel to the Jewish People," Pew Research Center, October 3, 2013, http://www.pewresearch.org/fact-tank/2013/10/03/more-white-evangelicals-than-american-jews-say-god-gave-israel-to-the-jewish-people/.

41. Walter Russell Mead, "God's Country?" *Foreign Affairs* 85, no. 5 (2006): 40.

42. Pew Research Center Global Attitudes Project, *Anti-Americanism: Causes and Characteristics* (Washington, D.C.: Pew Research Center, December 10, 2003), http://www.pewglobal.org/2003/12/10anti-americanism-causes-and-characteristics/.

43. Lipset, *American Exceptionalism*, 18.

44. Samuel Huntington, *American Politics: The Promise of Disharmony* (Cambridge, Mass.: Harvard University Press, 1981), 25.

45. Sacvan Bercovitch, *The American Jeremiad* (Madison: University of Wisconsin Press, 1978), 176.

46. Hartz, *The Liberal Tradition in America*, 78.

47. Robert L. Heilbroner, *The Future as History* (New York: Grove Press, 1961), 52.

48. Hartz, *The Liberal Tradition in America*, 306.

49. Frances FitzGerald, *Fire in the Lake: The Vietnamese and the Americans in Vietnam* (Boston: Little, Brown, 1972), 16.

50. Ibid. See also Doris Kearns, *Lyndon Johnson and the American Dream* (New York: Harper and Row, 1976), 265.

51. Robert S. McNamara, *In Retrospect: The Tragedy and Lessons of Vietnam* (New York: Times Books, 1995), 322.

4. THE SUCCESSFUL SOCIETY

52. Pillar, *Intelligence and U.S. Foreign Policy*, 101.

53. Michael C. Desch, "America's Liberal Illiberalism: The Ideological Origins of Overreaction in U.S. Foreign Policy," *International Security* 32, no. 3 (2007–2008): 10.

54. Lipset, *American Exceptionalism*, 26.

55. Lieven, *America Right or Wrong*, 49.

56. G. John Ikenberry, "Woodrow Wilson, the Bush Administration, and the Future of Liberal Internationalism," in G. John Ikenberry, Thomas J. Knock, Anne-Marie Slaughter, and Tony Smith, *The Crisis of American Foreign Policy: Wilsonianism in the Twenty-First Century* (Princeton: Princeton University Press, 2009), 11–12.

57. Francis Fukuyama, "The End of History?" *National Interest*, no. 16 (Summer 1989): 3–18.

58. Desch, "America's Liberal Illiberalism," 25.

59. Alexis de Tocqueville, *Democracy in America*, 2 vols., trans. Henry Reeve (New York: Schocken, 1961), 2:37–39.

60. President George H. W. Bush, address at Maxwell Air Force Base, April 13, 1991, *Vital Speeches of the Day* 57, no. 15 (1991): 452.

61. Jeremi Suri, *Liberty's Surest Guardian: American Nation-Building from the Founders to Obama* (New York: Free Press, 2011), 6.

62. Dominic Tierney, *How We Fight: Crusades, Quagmires, and the American Way of War* (New York: Little, Brown, 2010), 7–8, 36–40, 45.

63. Pillar, *Intelligence and U.S. Foreign Policy*, 15–20.

64. W. Patrick Lang Jr., "What Iraq Tells Us About Ourselves," *Foreign Policy*, February 2007, http://www.foreignpolicy.com/story/cms.php?story_id=3734.

65. David M. Potter, *People of Plenty: Economic Abundance and the American Character* (Chicago: University of Chicago Press, 1958), 141.

66. President George W. Bush, Address to the Nation, September 20, 2001, http://www.presidentialrhetoric.com/speeches/09.20.01.html.

67. Stephen M. Walt, *Taming American Power: The Global Response to U.S. Primacy* (New York: Norton, 2005), 81.

68. Hunt, *Ideology and U.S. Foreign Policy*, 116.

69. George F. Kennan, *American Diplomacy*, exp. ed. (Chicago: University of Chicago Press, 1984), 96.

70. Ibid.

71. See, for example, Fred Hiatt, "Obama's Foreign Policy Reveals the Effects of Disengagement," *Washington Post*, July 27, 2014, http://www.washingtonpost.com/opinions/fred-hiatt-obamas-foreign-policy-reveals-the-effects-of-disengagement/2014/07/27/4c0f9452-1284-11e4-8936-26932bcfd6ed_story.

72. Potter, *People of Plenty*, 138.

5. SEARCHING FOR MONSTERS TO DESTROY

1. Samuel P. Huntington, "The Erosion of American National Interests," *Foreign Affairs* 76, no. 5 (1997): 30.

2. Jürgen Heideking, "The Image of an English Enemy During the American Revolution," in Ragnhild Fiebig-von Hase and Ursula Lehmkuhl, eds., *Enemy Images in American History* (Providence, R.I.: Berghahn, 1997), 103–5.

3. Peter Beinart, *The Icarus Syndrome: A History of American Hubris* (New York: Harper, 2010), 6.

4. Richard W. Stewart, ed., *The United States Army and the Forging of a Nation, 1775–1917*, vol. 1 of *American Military History* (Washington, D.C.: Center of Military History, United States Army, 2005), 107, 113, 116.

5. Alexis de Tocqueville, *Democracy in America*, 2 vols., trans. Henry Reeve (New York: Schocken, 1961), 1:341.

6. Walter Russell Mead, *Special Providence: American Foreign Policy and How It Changed the World* (New York: Routledge, 2002), 254.

7. Dominic Tierney, *How We Fight: Crusades, Quagmires, and the American Way of War* (New York: Little Brown, 2010), 260–61.

8. Michael H. Hunt, *Ideology and U.S. Foreign Policy* (New Haven: Yale University Press, 1987), 14.

9. Yuen Foong Khong, *Analogies at War: Korea, Munich, Dien Bien Phu, and the Vietnam Decisions of 1965* (Princeton: Princeton University Press, 1992), 32–36.

10. John Quincy Adams, speech to the U.S. House of Representatives, 17th Cong., 1st sess., July 4, 1821.

11. Quoted in Richard T. Hughes, *Myths America Lives By* (Urbana: University of Illinois Press, 2003), 164. See also Merle Curti, *The Roots of American Loyalty* (New York: Columbia University Press, 1946), 232–35.

12. Quoted in David Fromkin, *A Peace to End All Peace: The Fall of the Ottoman Empire and the Creation of the Modern Middle East* (New York: Holt, 1989), 5.

13. Richard W. Stewart, ed., *The United States Army in a Global Era, 1917–2008*, vol. 2 of *American Military History*, 2nd ed. (Washington, D.C.: Center of Military History, United States Army, 2010), 55–57.

14. Mary L. Dudziak, *War Time: An Idea, Its History, Its Consequences* (New York: Oxford University Press, 2012), 61–62.

15. Carl von Clausewitz, *On War*, trans. and ed. Michael Howard and Peter Paret (Princeton: Princeton University Press, 1984), 87.

16. Robert Kagan, *Of Paradise and Power: America and Europe in the New World Order* (New York: Vintage, 2004).

17. Mary N. Hampton, *A Thorn in Transatlantic Relations: American and European Perceptions of Threat and Security* (New York: Palgrave Macmillan, 2013), 4–5.

18. Tom Brokaw, *The Greatest Generation* (New York: Random House, 2004).

19. Walter Lippmann, *The Cold War: A Study in U.S. Foreign Policy* (New York: Harper, 1947).
20. Mead, *Special Providence*, 62–64.
21. Walter Lippmann, *U.S. Foreign Policy: Shield of the Republic* (Boston: Little, Brown, 1943), 11–26.
22. For such challenges, see, for example, William Appleman Williams, *The Tragedy of American Diplomacy* (Cleveland: World, 1959); Gar Alperovitz, *Atomic Diplomacy: Hiroshima and Potsdam, the Use of the Atomic Bomb, and the American Confrontation with Soviet Power* (New York: Simon and Schuster, 1965).
23. The dispute between historians on the start of the Cold War has also concerned the historians' own methods. See Robert James Maddox, *The New Left and the Origins of the Cold War* (Princeton: Princeton University Press, 1973).
24. Charles Krauthammer, "The Unipolar Moment," *Foreign Affairs* 70, no. 1 (1990–1991): 23–33.
25. John J. Mearsheimer, "Why the Ukraine Crisis Is the West's Fault: The Liberal Delusions That Provoked Putin," *Foreign Affairs* 93, no. 5 (2014): 77–89.
26. Arthur M. Schlesinger Jr., *The Cycles of American History* (Boston: Houghton Mifflin, 1986), 54–55.
27. Zbigniew Brzezinski, speech given at the conference "New American Strategies for Security and Peace," October 28, 2003, http://www.informationclearinghouse.info/article5132.htm.
28. Paul R. Pillar and Christopher A. Preble, "Don't You Know There's a War On? Assessing the Military's Role in Counterterrorism," in Benjamin H. Friedman, Jim Harper, and Christopher A. Preble, eds., *Terrorizing Ourselves: Why U.S. Counterterrorism Policy Is Failing and How to Fix It* (Washington, D.C.: Cato Institute, 2010), 61–81.
29. Bruce Hoffman, *Inside Terrorism*, rev. ed. (New York: Columbia University Press, 2006), 83–84.
30. Paul R. Pillar, *Intelligence and U.S. Foreign Policy: Iraq, 9/11, and Misguided Reform* (New York: Columbia University Press, 2011), 203–5, 294–95, 300–302.
31. Paul R. Pillar, "Forgotten Lessons of Counterterrorism," *National Interest*, October 8, 2014, http://nationalinterest.org/blog/paul-pillar/forgotten-lessons-counterterrorism-11438.
32. Robin Wright, "From the Desk of Donald Rumsfeld," *Washington Post*, November 1, 2007, http://www.washingtonpost.com/wp-dyn/content/article/2007/10/31/AR2007103103095.html.
33. Chicago Council on Global Affairs, *Worldviews 2002: American Public Opinion and Foreign Policy* (Chicago: Chicago Council on Global Affairs, 2002), 10.
34. Pew Research Center, *Most Expect "Occasional Acts of Terrorism" in the Future* (Washington, D.C.: Pew Research Center, April 23, 2013), http://www.people-press.org/files/legacy-pdf/4-23-13%20Boston%20Release.pdf.

35. Director of Central Intelligence George J. Tenet, "Worldwide Threat 2001: National Security in a Changing World," statement to the Senate Select Committee on Intelligence, 107th Cong., 1st sess., February 7, 2001, https://www.cia.gov/news-information/speeches-testimony/2001/UNCLASWWT_02072001.html.

36. Philip Jenkins, *Images of Terror: What We Can and Can't Know About Terrorism* (New York: Aldine de Gruyter, 2002), 35–36.

37. President George W. Bush, Address to Congress, 107th Cong., 1st sess., September 20, 2001, http://georgewbush-whitehouse.archives.gov/news/releases/2001/09/20010920-8.html.

38. Stephen M. Walt, *Taming American Power: The Global Response to U.S. Primacy* (New York: Norton, 2005), 107.

39. James J. F. Forest, ed., *Root Causes*, vol. 3 of *The Making of a Terrorist: Recruitment, Training, and Root Causes* (Westport, Conn.: Praeger Security International, 2006).

40. David D. Kirkpatrick, "A Deadly Mix in Benghazi," *New York Times*, December 28, 2013, http://www.nytimes.com/projects/2013/benghazi/?hp#/?chapt=0.

41. Fawaz A. Gerges, *The Far Enemy: Why Jihad Went Global* (New York: Cambridge University Press, 2005), esp. chap. 4.

42. Paul R. Pillar, "The Diffusion of Terrorism," *Mediterranean Quarterly* 21, no. 1 (2010): 1–14.

43. Office of the President, *National Strategy for Counterterrorism* (Washington, D.C.: U.S. Government Printing Office, June 2011), http://www.whitehouse.gov/sites/default/files/counterterrorism_strategy.pdf.

44. David C. Rapoport, "The Four Waves of Modern Terrorism," in Audrey Kurth Cronin and James M. Ludes, eds., *Attacking Terrorism: Elements of a Grand Strategy* (Washington, D.C.: Georgetown University Press, 2004), 46–73.

45. I am indebted to Bruce Hoffman for pointing out this contrast.

46. See, for example, Gabriel Schoenfeld, "Could September 11 Have Been Averted?" *Commentary*, December 2001, 21–30, and the responses to this article in *Commentary*, February 2002, http://www.commentarymagazine.com/article/counterterrorism-before-september-11/.

47. President Barack Obama, "Weekly Address: We Will Degrade and Destroy ISIL," September 13, 2014, http://www.whitehouse.gov/the-press-office/2014/09/13/weekly-address-we-will-degrade-and-destroy-isil.

48. Pillar, *Intelligence and U.S. Foreign Policy*, 55–59.

49. John D. Banusiewicz, "Wolfowitz Discusses Iraq in Series of Radio Interviews," *DoD News*, March 18, 2004, http://www.defense.gov/news/newsarticle.aspx?id=27049.

50. Flynt Leverett and Hillary Mann Leverett, *Going to Tehran: Why the United States Must Come to Terms with the Islamic Republic of Iran* (New York: Metropolitan, 2013), chap. 6.

51. Edward Vose Gulick, *Europe's Classical Balance of Power* (New York: Norton, 1967).

52. Quoted in Wilson D. Miscamble, *From Roosevelt to Truman: Potsdam, Hiroshima, and the Cold War* (Cambridge: Cambridge University Press, 2007), 49–52. See also Seymour Martin Lipset, *American Exceptionalism: A Double-Edged Sword* (New York: Norton, 1995), 66.

53. Michael C. Desch, "America's Liberal Illiberalism: The Ideological Origins of Overreaction in U.S. Foreign Policy," *International Security* 32, no. 3 (2007–2008): 10.

54. Robert Jervis, *Perception and Misperception in International Politics* (Princeton: Princeton University Press, 1976), 117.

55. Bush, Address to Congress, September 20, 2001.

56. Paul R. Pillar, *Terrorism and U.S. Foreign Policy* (Washington, D.C.: Brookings Institution Press, 2001), 178.

57. For more on the democratic peace theory, see the essays in Michael E. Brown, Sean M. Lynn-Jones, and Steven E. Miller, eds., *Debating the Democratic Peace* (Cambridge, Mass.: MIT Press, 1996).

58. Such explanations are what Kenneth N. Waltz called "second image theories" of war (*Man, the State, and War: A Theoretical Analysis* [New York: Columbia University Press, 1959], chap. 4).

59. Edward D. Mansfield and Jack Snyder, "Democratization and War," *Foreign Affairs* 74, no. 3 (1995): 79–97.

60. Jervis, *Perception and Misperception in International Politics*, 319–29.

61. Robert Malley and Peter Harling, "Beyond Moderates and Militants," *Foreign Affairs* 89, no. 5 (2010): 19, 26.

62. Norman D. Palmer, *The United States and India: The Dimensions of Influence* (New York: Praeger, 1984), 21.

63. Quoted in Andrew J. Rotter, *Comrades at Odds: The United States and India, 1947–1964* (Ithaca: Cornell University Press, 2000), 57.

64. Glenn D. Paige, *The Korean Decision* (New York: Free Press, 1968), 51.

65. Robert S. McNamara, *In Retrospect: The Tragedy and Lessons of Vietnam* (New York: Times Books, 1995), 30.

66. Lyndon Baines Johnson, *The Vantage Point: Perspectives of the Presidency 1963–1969* (New York: Holt, Rinehart, and Winston, 1971), 134.

67. Jervis, *Perception and Misperception in International Politics*, 125.

68. Thomas J. Christensen, *Worse Than a Monolith: Alliance Politics and Problems of Coercive Diplomacy in Asia* (Princeton: Princeton University Press, 2011), 21, 67–68, 72–73.

69. Ibid., 24–25.

70. Pillar, *Intelligence and U.S. Foreign Policy*, 110–12; Christopher Van Hollen, "The Tilt Policy Revisited: Nixon–Kissinger Geopolitics and South Asia," *Asian Survey* 20, no. 4 (1980): 350–52.

71. Pillar, *Intelligence and U.S. Foreign Policy*, 112–15; Ralph K. White, *Fearful Warriors: A Psychological Profile of U.S.–Soviet Relations* (New York: Free Press, 1984).

72. Sacvan Bercovitch, *The American Jeremiad* (Madison: University of Wisconsin Press, 1978), 178–79.

73. Curti, *The Roots of American Loyalty*, 226–27.

74. Michaela Hoenicke Moore, *Know Your Enemy: The American Debate on Nazism, 1933–1945* (Cambridge: Cambridge University Press, 2010), 345.

75. Ernest R. May, *"Lessons" of the Past: The Use and Misuse of History in American Foreign Policy* (New York: Oxford University Press, 1973), 84–85.

76. Harry S. Truman, *Years of Trial and Hope*, vol. 2 of *Memoirs* (Garden City, N.Y.: Doubleday, 1956), 332–33.

77. Khong, *Analogies at War*, chap. 7; Johnson, *Vantage Point*, 46; McNamara, *In Retrospect*, 195.

78. Quoted in Alexander Dallin, "Learning in U.S. Policy Toward the Soviet Union in the 1980s," in George W. Breslauer and Philip E. Tetlock, eds., *Learning in U.S. and Soviet Foreign Policy* (Boulder: Westview Press, 1991), 407.

79. See Paul Wolfowitz's description of his own use of the analogy as quoted in Derrick Z. Jackson, "A Fatal Distraction," *Boston Globe*, March 26, 2004, http://www.boston.com/news/globe/editorial_opinion/oped/articles/2004/03/26/a_fatal_distraction/.

80. Harry Truman, speech in Laramie, Wyoming, May 9, 1950, http://www.trumanlibrary.org/publicpapers/index.php?pid=742.

81. Ronald Reagan, speech to the National Association of Evangelicals, March 8, 1983, http://voicesofdemocracy.umd.edu/reagan-evil-empire-speech-text/.

82. George W. Bush, State of the Union Address, January 29, 2002, http://georgewbush-whitehouse.archives.gov/news/releases/2002/01/20020129-11.html.

83. Both Cheney and Rice quoted in Dan Murphy, "Bad Reason to Invade Iraq No. 1: Saddam Was 'Evil,'" *Christian Science Monitor*, March 18, 2013, http://www.csmonitor.com/World/Backchannels/2013/0318/Bad-reason-to-invade-Iraq-No.-1-Saddam-was-evil.

84. George F. Kennan, *American Diplomacy*, exp. ed. (Chicago: University of Chicago Press, 1984), 164.

85. For a more detailed treatment of American perceptions of Iran, see Paul R. Pillar, "The Role of Villain: Iran and U.S. Foreign Policy," *Political Science Quarterly* 128, no. 2 (2013): 211–31.

86. Michael A. Ledeen, *Accomplice to Evil: Iran and the War Against the West* (New York: Truman Talley, 2009).

87. Jim Inhofe, "To Defeat Iran, Drill for Energy at Home," *Investors Business Daily*, May 10, 2013, http://news.investors.com/ibd-editorials-viewpoint/051013-655687-to-defeat-iran-drill-for-american-energy.htm.

88. Richard E. Nisbett and Lee Ross, *Human Inference: Strategies and Shortcomings of Social Judgment* (Englewood Cliffs, N.J.: Prentice Hall, 1980), 122–23.

89. Chicago Council on Global Affairs, *Foreign Policy in the New Millennium* (Chicago: Chicago Council on Global Affairs, 2012), 30.

90. Ronald Reagan, *An American Life* (New York: Simon and Schuster, 1990), 605–6; George P. Shultz, *Turmoil and Triumph: My Years as Secretary of State* (New York: Scribner, 1993), 490; Robert M. Gates, *From the Shadows: The Ultimate Insider's Story of Five Presidents and How They Won the Cold War* (New York: Simon and Schuster, 1996), 281.

91. Anatol Lieven, *America Right or Wrong: An Anatomy of American Nationalism*, 2nd ed. (New York: Oxford University Press, 2012), 163.

92. Ira Chernus, *Monsters to Destroy: The Neoconservative War on Terror and Sin* (Boulder: Paradigm, 2006), x.

93. Paul R. Pillar, "ISIS in Perspective," *National Interest*, August 25, 2014, http://nationalinterest.org/blog/paul-pillar/isis-perspective-11150.

94. Robert Legvold, "Managing the New Cold War: What Moscow and Washington Can Learn from the Last One," *Foreign Affairs* 93, no. 4 (2014): 74–84.

95. John Mueller, "The Iraq Syndrome," *Foreign Affairs* 84, no. 6 (2005): 44–54.

96. See John Mueller's further thoughts on this subject in "The Iraq Syndrome Revisited: U.S. Intervention, from Kosovo to Libya," *Foreign Affairs*, March 28, 2011, http://www.foreignaffairs.com/articles/67681/john-mueller/the-iraq-syndrome-revisited.

6. UNENDING MISPERCEPTION

1. Walter Lippmann, *The Public Philosophy* (New York: New American Library, 1956), 23–24.

2. Paul R. Pillar, *Intelligence and U.S. Foreign Policy: Iraq, 9/11, and Misguided Reform* (New York: Columbia University Press, 2011), esp. chap. 8.

3. Richards J. Heuer Jr., "Computer-Aided Analysis of Competing Hypotheses," in Roger Z. George and James B. Bruce, eds., *Analyzing Intelligence: Origins, Obstacles, and Innovations* (Washington, D.C.: Georgetown University Press, 2008), 251–65.

4. Pillar, *Intelligence and U.S. Foreign Policy*, 55–59, 100–107.

5. Elihu Root, "A Requisite for the Success of Popular Diplomacy," *Foreign Affairs* 1, no. 1 (1922): 5.

6. Harry Harding, *A Fragile Relationship: The United States and China Since 1972* (Washington, D.C.: Brookings Institution Press, 1992), 35, 40.

7. Theodore J. Lowi, *The End of Liberalism: Ideology, Policy, and the Crisis of Public Authority* (New York: Norton, 1969), 170–86.

8. Dana Milbank and Claudia Deane, "Hussein Link to 9/11 Lingers in Many Minds," *Washington Post*, September 6, 2003, A1.

9. Michaela Hoenicke Moore, *Know Your Enemy: The American Debate on Nazism, 1933–1945* (Cambridge: Cambridge University Press, 2010), 8–9.

10. E. J. Dionne Jr., *Our Divided Political Heart: The Battle for the American Idea in an Age of Discontent* (New York: Bloomsbury, 2012), 226–27.

11. Gabriel A. Almond, *The American People and Foreign Policy* (New York: Harcourt, Brace, 1950), 27–28.

12. James A. Baker III, *The Politics of Diplomacy: Revolution, War, and Peace, 1989–1992* (New York: Putnam, 1995), 273.

13. Mary N. Hampton, *A Thorn in Transatlantic Relations: American and European Perceptions of Threat and Security* (New York: Palgrave Macmillan, 2013), 47.

14. Seymour Martin Lipset, *American Exceptionalism: A Double-Edged Sword* (New York: Norton, 1995), 67.

15. President Dwight D. Eisenhower, Farewell Address, January 17, 1961, http://coursesa.matrix.msu.edu/~hst306/documents/indust.html.

16. Anatol Lieven, *America Right or Wrong: An Anatomy of American Nationalism*, 2nd ed. (New York: Oxford University Press, 2012), 4.

17. Arthur M. Schlesinger Jr., *The Cycles of American History* (Boston: Houghton Mifflin, 1986), 60.

18. Robert Malley and Peter Harling, "Beyond Moderates and Militants," *Foreign Affairs* 89, no. 5 (2010): 27.

19. Michael H. Hunt, *Ideology and U.S. Foreign Policy* (New Haven: Yale University Press, 1987), 191; Paul R. Pillar, "The Age of Nationalism," *National Interest*, no. 127 (September–October 2013): 18–19.

20. Stephen Brooks, *As Others See Us: The Causes and Consequences of Foreign Perceptions of America* (Peterborough, Canada: Broadview Press, 2006), 13.

21. Alexander L. George, *Presidential Decisionmaking in Foreign Policy: The Effective Use of Information and Advice* (Boulder: Westview Press, 1980), 77.

22. Bernard Lewis, *What Went Wrong? Western Impact and Middle Eastern Response* (New York: Oxford University Press, 2000).

23. Lewis Hartz, *The Liberal Tradition in America* (New York: Harcourt, Brace & World, 1955), 10–11.

24. Robert L. Heilbroner, *The Future as History* (New York: Grove Press, 1961), 16, 51.

25. On paradigm shifts in science, see Thomas S. Kuhn, *The Structure of Scientific Revolutions*, 3rd ed. (Chicago: University of Chicago Press, 1996).

26. For such lumping, see, for example, Norman Podhoretz, *World War IV: The Long Struggle Against Islamofascism* (New York: Vintage Books, 2007).

27. Peter R. Feaver and Christopher Gelpi, *Choosing Your Battles: American Civil–Military Relations and the Use of Force* (Princeton: Princeton University Press,

2004), 63. Cross-national research has pointed to previous combat experience as inclining leaders against the initiation of military conflict (Michael C. Horowitz and Allan C. Stam, "How Prior Military Experience Influences the Future Militarized Behavior of Leaders," *International Organization* 68 [Summer 2014]: 527–59).

28. For the costs of the Iraq War, see Joseph E. Stiglitz and Linda J. Bilmes, *The Three Trillion Dollar War: The True Cost of the Iraq Conflict* (New York: Norton, 2008).

29. U.S. Senate, Select Committee on Intelligence, *Committee Study of the Central Intelligence Agency's Detention and Interrogation Program* (Washington, D.C.: U.S. Government Printing Office, December 3, 2014), http://www.intelligence .senate.gov/study2014/sscistudy1.pdf.

30. For another source that received little attention, see the Central Intelligence Agency's analysis of the Senate committee report at https://www.cia.gov /library/reports/CIAs_June2013_Response_to_the_SSCI_Study_on_the_Former _Detention_and_Interrogation_Program.pdf.

31. George F. Kennan, *American Diplomacy*, exp. ed. (Chicago: University of Chicago Press, 1984), 166.

32. Paul R. Pillar, "The Damaging Myth About 'Winning' the Iraq War," *National Interest*, November 17, 2014, http://nationalinterest.org/blog/paul-pillar/the -damaging-myth-about-winning-the-iraq-war-11695.

33. President Barack Obama, remarks at the National Defense University, May 23, 2013, http://www.whitehouse.gov/the-press-office/2013/05/23/remarks -president-national-defense-university.

34. Walter Russell Mead, *Special Providence: American Foreign Policy and How It Changed the World* (New York: Routledge, 2002), 216.

35. Ibid., 226.

36. Ibid., 331.

37. Chicago Council on Global Affairs, *Foreign Policy in the New Millennium* (Chicago: Chicago Council on Global Affairs, 2012), 46.

38. Dana Milbank, "Bottom Feeders," *Washington Post*, February 14, 2008, A2.

39. See, for example, the data on civilian casualties from violence in Iraq compiled by the Iraq Body Count project at https://www.iraqbodycount.org/database/.

40. Lieven, *America Right or Wrong*, 11.

41. Alexis de Tocqueville, *Democracy in America*, 2 vols., trans. Henry Reeve (New York: Schocken, 1961), 1:310.

42. Peter Beinart, *The Icarus Syndrome: A History of American Hubris* (New York: Harper, 2010), 378, 384.

INDEX